Also by Joseph N. Manfredo

Only the Living
(A memoir)

After Midnight
(Poems and Pontifications)

The Trained Killers
(A Memoir)

AS I Recall

THE STORY OF A BIKE RIDE

Joseph N. Manfredo

Order this book online at www.trafford.com
or email orders@trafford.com

Most Trafford titles are also available at major online book retailers.

This work of fiction is drawn from real events, people, and places. A few
names, venues, and events have not been changed and are recognizable. The
balance, however, is fictionalized. Rest assured that any similarity to people,
places, or events that would generate controversy or any other nasty thing like
libel or slander are positively and unquestionably purely coincidental.

Printed in the United States of America.

ISBN: 978-1-4907-4276-2 (sc)
ISBN: 978-1-4907-4275-5 (hc)
ISBN: 978-1-4907-4277-9 (e)

Library of Congress Control Number: 2014913253

Trafford rev. 07/25/2014

 www.trafford.com
North America & international
toll-free: 1 888 232 4444 (USA & Canada)
fax: 812 355 4082

For a while he looked down at the beach and out to the small breakers, scanning for the dolphins that sometimes played and fed along this beach. *Photo by EM Clark.*

To Mr. Senatro D. La Bella who taught English and Composition at Thomas R. Proctor High School. He critiqued our fledgling writings, offered advice and encouragement, and wrote across the top of my last composition, "You should continue to write for your own pleasure."

Thank you, Mr. La Bella. I did.

"Old age is a tyrant who forbids, upon pain of death, all the pleasures of youth."

—La Rochefoucauld, *Maxims*

"Alonso of Aragon was wont to say in commendation of age, that age appears to be best in four things—old wood best to burn, old wine to drink, old friends to trust, and old authors to read."

—Francis Bacon, *Apothegms*

What though the radiance
which was once so bright
Be now for ever taken from my sight,
Though nothing can bring back the hour
Of splendour in the grass,
of glory in the flower,
We will grieve not, rather find
Strength in what remains behind;
In the primal sympathy
Which having been must ever be;
In the soothing thoughts that spring
Out of human suffering;
In the faith that looks through death,
In years that bring the philosophic mind.

—William Wordsworth

Contents

Illustrations

Acknowledgments

My thanks to Dominick (Dick) Morelli, who shared with me the incredible yet true stories of his experiences in the Pacific Theatre campaign against the Japanese Empire during World War II.

Thanks also to former schoolmate, Genevieve La Colla Grosbaum, for her recollection of names, places, and events during those early years.

The story of the Tonopah Cotton Gin would not have been complete without certain historical information provided by Shirley Caudillo of the Tonopah Tribune, Tonopah, Arizona.

Many thanks to Liz Caldwell, Jo Ann St. Claire, and Pati Manfredo Wilkinson. They were kind enough to read the penultimate draft and courageous enough to offer constructive advice.

Thank you to good friend and talented photographer, EM Clark, for the cover and frontispiece photographs.

And finally my thanks to Guido, a rescued cat, who spent many affectionate hours curled at my feet or lying on my desk, directly in front of my work, while I fussed with the drafts of this book. His support was unwavering although sometimes annoyingly in the way. Not unlike some people I know.

To those I missed, please accept my apology and know that in our next life I will sing your praises—or not—depending, of course, on whether or not I will be in a position to sing at all.

1

Rat Beach

He was eighty years old, and he could still ride his bicycle for significant distances. But now he stayed as much as possible on the strand along the beach, away from the busy streets of greater Los Angeles. The sound and smell of the sea was soothing, and studying people along the beach gave him great pleasure. He sometimes tried to imagine the life story behind the more striking ones—the old and feeble, the young and nubile, and those few regulars who appeared homeless, all their worldly possessions piled on a stolen shopping cart or strapped onto a sea-air rusted bicycle.

He had parked his car on a bluff overlooking the start of the paved bicycle path in Torrance Beach. His bicycle was mounted on a rack behind the trunk of the sedan.

For a while he looked down at the beach and out to the small breakers, scanning for the dolphins that often played and fed along this beach. Southward, the shoreline curved slightly in a long arc that turned westward toward Catalina Island. It formed a cove that was very popular with the local teenagers. The cove became known as Rat Beach, an acronym for "right after Torrance beach." The paved bicycle path started here and ran northerly up the coast.

With practiced movements, he opened the trunk, pulled out the front wheel, mounted it to the front fork, tested the brakes, lifted the bike off the rack, removed the rack, and stored it inside the trunk, closing it with a muffled *thunk*. He zeroed the small speedometer-odometer mounted to the front handlebar. Taking one last look at his wristwatch, he tossed a leg over the crossbar and set out across the parking lot and down the slanting concrete ramp that traversed the steep cliffside and led to the paved bike path which cleaved through the sand. The long steep ramp was lined with signs that said "No Skateboards, Roller Skates, Bicycles on Ramp." But he, like all the other skaters and bikers, ignored the signs.

This path extended all the way to Will Rogers State Beach in Pacific Palisades. There was a time when he would have ridden its whole length, a round trip of around forty-four miles. Now he often turned around earlier—especially if the wind became adverse, the crowds grew too thick, or some part of his body began to warn him that it was unhappy.

The cloudless, light-blue sky stretched from the Los Angeles skyline in the east clear out to the Pacific Ocean horizon in the west where it dipped softly behind the deep, dark-blue water. The wind hadn't come up yet. When it did, he would smell the sea and taste the salt spray. But for now it was silent, except for the occasional call of a gull or the splash of a diving cormorant or pelican. There were no sailboats out on the water. Sails would appear later when the wind came to life.

The first mile or so went easily. The bike path sloped slightly downhill, and with no wind to interfere, the bike rolled effortlessly. Up ahead, where Avenue C ended its run through the city of Redondo Beach, a concrete flight of steps was filled with chattering little children. A school bus had just emptied a large group of children for one of the many field trips so common in the Los Angeles Unified School District. He braked gently to a stop and watched as the teachers herded what appeared to be second or third graders across the path to the wide sand beach.

A young man on a shiny new Schwinn pulled up next to him. "Lucky kids," he said. "They get to spend a school day at the beach."

The Old Man nodded in agreement. Leaning on his handlebars, he turned to speak. Just as he did so, the other man spotted a break in the line of children and sped off, leaving him with his unspoken thoughts.

He spoke anyway—to himself, in his head—as the children ran, shrieking and laughing, down to the sand-lapping wavelets.

We didn't have day trips when I started school. We never got to visit a museum or a beach. We had recess. That was it. File outside, play for a while, and file back inside. The three Rs: 'Readin', 'Rittin', 'Rithmatic. Art. Music. Gosh, that was over seventy-five years ago. It was a different world. I recall that first, exciting day...

And all the memories slipped softly out of their hiding places.

Brandegee

September 1937 was the start of an especially colorful autumn. Tree leaves had begun turning to outrageously beautiful shades of red, auburn, yellow, and brown—a fireworks display to announce the beginning of the fall season.

We talked excitedly during breakfast—the usual bowl of hot milk, colored with a touch of coffee, filled with chunks of Italian bread, and sprinkled with sugar.

Mama washed my face; her hands, so soft and gentle, rinsing the soap away with silky smooth palms. She helped me get dressed and combed my hair, still wet, while delivering admonishments, primarily about being a good boy and doing what the teacher told me to do. Today she would take me to be enrolled in kindergarten. I gripped her hand tightly as we left our apartment, knowing that as long as she had hold of me, I was going to be okay. Barely four blocks from our small apartment building was the strange and intimidating new world of Brandegee Grade School.

The two-story building covered half a city block. Dark red bricks with light-colored cement trim around doors and windows gave the structure an imposing, authoritative look. Tall windows glared menacingly down at us as we walked the narrow walkway to the immense double doors that were propped open that first day.

Administrative offices and kindergarten through fourth grade occupied the first floor. Grades five through eight were upstairs. A wood shop and drafting design classes were held in the basement. Also in the basement was the boiler room where a furnace generated steam heat for the building. This was also where children clapped blackboard erasers to get rid of chalk dust. Without realizing it, we would be taught a metaphor for life. Physical labor was at the lowest level and higher education took us to higher levels.

KINDERGARTEN

We entered the kindergarten classroom. Mrs. Woolis, a white-haired, well-dressed woman greeted us warmly, shaking my mother's hand. Crouching down to my level, she placed a bracelet-clad arm around my shoulders and gave me a brief hug of welcome. It was strange to be hugged by a complete stranger, and warm feelings flooded my small being. She and Mama chatted while I stared in awe at the small dark wooden chairs and tables.

Other children stood, staring around with curiosity. Along the windowsills were small pots with little plants, reaching for sunlight. Several tall vases, filled with water, held pussy willow stems bearing small, gray, furry willow buds that felt like rabbit fur to my tiny inquisitive fingers. I was drawn to these, and though I had seen them many times, growing wild in the marshes surrounding the outskirts of East Utica, I had never thought of them as indoor plants. I immediately connected Mrs. Woolis with these soft willow buds and would recall them with fondness the rest of my life. She, like them, was soft, tender, and comforting. It was several months before I stopped calling her Mrs. Willow.

One by one the mothers left. I felt a profound sadness when Mama left, but Mrs. Woolis seemed to sense this and took me in her arms ever so gently. I felt warm and safe. That empty feeling of abandonment faded away as I became engrossed in the children and sounds around me.

Of the many little boys and girls I met that first day, I recall most vividly little Lucy Santos, freckle-faced, teary-eyed, runny-nosed, and with naturally curly dark hair. She cried inconsolably that first day despite our teacher's efforts to comfort her. It was a sadness that seemed to shadow her in the coming years. A couple grades later, when we were being introduced to pen points and ink wells, Lucy suffered a severe scratch when a passing child accidentally scraped a wet ink pen across Lucy's forearm. I remember the bleeding and the tears and the long permanent tattoo it left on her arm. It was Lucy's home, just a few years later, which bore a Scarlet Fever seal on the front door, warning others away from this highly contagious disease. She was not allowed to come back to school for some time. The stigma followed her for a while. Over thirty years later, I received a newspaper clipping in a letter from home. A barroom brawl had resulted in gunfire. One Lucy Santos had been shot and killed. No details were available. As I read it, I pictured again that teary-eyed, freckle-faced, curly-haired, agonizingly sad little girl who sat next to the pussy willows and cried.

Later that first week, a photographer showed up and took pictures of us in groups of three. My group included Salvatore and Felix. We sat side by side, me in a red-and-white, horizontally striped, long-sleeved sweater. Next to me was Salvatore in a blue sailor suit with large white buttons and white beading trim and Felix in a white shirt and tie. All three of us wore shorts and full-length, heavy cotton stockings that started under our shorts and went down into the tops of our high-top shoes. It would be several years before we were considered old enough to wear knickers instead of shorts and a few years more before we graduated to long pants.

Looking at that old photo revealed, in the way we sat, our individual personalities. I was leaning back, a wistful look on my face, feet apart, toes up, shoes resting on their heels, loosely clenched fists lying in my lap. Salvatore, rigidly posed, stared dutifully straight at the camera, feet flat on the floor, knees and legs tightly together, hands lying flat on his lap, palms down, one on top of the other. Felix held both of his hands tucked under his thighs, feet and legs were splayed, the bottom of his father's long necktie was tucked into his shorts. The three male muses of East Utica.

FIRST GRADE

Our days in kindergarten passed quickly, and we were excitedly ushered down the hall to our first grade class. Now instead of small chairs lined up at tables, we had our very own desks. The lids were hinged and lifted to reveal a storage space, though we still had nothing to put into them. In the front of the room, behind the teacher's desk, ran a clothes closet the full width of the room—like a hidden passageway—with a door at either end. In here we encountered the wonder of our very own clothes hooks. Clothes and lunches were stored in this dimly lit alcove.

Our teacher encouraged us to bring interesting things to school to share. I thought of my uncle Bob's World War I souvenirs. Uncle Bob had fought in that war. He brought back a French bayonet and a pair of German aviator goggles. Dad inherited both when Uncle Bob died. I begged him to let me take the bayonet to school. He wisely declined and offered to loan me the goggles instead. I promised to "take good care of them." My class was impressed. I let some of the boys try them on and hung them back on my clothes hook afterward. They disappeared by the end of the day, along with my innocence.

I don't recall the name of the first grade teacher or any of my classmates, except for one. She sat at the desk to my right. Lovely Katherine had long, honey-colored, Shirley Temple curls set about a very pretty, fair-skinned face with dark eyes framed by long eyelashes. She was smart, polite, and exuded a self-confidence that exceeded her years. I was entranced by her poise and intelligence. I was discovering puppy love.

On certain days of the week, our teacher passed out colored crayons and sheets of heavy drawing paper. She put up a sample drawing or an object for us to copy—some days a still life, others a landscape or pictures of animals or people. Katherine's drawings were always colorful, flowing scenes closely resembling what the teacher had on display. By contrast, everyone else's work, including mine, seemed simplistic and crude.

One special day, our teacher gave each of us an unusually large sheet of drawing paper. It covered my entire desktop. This was to be a humungous drawing. She told us to use our imaginations and draw whatever we wished. I was excited. I scoured my mind for an idea but kept looking out of the corner of my eye to Katherine's paper. I knew she would do something outstanding. I decided I would try to draw whatever she chose to draw today. It would, it seemed to me, draw me closer to her.

Beautiful Katherine, who was creative and imaginative and so very pretty, picked up a red crayon. I picked up my red crayon. She put it back down and picked up a black crayon. I put down my red and picked up my black. She placed the tip of her crayon at the upper left-hand corner of the desk-sized drawing paper and carefully, with a steady hand, drew a long, straight dark line down to the right-hand corner. What would this be? How intriguing. Perhaps a hillside in the Italian Alps or a ski slope winter scene? I carefully drew a long dark line, diagonally, upper left to lower right, from corner to corner.

Katherine seemed to think for a minute then placed her crayon tip at the upper right-hand corner of her paper and, with a steady hand, drew a perfectly straight diagonal line down to the lower left-hand corner. I was puzzled. Oh, wait, maybe it was an aerial view of a crossroad in the countryside or the intersection of Genesee and Bleecker Streets right here in our own hometown. I did my best to copy exactly what she had just done.

She set down her black crayon. I set down my black crayon. I sat back and waited to see what color she would select next and what delightful creation she would make of this when she raised her arm straight up and waved at the teacher.

"May I please be excused to go to the bathroom?"

She stood and left the room. I waited for her return, sitting back and looking from her paper to mine. What would it be?

Slowly, as I looked, it seemed to come into focus, and I saw what we had drawn. A very large black X filled her paper and, by imitation, mine too. My wonderful, oversized drawing paper had been cancelled by a big black X. I could have done so much with it. The possibilities leapt about in my mind, but now it was ruined.

When Katherine returned, she set her crayons to one side, folded her paper in half, and slid it beneath her crayons; my disappointment was complete. I vowed never to be misled and disappointed by a beautiful girl again. But of course, I would.

Second Grade

The next year, we moved right next door to second grade. I had looked into that doorway each day and was so very impressed by the spindle back stools the color of blond wood that lined the front of the classroom. They looked so adult. Now we would sit in those stools as we waited our turn to read to the class or perform a show and tell.

It was in this classroom that Katherine completely stole my heart. She consistently got the highest grades and delivered dramatic presentations. Her parents were giving her the best of private tutoring, and soon she was standing before us delivering classical soliloquies. She recited portions of the balcony scene from "Romeo and Juliet," Edgar Allen Poe's poem, "The Raven," and Hamlet's "To be or not to be" soliloquy in its entirety. And most impressive was her rendition of Juliet's soliloquy from act IV, Scene III where Juliet drinks the sleeping potion. I can still see her, holding the imaginary vial upward at arm's length, before her as she recited, "Romeo, I come! This do I drink to thee." She drew the vial to her sweet lips then, lowering it, lay slowly back across three of the blond, wooden spindled chairs, her right arm across her eyes, her left dangling downward toward the floor, her body in repose. The stage presence, gestures, and inflections were professional. I was thunderstruck. I spoke to her every chance I got. She was politely responsive.

At the end of that school year, her family sold their pretty little home, which was just across the street from our school, and moved to the south side of the city, a more prosperous and higher-priced neighborhood. I was devastated. My little heart ached each day as I passed her old home. I lost track of her.

We moved to the third grade just down the hall. Ms. McCalmont taught us—among other things—cursive writing using the Palmer method of repeated rows of push-pulls and ovals, rolling on the muscle of our forearm. Each desk had an ink well that was filled from a large ink bottle by Ms. McCalmont herself. Our wooden penholders had a replaceable pen tip. When we received a new pen point, we sucked on it for a moment to dissolve some sort of preservative coating; then we wiped it with our little square ink cloth to dry it before dipping and again after each use. It was all so new.

THE VIOLIN

I wanted to take piano lessons, as my older brother had done some years earlier, but we sold the piano when we moved to a smaller apartment. Friends offered to loan me a used violin, and I took lessons from our school music teacher at 25¢ a week. Soon I mastered the standards like "Pomp and Circumstance" and could render a mean "Turkey in the Straw." I earned second violin position in the school orchestra. Angela, who took private lessons from an outside teacher, played first violin, the most prestigious seat in the orchestra. We played exactly the same music, but her technique was much better than mine. She bathed in the glory of that first seat while I sat—invisible—in her shadow.

On the day of our first performance in front of the school assembly, Angela was out sick, and I sat in her first position seat. It was exhilarating. The conductor made eye contact with me now. I led the strings. From then on, when special performances approached, I whispered a little prayer that Angela would catch a cold or develop a stomachache—just something small to keep her home that day. But she never did again. Eventually, Angela went on to the Julliard School of Music in New York City and became a professional musician. She joined the prestigious Curtis Institute of Music in Philadelphia, studied under a well-known Russian violinist, Ivan Galamian, and enjoyed an illustrious career in music.

One day, my violin teacher called me aside and explained that she had gone as far as she felt qualified to teach and encouraged me to take private lessons outside the school. As a reward for my completion of her classes, she gave me a shiny enameled pin. She had wanted to find a violin pin, but the local jewelry store was out of them, so she gave me a red, white, and silver enameled drum pin. I wore that drum pin proudly at our orchestral performances.

Carrying a violin case to and from school was hazardous. It meant drawing the attention of some of the school roughnecks who interpreted this as a sign of weakness— like the time I was walking home after school one winter day. A group of boys I knew vaguely were playing King of the Hill. King of the Hill is a simple game. The object is to climb to the top of a high pile of hard packed snow and throw everyone else off. Once on top, you were the King of the Hill. Everyone else would try to throw you off. I put down the violin case and joined in. I was at the top and struggling to keep my "King" position when a bigger kid got a good head grip on me and dragged me off the pile. Once at the bottom, he should have let me go and run to the top before the others beat him to it. But he didn't. Instead, he began to squeeze my neck with the arm that encircled my throat. I was facing the ground and could not see him.

"Let go!" I croaked. "Lemme go!"

He laughed, and a couple of his friends snickered. One of them kicked the violin case.

"Leggo!" I gasped. I doubled a fist and swung it blindly upward to a point above my head where I thought his head might be.

I heard a sickly crack and was instantly released. I fell backward against the snow pile. Blood gushed from his nose. He swore at me. His two friends went from astonishment to rage. I grabbed the violin case and began to run. As I reached the street corner, I could hear the pounding boots and yelling voices behind me. The violin thumped and rattled inside the case as I ran. I was sure they'd catch me in another half block because running with that case was so awkward. Just around the corner was a set of concrete steps with concrete railings leading up to the front door of a candy shop. I ducked behind the steps and waited. The boot stomps and voices grew louder quickly, and as the first pursuer reached the steps, I swung the violin case blindly around the low concrete railing. The solid impact was followed by a grunt, and as he fell, I stepped out and kicked wildly at the second kid. He doubled over, holding his groin.

The third guy came around the corner just as an adult voice shouted, "Hey! What the heck is going on here?" Guy number three stopped in his tracks and stared toward the curb where a car had pulled up and a big man was stepping out of the car. The man strode menacingly toward us. The third kid turned and ran back the way he had come, followed closely by the other two.

The man looked somewhat familiar. He turned to me, smiled, and said, "You're Al's kid brother, ain'tcha? Get in. I'll drive ya home." I recognized him then as one of the guys who hung out with my elder brother and I accepted the ride. I lived for another day.

THE BULLY

Bullying was a normal part of our young lives back then. Every school had at least one bully. We had Frankie Bruno. Frankie was a stocky, muscular kid whose rough behavior put off most of the children. He was usually alone. He was not a good student, and his overtures to join in our games or conversations were brusque and hurtful. It was as if he had never learned to play with others.

An oft-repeated scenario went like this: Frankie would walk up to a small group of boys and try to join in whatever was going on. They often ignored him. When they did, he'd saunter a short distance away then come silently back, unseen, from behind and deliver what we called a Charlie Horse to the nearest boy. That was a blow, with his knee, to the side of either leg. He was very good at it. The pain was excruciating and sometimes led to crying. Frankie laughed and looked at the others to see if they were impressed. The others failed to see the humor in what he had just done and walked away from him. Frankie stood alone for a moment and then left in search of another group to play with.

Eventually, the boys learned to keep one eye on Frankie and avoided his sneak attack. He changed tactics. One afternoon as we were leaving school, I watched him as he walked up to one boy after another, made small talk, then unexpectedly delivered a closed-fist punch to the stomach, causing them to double over, gasping for breath. I hesitated inside the doorway, knowing I would have to walk the gauntlet in order to go home. I took my hard-covered notebook and put it inside my shirt and short pants. When I walked out, he strolled up to me and said, "Hey. How ya doin'?" then threw a stiff punch to my stomach. There was a solid *thunk* sound as his knuckles cracked against the hidden stiff-covered notebook. I stepped around him and walked off while he rubbed his knuckles and stared after me with a puzzled look on his face.

A few months later on a wet spring weekend, Frankie wandered to Proctor Park where a rain-swollen creek rushed over rocks under a stone bridge and eventually entered a deep channel that swirled into a tunnel which disappeared into a hillside. He was alone as usual. He attempted to cross the torrent on a makeshift raft and fell off. Frankie could not swim. Nearby people rushed to the stream's edge but watched helplessly as he was swept into the tunnel. His body was found where the creek emerged from the tunnel and emptied into the Mohawk River.

A few days later, our teacher announced what had happened and told us Frankie could be viewed in his family living room for two days. She suggested it would be kind to stop by and pay our respects.

My friends and I did not like Frankie. We did not understand his cruel behavior and would not miss him. But our morbid curiosity overcame us. His house was right on our way home, just two blocks from the school. We approached the front porch timidly. The door stood open. His Italian grandmother came to us, dressed in black, with a black lace kerchief over her head and a black veil over her weathered, tearful face.

"*Vieni dentro, venire.* Come in-a, come in-a," she beseeched. "Come-a see Frankie."

She turned to the casket, which sat just a few feet from the door, its lid raised. Frankie seemed asleep. His throat seemed swollen. His large thick hands were folded neatly on his chest. We'd never seen him looking so peaceful. This was not the troubled Frankie we had learned to fear and avoid.

With tears streaming down her face, his grandmother spoke to him. "See, Frankie? You' frien's, they come-a see you. But you no see them. See, Frankie? You no see them no more."

She turned her head to us, a bunched handkerchief held tightly in one hand.

"*Povero figlio sfortunato.* My poor child." She pressed her trembling hands against her chest. "He lose-a his mamma an'a papa when he was a baby. *Sempre solo.* Always alone. He 'ave nobody. *Solamente me.* Just-a me."

She turned back to look at him, gesturing toward him with one hand. "Now I 'ave nobody."

Our sensibilities were stunned. She wept quietly while we stared at the sleeping Frankie. After what seemed to be a long awkward time, we mumbled our regrets to her.

As we turned to go, she said to him, "They leave-a now, Frankie. *Dite addio ai vostri amici.* Say go-bye you' frien's, Frankie."

She stood on the front porch as we walked down the front steps. "Thank you, you come-a see my Frankie… you come-a say go-bye a-my Frankie."

We walked away in silence, each of us lost in thought. As we turned the corner, I looked back. She was still standing on the porch, looking after us through her black lace veil, a kerchief pressed to her lips.

We had not known that Frankie had no parents or siblings, that he had been raised by his widowed grandmother. No one to read bedtime stories to him, play catch with a ball, teach him to ride a bike. We knew nothing about him. We knew only what we saw at school. We saw a bully. We did not see the lonely misfit, hungry for our attention, the lonely little boy.

For the first time in my young life—but not the last—I experienced a flush of remorse and guilt, wondering if there was more I could have done—should have done—had I known.

Had I only known.

Ms. Arthur

In the fifth grade, I met my second schoolboy crush. Ms. Leona Arthur taught our class to appreciate music and, inadvertently, to appreciate female beauty. She was a strikingly lovely, well-dressed, and cosmetically made-up young teacher with provocative bright red lipstick and very white, even teeth. She explained the classics and played black vinyl records on a portable player she carried from class to class. I could not take my eyes off her mouth as she explained then played excerpts from such classics as "The Unfinished Symphony," "Beethoven's Fifth," "Brahm's Lullaby," "The Nutcracker," and of course, the exciting overture to the "William Tell" opera.

I drank in the vision and the music.

We broke off school for summer vacation, and I dreamed about her while playing with friends and reading borrowed books from the East Utica Public Library, anxiously awaiting our first Music Appreciation class in the new school year.

She entered the classroom, set up her record player, turned to us, and with that beautiful, enchanting, red-lipped mouth, announced, "Boys and girls, my name is now Mrs. Mandeville." She smiled that painfully piercing smile, turned again, and as if to make it permanent, carefully wrote the name on the blackboard in stark white chalk. I was crushed. I felt betrayed. She had not waited for me. Years later, I learned that every other young boy in those classes felt the same way.

I soon found a new teacher who stole my complete attention and admiration for a totally different reason. Today I recall her as Mrs. Smith—short, rotund, and well-spoken. She taught us to appreciate poetry and classic literature. She read to us with patience, using proper inflections and timing so the complex wording suddenly made sense. Mrs. Smith explained the meaning of words and phrases in a way that made the poems come to life. To this day, I can hear her explaining the meaning of "ermine too dear for an Earl" and "sheds new-roofed with Carrara" from "The First Snowfall." She did the same with "In Flanders Field," "A Tree," and "The Children's Hour." She introduced us to Edgar Allen Poe and Shakespeare. Her impact on my understanding opened wide the doors of literature.

Time passed. We lived through frightening outbursts from our drafting and wood shop teachers when the boys got out of hand in basement classrooms. We learned gymnastics and basketball from Mr. Cook and the art of dribbling a soccer ball from a visiting Italian soccer player. We giggled to ourselves as tall thin wizened Ms. McVey, overwrought several times a day by her sixth- and seventh-grade classes, shouted, "Wait a minute. I don't have forty hands, you know!"

We froze our hands as we crouched in the snow, shooting marbles and losing to Johnny P., a blond, blue-eyed kid who played clarinet and was the marble king. We threw snowballs and played King of the Hill in the winter and walked warm summer days under chestnut trees on Jay Street, arguing over such important issues as whether or not our parents "did it" to "have us."

And so I traveled happily through the sixth, seventh, and eighth grades.

The Recital

As the eighth and last grade in Brandegee School drew to a close, our orchestra put on a final concert in the gymnasium/auditorium. After the concert and a small graduation ceremony, our orchestra teacher called a few of us aside. She gave each of us a special invitation to attend a stringed quartet concert at one of the upscale, uptown schools the following week. Just a few children from each of the city grade schools would be invited based on their outstanding accomplishment in music.

Our auditorium in Brandegee School consisted of the flat gymnasium floor with a small raised stage at one end. During concerts or assemblies, the audience sat on folding chairs. But the auditorium we visited for the stringed quartet recital had stadium seating, each row slightly higher than the one in front. At the foot was a slightly elevated orchestra stage. As the lights came up, we saw the stringed quartet—two violins, one viola, and one cello. The musicians were seated in a semicircle facing the audience. And there she was, beautiful Katherine, her long coiled tresses just as curly, eyes and lips just as enchanting as I remembered from first and second grade.

The music was exquisite, made even more enchanting by her beauty. I sat transfixed as she played a different instrument with each number. Were her talents unlimited? Was there nothing she could not do? My heart pounded.

After the last number, we were invited to come down and meet the players before the buses took us back to our respective schools. I made a beeline for the stage, arriving well ahead of all the other kids. Approaching Katherine, who was still seated, I excitedly recited the short speech I had composed in my head as I rushed down the aisle.

"Hi, Katherine. Remember me? We were in the first and second grades together at Brandegee!"

She smiled politely and rose to her feet. And rose... and rose... and rose... until I was staring directly at her breasts, which were level with my nose. Where had she gone? I looked upward, and there, a good foot above my head, was that lovely face. I was looking up into her nostrils. She had done it to me again. I was shocked and disappointed, just as I had been when I realized my drawing paper was ruined because I had imitated her big black X.

With aching neck, I made small talk for another minute and then beat a hasty retreat. I guess you could say that Katherine had outgrown me.

THE RETURN

Many years later, I visited the old hometown, rented a car, and retraced the route my mother and I had walked to kindergarten on that first day. I drove east on Bleecker Street, crossed Mohawk, continued one block, turned south on Hubbel, made a right turn on Jay Street, and there it was. The same two-story building that covered half a city block. Dark red bricks with light-colored cement trim around doors and windows still gave the structure an imposing, authoritative look. But the school yard was gone, replaced by a paved parking lot and a patch of weedy green grass. The windows were smaller and had curtains in them.

I looked at the large double doors at the main entrance, the same doors where Frankie the bully waited outside to pick on us. Above it was a new sign that read "Brandegee Garden Apartments."

The school—like all those teachers and little children who walked those halls for so many years—was gone.

3

Torrance Boulevard

When the Old Man looked up from his reverie, the last of the little children had crossed over to the sand. He resumed his ride. It remained fairly quiet until he approached Redondo Pier. Here, below the foot of Torrance Boulevard, the crowd increased dramatically. He weaved around couples walking hand in hand, kids riding skateboards, mothers jogging behind three wheeled strollers, girls walking dogs, and surfers carrying boards from their cars to the surf. Torrance Boulevard served as a funnel channeling people from the inner city and the nearby beach communities. It ends at a multistoried parking garage. Busy groups gathered here, where the sand snuggles against the pilings of this large, horseshoe-shaped pier. Families of all sizes carry down blankets and coolers. Others wander onto the pier to fish, stroll through the souvenir shops, or grab a meal at one of the restaurants or fast-food stands.

Signs warn bikers to walk their bikes in this area. He stopped, dismounted, and stood for a few minutes watching the crowd that was growing on the sand. His eyes drifted to two little boys, about five years old, off by themselves. They brandished plastic swords bearing the name of a popular dinner show in Orange County called *Medieval Times*. Imitating what they had seen at the show, they engaged in an awkward style of swordfighting consisting mostly of little cries of "Hah!" accompanied by the clack of plastic on plastic. One of them was just an inch taller and had chubby cheeks. The smaller, darker-skinned, wiry one moved faster, took wilder slashes, and made more noise. Both stopped, now and then, laughed, or argued over who was winning.

The Old Man wondered to himself:

Are they best friends? Best friends like Chickie and I were best friends? Best friends forever? Will they go to the same schools, share similar dreams?

It all passed so quickly. Will they take different paths in life as they grow up? And will they reminisce together about their youth when they are older?

Like we did? Back then, on Bleecker Street, all those years ago?

And he was back there, remembering the sights and sounds of mortal combat...

Best Friends Forever

The blades clanged and swirled in the air as the swordfight grew in intensity. The adversaries fiercely dodged and weaved around each other, slashing and lunging in deadly battle.

"Hah! Gotcha! You're dead!"

"No, ya' didn't!"

"I got your arm."

"That was just a flesh wound!"

We circled each other warily, holding our swords menacingly at our sides. It was a sultry summer day, and we had been playing war with these broken wooden slats, using them as rifles or swords as the spirit moved us. We were hot, tired, and thirsty.

"Let's get a drink," I said.

"Good idea," Chickie answered. We went to the rusty hose bib on the back wall of the building next door and took turns drinking out of our cupped, dirty hands. Anthony J. La Porte was my very best childhood friend. He was a chubby, cuddly baby and reminded his mother of a rotund, fluffy baby chick, so she gave him the nickname which he later despised but which stuck all the way through high school. She called him

Chickie. I did too. So did most of his close boyhood friends. Sometimes it was shortened to Chick.

Our families lived in apartments on the third floor of a building near the corner of Bleecker and Mohawk Streets. A short hallway separated us. We were born in those apartments—not in a hospital—just a few feet and eleven months apart.

Chick was smart. He got top grades in St. Mary of Mount Carmel, the local Catholic grade school. I was fascinated when he shared stories of the nuns, their strict discipline and expectation of high levels of performance. I attended the public grade school, but I lived the Catholic school experience through his stories.

He was a handsome, gentle, easy-going, likable person. Unobtrusive, he deferred to other people's wishes when we played games or invented adventures. He was taller than me and heavyset, fun to be around, and easy to enjoy. He had one peculiar idiosyncrasy. Every so often, as if to relieve some inner stress, he would take a deep breath and utter, "Oh, dear, bread and beer. If I were somewhere else, I wouldn't be here." It seemed to be a way of releasing something pent-up. It was something that only he understood.

We played together every chance we got. During most non-school days, we hung out together, usually in the alleys between buildings or in the fenceless backyards. We had pretend sword- or gun-fights, built club houses, formed clubs with our little friends, and held sand lot ball games. We shot and killed each other over and over again. During one war game, he hid behind a shed in the backyard of our apartment building. He popped out and shot at me with his stick—"pow!"—then ducked back. I lobbed a hand grenade, in the form of a small rock, in his general direction. It should have landed on the ground while I made a loud, explosive "pppkrrrr!" sound with my mouth. While the grenade was still airborne, he stuck his head out to take another shot and got nailed by my hand grenade. He was bleeding profusely but resisted going upstairs. He pressed his hand hard over the cut, but when the blood started to seep through the spaces between his fingers, run down his arm, and drip from his elbow, he gave in and went up those stairs. He returned later to resume the battle with a bandage on his head.

We made scooters out of old boards, orange crates, and broken skates. Our headlights were tin can tops or bottle caps nailed on the front. We played with yo-yos and glass marbles. He was a superb marble player, less adept at ball games because of his extra weight. We didn't own cap guns. When we could get caps, we scrounged in the basements and cellars and tool boxes of our families to find a large metal nut and two matching bolts. Then we removed all the extra paper around the small powder charges, stuffed one or two into the nut, and screwed one bolt into each end of the nut. We hand-tightened them against each other until the pressure on the powder charge was as much as we dared. If the bolts were not screwed tightly enough, it did not explode upon impact; too tight and the mini-bomb exploded in your hand. We tied the bolts together with string to avoid losing them and tossed the contraption high into the air. If it was done right, there would be a terrific explosion when it hit the concrete sidewalk.

Around the Fourth of July, firecrackers appeared, and the older kids lit them off. Sometimes half a stick would remain unburned, and after the older kids left, we retrieved it, trimmed it to reveal a stub of fuse, and stuffed it into a crack between the bricks of our building with the short fuse exposed. It was tricky to get it lit and duck out of the way quickly. To do so successfully and boldly was a rite of passage.

We did not return indoors voluntarily. If and when nature called, we found someplace outdoors to go or held it until our eyes watered and we shivered with agony because, once inside, our moms often said we had played long enough and made us stay home. But as long as we remained outside, we were free until called. When they wanted us to come home, they raised a third-floor window sash and yelled our names. And we'd better answer by the third yell. We entered the rear door together and ran up the three flights of stairs. Once on the third floor landing, we parted, going into the opposing apartment doors. Before closing his door, he'd say, "Oh, dear, bread and beer. If I were somewhere else, I wouldn't be here."

Attached to the rear of the three-storied brick building next door stood a dirt-floored, wooden shed with a sloping roof, boarded-up windows, and two doors. One door opened to the outside and was always locked from the inside. The other opened into the rear hallway of the brick building. This inside door was always unlocked. The older boys told us that the shed used to be the original location of a gelato store, a place that made and sold Italian lemon ice through the now boarded-up windows. Now it served as a storage shed. Old Mr. Bosco lived on the second floor with his son's family. He wandered the streets collecting paper and metal from other people's trash barrels. This he stored inside the shed and eventually took it to be sold at a scrap collection center.

On one rainy day, Chick and I stood restlessly under the overhanging wooden roof of the shed. We saw Mr. Bosco leave carrying an umbrella and pulling his little wagon. He was going trash hunting. After much discussion, we entered the rear hallway of the brick building, opened the unlocked rear door of the shed, and rummaged through old Mr. Bosco's collection. We found little of interest and were about to leave when it happened: we struck gold.

Buried beneath a pile of old newspapers, we came across a stack of magazines entitled *Sunshine and Health*. We opened one. And there, smiling at us, was a young family—husband, wife, and two children—totally nude. It was a monthly nudist colony publication. Total nudity, even in black and white, was a treasure find for two young boys. There was page after page after page of happy, sunburned, healthy-looking naked people. After that day, we sneaked in periodically in search of new issues. Mr. Bosco did not part with the older ones. They never got to the recycle center. Our hidden treasure of prurient material grew. Chick and I did not share this find with our numerous friends. It rivaled, in intrigue and value, Chick's comic book collection.

Chick's father had the best job on the block, and it made Chick the luckiest and most revered kid in the neighborhood. His father worked for Wolf News Service. He loaded trucks with newspapers, magazines, and comic books for delivery to the local outlets. Every month, he brought home one of every issue of the latest comic books. Chick had boxes full of them, new and shiny, in his bedroom. When he tired of reading them, he gave them away. For the rest of us poor guys who could not dream of affording to buy comic books, Chick's handouts were a treasure.

Being his best friend and next-door neighbor, I was often the first recipient of the latest comic books as he tired of them. This gave me a measure of power and influence with the rest of the gang.

We regarded Chick as an authority on the facts surrounding the then ongoing World War II. He told us how the Nazis stabbed babies and how the Japanese would die before surrendering but were lousy shots, and we believed him because he had all these literary sources. When Chick lauded the technical prowess of the Germans and how well they built tanks or submarines or airplanes, we listened. He should know. He had all the latest propaganda. If Superman or Captain Marvel said so, it must be true. Boy, did we envy him. When we went home to our families, he went home to his comic books.

Chickie's dad worked the swing shift from late afternoon to midnight and slept late in the morning. His work hours did not allow for much father-son time. How this played out in Chickie's life, I will never know. But I suspect that it robbed him of some of the self-confidence that this intelligent young boy, soon to be a "man," needed to move forward confidently in life.

We attended the same high school together. It was the newest school in town, large with a beautiful campus. Each morning, we met in front of our alley and walked to the corner where we waited for Sammy to come walking up Mohawk Street. We walked to school together, ate lunch together, and walked home together, parting from Sammy at the same corner.

Sometimes Hank Maggio, our shortest buddy, joined us. One Friday afternoon, we lingered on our corner longer than usual because Hank didn't want to go home. A girl with a loose reputation had told his mother she was "in the family way" and that it was Hank's baby. Hank denied that he ever touched her. He denied even knowing her very well. We believed him because, for sure, he would have boasted about it long before this. But she was in trouble, and she liked him. Hank feared that when his father learned of the girl's claim, he would, no doubt, kill Hank. We lingered as long as we could, trying to give him some form of moral support, then watched as he walked, with hesitant steps, down the street and turned the corner with one last look back and a small wave. Would we see him alive again?

On Monday morning, Chick and I waited on the corner for Sammy and were delighted to see Hank skipping up the street with him. As it turned out, the troubled girl wasn't pregnant after all. She withdrew her accusation. His father didn't have to kill him.

During our senior year, we talked about what we would do after graduation. As the time drew closer, I became aware of an opportunity to compete for what amounted to a scholarship to an engineering school. With Chick's brains, I felt sure he could pass the exams and go with me. His grades were consistently better than mine. He was a much better student than I was.

We agreed to take the entrance exams together. We speculated on how good life would be—how we would build marvelous things as engineers, maybe leave Utica forever, and become famous. We talked about it with the counselors and with his mother. Everything appeared in order. But on the day before the test, he changed his mind. I tried desperately to convince him to go with me to the exams. No amount of cajoling could convince him. He seemed to lack confidence. "Why?" I asked. "Oh, nothing," he replied, then he added, with a grin, "Oh, dear, bread and beer. If I were somewhere else, I wouldn't be here." Something had happened that last night before the entrance exams. Try as I might, I never found out what transpired behind the door of that little rear apartment to change his mind.

I went off to college. Chick remained behind and was drafted into the US Army as the Korean War exploded. We did not see each other for four years. When Chick was discharged, I again tried to arrange for him to apply for the same scholarship. Chick waffled and declined. He got a job at United Parcel Service and later with an air conditioning firm.

We lost touch for a few more years. After college, I spent two years on active military duty. Upon discharge, my civilian employer transferred me to Los Angeles.

One day, during one of my trips to Utica, I met Chickie at Union Railroad Station where he worked as a baggage handler. He insisted I call him Tony now. That night we went out for a beer. He was married and had a child. We walked the route we did as kids—over Bleecker Street to Third Avenue up to Mary Street back to Mohawk Street and down to Bleecker Street again. We joked and exchanged stories of our experiences during those years during which we had been away from each other. We walked in military march step, Tony calling out the cadence, fooling around, laughing. We were delighted to find we both knew the same commands and responses. We marched sharply, crisply executing, side by side, each command he gave until he called, "By the left flank... Hoo!" I executed a sharp left turn on "Hoo" as we had been taught. But he kept marching and completed the sentence by shouting "...told you to move?" It was an old basic training trick some drill sergeants used to annoy the troops. We both stopped and laughed. He smiled and added, "Oh, dear, bread and beer. If I were somewhere else, I wouldn't be here."

A few years later, I again visited Utica. I phoned Tony. He was working as a security guard at a local warehouse and storage facility. He was divorced and lived with his widowed mother. He spoke about his son. We went to a few bars and consumed a few beers. I could not keep up with his rapier wit or his rate of consumption. As the evening wore on, it became evident that he was going through a difficult time because of his divorce. He seemed to become more somber, drank more heavily, and was in a hurry to make everything numb. One moment he was humorous and philosophical, a moment later he became condemning, critical, and cynical. He talked of political conspiracies and dangerous threats, whispering to me and pointing to strangers across the room that he seemed to know something menacing about.

I ordered a pizza at one saloon and offered pieces to others who sat at nearby barstools. A woman sauntered up, smiled, and reached across in front of Tony for a slice. Tony rebuked her angrily, frightening both of us. She scuttled away.

We decided we had enough to drink. We went for a long walk, slowly this time, remembering our childhood and our old school chums. He mellowed, became gentle, melancholy, and sentimental. The night was clear and warm. Stars shone overhead with a half moon lighting the dark streets. It was the same sky he and I had sauntered under a hundred times as kids. We spoke of long past friends and events. We laughed, remembering the time Hank— he loved cops-and-robbers movies—told us that when it was time for him to die, he wanted to be shot with a machine gun while standing at the edge of a cliff so he could slowly and dramatically collapse over the edge, admired and mourned by all. We reminisced about Sammy and how embarrassed he was when, one day, we insisted on having him describe how his father's pigeons mated. Sammy blushed as he answered our questions, just as he did if a girl flirted with him, which they sometimes did.

We walked the same streets we used to walk on those many warm, summer nights and those crisply cold, snow-blanketed winter days so many years ago when we were children, when life lay long and promising ahead of us. We were childhood buddies again. We recaptured, for a little while, that close, relaxed, intimate feeling little kids have with their "best friend." I felt again the wonder we had about the future and remembered the hopes and beliefs we shared that the world would someday be ours.

I drove him home about 3:00 am. We said good-bye on the front porch of his mother's home on Mary Street. His speech was thoughtful, and he was apologetic for his earlier mood. We shook hands and promised to write each other. This time, we swore we would not lose track of one another.

"Take care, Tony," I said. He smiled and answered, "Oh, dear, bread and beer. If I were somewhere else, I wouldn't be here." Then he ducked inside.

I wrote once. He didn't answer. I learned from my mother that his mother had died and he had moved. Mom didn't know where he lived.

I wondered for many years where he was and if he still lived alone. Was he happy? How large was his family now? I searched the Internet and tried several search engines to no avail. I found several La Porte families in the Utica area and wrote letters to them but received no replies. I hoped to someday go back there and try to find him.

Recently I was contacted by an old high school friend I had not heard from in sixty years. She sent me a copy of an obituary dated July 2011. Anthony J. La Porte had passed away with his family by his side.

My relatives and friends are almost all gone from Utica—moved on or passed away. I don't really have a compelling reason to go there now. Still, from time to time, I sense the pull of my "very best friend" and yearn to feel those feelings and hear those voices and dream those dreams one more time.

Just one more time.

5

Redondo Pier

The two little boys the Old Man had been watching stopped their battle as if struck by lightning and turned swiftly at the sound of a mother's call. "Who wants ice cream?" He watched as they rushed up the sandbank to the vendor whose ice cream cart sat at the confluence of the pier and the sand. His thoughts returned to his own purpose, which was to ride as far as Marina Del Rey and back today.

He pushed his bike down the slight incline to the pier, made a short left turn, and faced Charlie's Place. Charlie was of Asian extraction and had owned this fast-food place for almost thirty years. He wasn't there today, but his employees were busily cooking deep fried seafood and pouring beer for customers. This was a favorite stopping place for the Old Man. He bought a diet soda, sat at one of the outside tables, and nursed it while watching and listening to the customers.

The Redondo Pier was first built as a group of disjointed wharves in the late 1890s. It was rebuilt a number of times following severe storm damage, each time acquiring new features, new names, and more shops. In 1988, it burned to the waterline and was rebuilt one last time in 1993 with steel reinforced, concrete pilings in an artistic horseshoe-shape sometimes dubbed the "Endless Pier."

The movie and television industries liked to shoot scenes in and around the pier. He recalled one day, a few years ago, when he had ridden onto the pier and stopped to watch a scene being set up against the rear patio of Charlie's Place. That section of the pier had been converted to a faux outdoor cocktail lounge complete with tables, chairs, linen, waitresses, and customers. Potted plastic palm trees and silk flower bushes completed the tableau beneath a sign, screwed to the back of Charlie's Place that said "Coconut Lounge." He watched as lights and reflectors were adjusted, cameras ran while couples sat down and the waitress brought them drinks, over and over, until the director was satisfied. Once that was over, the actors sat or stood around, chatting. One of the actors, dressed neatly in suit and tie, leaned lazily against the pier railing just next to the Old Man, his arms folded. He caught the actor's eye and asked, "Are you going to shoot any more today?"

"Oh, sure," the talent said, "but we're waiting for the tide to come all the way in. I've gotta' dive off the pier in the next scene, and we want to be sure the water is plenty deep."

That was some time ago, but today there was little going on, except for the regulars. Charlie's customers were mostly tourists, but his main revenue came from selling beer to a dozen regulars. On some days, only two or three regulars showed up at any one time, but on weekends they'd fill three or four tables. They didn't seem to have jobs, arriving at odd hours and leaving the same way.

One of the regulars was a muscular guy who wore sleeveless T-shirts that showed plenty of flesh and a few tattoos. His long hair hung out from under a slightly greasy baseball cap.

"That's a neat bike. Is it new?"

"No," he answered. "I've had it about three years now."

"Name's Frank," the regular said, extending a calloused hand.

"Good t'metcha," he said. "Your friends are late today, huh?"

"Yeah. They roll in whenever they feel like. Ought to be here soon, though. I'm su'prised Sarge ain't here."

"Which one's he?"

"He's the tall, quiet guy. Broad shoulders, big square jaw, always parks his bike against the beer counter over there. Sarge's usually the first to get here."

"Sarge? Is he in the military?"

"He was once. He wasn't no sergeant, though. He was a corporal in the Marines durin' the Vietnam War. When his hitch was up, they wouldn't let 'em reenlist. They gave 'em a medical discharge. Some kinda mental thing. Shell-shocked or somethin'. I figure he fried his brains on drugs over there in 'Nam. Anyways, he likes to say he coulda become a sergeant if they hadn't screwed him with that medical discharge. He says that all the time. The more beer he drinks, the madder he gets about it. We started callin' him "Sarge" just for fun, and it stuck."

The Old Man thought for a moment. "Funny, how people get stuck with nicknames, isn't it? I used to be called The General once, a long time ago. The Little General. But it didn't stick for very long."

"Was you in the army?"

"Not when they called me The Little General. I was just a kid."

He grew silent. *It was a very long time ago,* he thought.

The shoe store. Those wonderful people who worked there.

And all my little friends.

The Little General. That's what they called me.

They all did, for a while.

My gang of little friends... the people on Bleecker Street... The Little General.

And they saluted when they said it.

Well, some of them did.

6

The Little General

I was ten years old when I asked Mr. Flemma for a job, my first job. The Flemma Shoe Store was on the ground floor of the building we lived in. He humored me by agreeing to pay me $2 a week for doing odd jobs in the store. For two bucks a week, I hung out in the store, swept the floors, vacuumed the carpets, took out the trash, dusted shoe boxes, and shifted stock. Mostly I hung around. It was a loose arrangement. I made my own hours after school and on weekends.

We got paid on Saturday night, just before closing. The employees stood in line at the cash register as Mr. Flemma checked their sales receipts, toted up their base pay plus commissions, and doled out cash from the register. As the last adult employee took his pay and stepped aside, Mr. Flemma looked down to see me still standing there looking up at him. He opened the cash drawer again and ceremoniously picked out two $1 bills. I thanked him, folded them neatly in half, and shoved them deep down into the pockets of my short pants.

On the wall of the shoe store, facing the lined up chairs, hung a large sign located high above a full-length mirror. You had to raise your head up to see it. I read it countless times as I stood around waiting for something to do. It was a poem called "Cooperation" by J. Mason Knox that ended with:

> It ain't the individuals
> Nor the Army as a whole,
> But the everlasting Teamwork
> Of every bloomin' Soul.

On another wall close to his desk hung a horse whip, short and thick with a wrist loop at one end and several long, thin leather strips on the other end. When asked why it was there, he told the story of a certain Florsheim shoe wholesaler. The man with a silky tongue had cheated him out of a great deal of money. "One day, he will come here again, and when he does I want that horse whip to be close by."

The cash register receipts carried the original name of the store on them—The Beacon Boot Shop—with a drawing of a lighthouse and a beam of light shining out. Across the bottom read the admonition, "If you buy from someone else, we both lose."

Now and then I dragged the long, cylindrical Electrolux vacuum cleaner out from the back room and slid it around the store to vacuum the carpets. On warm summer days, I helped the older employees wash the front windows. The task was unbearable in the dead of winter, and I left it to the adults.

World War II was raging, and most males of eligible age were in the military. Those who remained behind had a physical handicap or were, as a song popular at the time said, "either too young or too old."

The shoe store had four employees other than me: Leonard, Gloria, Bunny, and Nick. Leonard was their most senior and their star salesman. He had already served in the US Air Force as the pilot of an F-5, better known as the P-38 fighter aircraft that had been retrofitted to fly photo reconnaissance missions over Germany. On his last mission, the plane received damage from enemy anti-aircraft fire. Due to that damage, or perhaps to a notoriously troublesome turbo-supercharged engine, it burst into flame as it landed back at its home base in England. The F-5/P-38 sat high on a tricycle landing gear. To climb down from the cockpit, Leonard had to crawl out onto the wing, open a small hatch, and lift a handle that lowered a narrow triangular ladder. The flames roared dangerously close. Fearing an explosion, Leonard scrambled past the hatchway and jumped from the high wing. He broke his ankle and was left with a permanent limp that earned him a medal and an honorable discharge.

Then there was lovely Gloria, ten years my senior, whose boyfriend was in the army serving somewhere in Europe. She could not stand the feel of peach fuzz which, of course, motivated me to sneak up on her from behind and stroke her cheek gently with a large peach. She smiled, thinking this little boy was being affectionate, and inclined her head slightly. She turned slowly against the peach, caught a glimpse of it, and let out a wide-eyed scream. Gloria avoided letting me get behind her after that.

Bunny Cameo had movie star looks, with a small, black, beauty mark on his cheek that women found irresistible and a beautiful wife who lit up the store when she came to visit him at work. He wore dark, horn-rimmed glasses, loved opera, and could be heard humming or softly whistling arias as he worked. His thick eyeglasses kept him out of the service.

Nick Amato, seventeen years old, was still too young to be drafted. He sold a lot of shoes by being creative and a bit daring in his sales technique.

The store had a number of tools in the back room that looked like instruments of medieval torture. Using these, we could stretch a shoe almost a full size or change its shape to fit your bunion or otherwise accommodate your abnormally shaped feet. If the customer needed a shoe size slightly smaller than the one we had in stock, we resorted to the insole. These thin, leather, sole-shaped strips were inserted to lie flat in the bottom of the shoe. Hence, a slightly oversized shoe could be made to fit more snugly.

If a particular shoe model was in stock too long, the letters PM were stamped on the box. This indicated a hefty 50¢ commission for the salesperson who sold it. We called them Peter Murphy's, and all our salespeople were highly motivated to sell them for the extra pay.

I recall one very old woman who desperately wanted a particular style which we did not have in her tiny foot size. That model was outdated and had been discontinued. The one pair we had was too large for her foot. But it was a Peter Murphy. Nick Amato inserted a pair of innersoles, brought it out, and put it on her foot. It was still too large. He encouraged her to walk in it. She insisted it was too loose. Nick took it to the back room, returned, and said, "Try this one." She did; too large. This procedure was repeated several times. Each time he returned, shoe in hand. and said, "Try this one." Finally she came back down the carpet smiling, satisfied that he had found her size.

At the cash register, as Nick was ringing up the sale, the little old gal could be heard muttering softly, "What is this? And what is this? And this? And this?" With each question, she was removing an insole. Altogether she removed seven insoles from each shoe. Nick lost the sale and the 50¢ commission. But he would do it again if given the chance.

On weekends, I was often outside playing with my friends rather than working in the store. The $2 seemed like a lot of money at first, but since I never bought anything with it, its power of appeal began to fade. I spent more time outside, playing, and less time inside the store, working. Mr. Flemma would see me as he came and went. He didn't seem to mind. One day, he remarked that I had many friends and that I seemed to be in charge of the games we played. That was true enough. For some unexplained reason, I was usually the one who organized and directed whatever it was that we were doing. There were about fifteen of us—sometimes more, sometimes less. We hung out together and played games. We played tag, dodge ball, tin can hockey, hide-and-go-seek, mumblety-peg with a knife—when somebody had one—marbles, touch football, and baseball. We played handball against the outside walls of stores and warehouses until someone came out and chased us away. I wonder if I can remember a few of them. Let's see...

Chickie was the kid next door and my constant companion.

Sammy, smart and studious, lived two blocks away and joined us when he could.

Nick, handsome, with perfect teeth, a dimpled smile, and a small chicken pox scar on his cheek.

Johnny P excelled at marbles, dodge ball, and playing the clarinet.

Hank M, the tough little guy you could depend on.

John B played the trombone, a manly instrument that befitted his tall, muscular looks.

Tony Z loved to play basketball and sneaked into the St. Mary of Mount Carmel gym to watch the boys' basketball games. He joined their school team when he got old enough.

Salvatore was the proud son of an AF of L/CIO Union official. He was a stickler for following the rules. He was the only kid in school who knew what AF of L and CIO stood for.

Mike and Jerry T were two brothers, attached at the hip, never apart. That worked out well because big Mike could protect little Jerry whose childish charm attracted the girls and angered their boyfriends.

Big Freddie and Tito D was another pair of brothers who squabbled a lot. They got along with everybody but each other. Big Freddie had a congenital condition called syndactyly. The middle two fingers on each hand were webbed together. He appeared to be proud of this abnormality because he gestured elaborately with either hand when he spoke. A few years later, when he had stopped growing, they were cut apart. He didn't gesture as much after that. Tito, his much smaller brother, resorted to whining to their parents when they quarreled, which usually resulted in Big Freddie being punished. One memorable day, the three of us—Freddie, Tito, and I—were standing out on the third-floor balcony of their apartment shortly after they had clashed over something. Freddie shoved Tito. Tito complained to his mother. She interceded. Freddie was grounded. She left to do some shopping. We watched, looking down from the third-floor balcony, as she walked away and disappeared around the corner, at which time Freddie unbuttoned his short pants and proceeded to pee on little Tito. Tito was cornered between the balcony railing and the wall and could only scrunch down on the floor, arms wrapped around his head, knees pulled up to his arms, crying and repeating, "I'm gonna tell Ma! I'm gonna tell Ma!" Freddie giggled insanely as he played the stream around so as to leave no dry spots on Tito. I left before their Mom got home.

I had just recently convinced the gang that we should form a club and give it a name. We agreed to meet every Saturday morning at nine o'clock in the empty lot behind Gaziano's Furniture Store on Mohawk Street. We made plans and organized games and adventures. One by one, all of the guys asked to join the club, even some who lived many blocks away. After a proper interview of some sort and a swearing in ceremony, they were accepted.

Flemma got wind of it and was intrigued. He gave me a lecture on organization theory and helped me to compose a name and a motto for the club. I asked him if I could have the bright yellow empty boxes that Dr. Scholl's arch supports came in. When I accumulated a couple dozen of them, I tediously hand-printed our club name and motto on the inside of each cover. I punched holes in the ends and laced shoulder straps through them using wrapping string from the shoe store. These boxes, I explained to the club members, were our official shoulder packs and were to be used only by members in good standing. In them we carried essentials, like sandwiches or candy or pencils or stones or whatever else would fit.

Before long, we had grown into a band of some twenty kids complete with titles of rank. We all had older relatives who were in the army or navy, and we had learned something about military protocol. We adopted what we had learned into our club structure.

I appointed myself the General. Chickie was my Major. I made Nick a Captain. Hank became a Lieutenant. Mike and Jerry, Big Freddie and Tito were Corporals. All of the others were designated Private until they had attended two meetings, after which they were promoted to Private First Class. I printed their names and ranks on the outside of their yellow Dr. Scholl's arch support boxes.

If someone did something I deemed outstanding, I would promote him. Conversely, I demoted some of them a few times. Promotions and demotions were made by an announcement at our Saturday morning formation. The deserving soldier was called forward. With eraser and pencil, I changed the designation on his Dr. Scholl's arch support box and sent him back to stand in formation.

It was all very formal and organized for the first few minutes of each meeting as they lined up before me at 9:00 am in that empty lot—Major Chickie in front, Captain Nick and Lieutenant Hank behind him, Corporals Mike, Jerry, Freddie, and Tito lined up in front of their platoons of Private First Class soldiers. After roll call, promotions, demotions, and announcements, we might march around for a while, shouting orders and issuing commands. When we tired of it, I called a halt and said something like, "Company dismissed!" Major Chickie and Captain Hank repeated that to the Corporals who repeated it to the troops. Everyone laughed and chattered and we started playing a game of dodge ball or whatever struck our fancy at the time.

I was surprised the first time I heard an adult in the shoe store refer to me as The Little General. It caught on and spread up and down the block. For some time thereafter, it remained my unofficial handle on the block. I liked it and enjoyed my newfound celebrity. "Here comes the Little General," one of the store proprietors or an employee would say as I walked by, and they would throw me a salute. At first I grinned shyly, but eventually I began returning the salute, which seemed to amuse them.

Slowly, over time, the club dissipated, the yellow boxes disappeared, and we returned to being little kids again.

Recently I came across an advertisement for Dr. Scholl's arch supports. They are now sold in sealed plastic bubbles attached to a black-and-blue hanging card on a rack at the local drugstores. A yellow swish streaks across the face of the card, reminiscent of the old, yellow, rectangular cardboard boxes. As I stared at the rack, sounds and images coalesced like fairy dust. Once again I could hear the distant trumpets of a huge army, the marching tramp of a thousand boots, and the snap of flags smartly fluttering in the wind—all those imaginary trappings of childhood glory that took place in the empty lot behind the Graziano building on Mohawk Street.

7

Charlie's Place

H is daydream was broken when Frank muttered something about Charlie's Place beginning to fill up fast. The stone tables on the rear patio faced the beach in one direction and the pier on the other. Directly across from the patio was a larger fast-food stand, Beach Cuisine. Its patio area was larger than Charlie's. Theirs had several signs warning that their tables were to be used by customers only. Charlie's Place, by default, was deemed to be friendlier because it lacked such signs.

To the left of Beach Cuisine was a two-story building with a night club downstairs and a bar upstairs that boasted ocean view windows. Stuffed between the night club and Beach Cuisine was a single, large glass window. Through the glass, a dozen little girls in brightly colored ballerina outfits were visible, bobbing around in no particular sense of order. The dance class was yet to start.

Frank pointed a snag-nailed finger at the window and asked, "Cute, ain't they? Seems like everybody's little girl takes dance classes anymore."

"Yeah. Dance classes for the girls, Karate classes for the boys."

"Well, I ain't ever met one that become a real dancer when they was grown, or a kid that become a Mixed Martial Arts champ, either."

As the Old Man was about to answer, Frank started waving hello to someone behind him and mumbled, "Well, look who's here, ole Sarge hisself,"

Big Sarge pulled up on his bike, swung off the seat, and leaned it against the beer order counter. He grinned back at Frank, held up two fingers for the beer guy to see, and came over to the table.

"Been here long?" he asked as he shook Frank's hand and nodded to the Old Man.

"'Bout a hour. We been watching the little Japanese kids going to their ballerina class over there." He gestured across the way. "I was just saying I doubt any one of 'em ever becomes a real dancer."

Sarge rubbed his whiskers with a hand whose gloves were missing fingertips. "Yeah," he said. "Guess they get interested in boys an' stuff an' lose interest. Ain't no money in it anyways."

"Oh, I don't know," said the Old Man. "I met one gal once who started dance lessons when she was quite small and went on to make it really big. She made a lot of money too."

"Anybody I'd of heard of?"

"I wouldn't be surprised if you did." The old guy smiled, drifting off into that treasure of memories that seemed to come back to him more often with every passing day.

I'll never forget the day I met her.
She was about four years old.
I was barely fourteen.
She probably doesn't remember me at all.
No, I guess she wouldn't... not after all these years.

The Little Ballerina

On Sunday mornings, as always, my parents and I walked to our church. It was located on a triangular lot about three blocks from our home. At the opposite corner was an Italian grocery store which we often visited after the church service. It was redolent with cheeses, spicy salamis, and those giant prosciuttos tightly bound in netting that hung from ceiling hooks. Two large brine barrels held black and green olives. Scores of exotic olive oils, wines, and Italian sauces nestled between shelves of pastas. Hot loaves of freshly baked bread beckoned from white bags stacked on a table next to the cash register.

I loved the smells and sights and relished the time we spent there while Mom picked and chose what she wanted to buy. I especially looked forward to the possibility that Carmen, the owner's dark-haired, olive-eyed teenage daughter, might be in the store. Running into her after church was the icing on church cake.

After our brief shopping stop, we proceeded home where Mom's spaghetti sauce was perking on the stove over a very low flame, awaiting another sumptuous Sunday afternoon meal.

On these walks home, we sometimes varied the route. Occasionally we wandered over to Milgate Street to visit Aunt

Mary before going home. If neighbors were sitting on their front porches along the way, we exchanged greetings.

One day—it had to be the summer of 1946 or so—a friendly couple sitting on their porch struck up a conversation with my parents. They introduced themselves as Virginia and Joseph and chatted for some time. As we took leave, they suggested we come by for coffee and a longer visit. They made a plan.

On the appointed day, we walked to their lovely home. They were waiting on their pillared veranda, greeted us warmly, and invited us in.

The adults completed their greetings, and after the usual salutations, we were led into the formal dining room. A lace covered table was set with coffee cups and an assortment of Italian biscotti. As we entered the room, Veronica called out for her daughter. "*Vieni qui, bellina*," she said. "Come here, little pretty one." In walked a very cute four-year-old, with dark eyes and dark flowing tresses held in place with a ribbon. She wore a soft, flared summer skirt and a white, buttoned blouse with fluffed short sleeves. Shyly she entered the room and walked to her mother. She smiled and greeted the adults as introductions were made all around. Her parents were clearly proud of her.

After a bit, the adults became lost in their own conversations. The little girl asked to be excused. She invited me to see her room and the rest of the house. All I recall is that her bedroom was well appointed in bright colors and girlish decor. I was impressed with her mature manners. She and I spent the rest of the visit making small talk while she showed me odds and ends that meant something to her.

We visited for about an hour, not longer. Virginia apologized for cutting our visit short but explained that her daughter must get ready for a dance lesson. She excused the girl to go into her room and change into her dance clothes.

Her parents walked us to the veranda. The usual last-minute chatter took place there. Everyone was smiling, laughing, saying "*Ciao*" and "*Arrivederci*" and "*Grazie*" and "*Ci vederemo ancora*." Italian, of course, for "so long, good-bye, see you soon, thank you, come again." Shortly, their pretty ballerina appeared in the doorway and announced she was ready. As my folks and I walked down the sidewalk, I turned and waved good-bye to her. She smiled and waved back.

I cannot recall details of subsequent visits. Eventually my parents stopped requiring that I accompany them. I think we would have been good friends if we had grown to know each other.

But I never saw the little dancer up close again.

Nine years later, around 1955, she magically appeared, not in person but on national television, in flickering black and white. I recognized her name before I recognized her. I stared openmouthed as she performed.

The show was on weekly for four years and popularized this talented young girl. As the years passed, she gained fame. She moved on to movies that epitomized young America, the beach scene, and what we all believed was how young boys and girls lived and loved in the California sunshine.

Way back in 1946, when I met her, I could not have imagined that she was destined to have a colorful playmate. One who was and is still known the world over. One with whom she became associated in the minds of millions of people.

No, I don't think she ever remembered me at all. But I always thought that maybe, someday, a faint recollection of a pleasant afternoon in Utica would come back to her, complete with the sound of Italian voices, the smell of hot, strong *café nero*, and the taste of fresh biscotti with anise seeds.

A few weeks ago, I read that she had passed away at the age of seventy after struggling with multiple sclerosis for many years. My heart ached as I recalled how pretty and charismatic she looked on that first black and white television show.

She wore a turtleneck sweater with "Annette" emblazoned across it, a pleated skirt, bobby sox, saddle shoes, and a funny black hat with oversized mouse ears on it. She sang and danced. At the end of the show, she and her friends sang, "M-I-C... see you real soon! K-E-Y... why? Because we love you! M-O-U-S-E."

Annette Funicello would never know that one day, many years ago, before she met Walt Disney and Mickey Mouse, she met a young boy whose parents thought she might grow up to be an excellent prospect for their unsuspecting son.

9

Pauly's on the Pier

The Old Man's thoughts returned to the present. He left the guys at Charlie's Place and wandered back to the bike path. He rode it through the parking structure and came out into the sunlight at the north end just above the weathered, odoriferous row of fish restaurants, shops, and bars along International Walkway.

He made several momentary stops above the walkway, looking down now and then on the tourists and inner city locals who swarmed below buying souvenirs and eating hot, fresh seafood with copious quantities of cold beer. Some bought tickets for the glass-bottomed boat tour. Others rented two- and four-place plastic pedal boats, irrationally paying good money to pedal around the small inner harbor, seeing things they could see on foot for free.

He rode the bike around Delzano's Restaurant and sped dizzily down the steep ramp leading to the lower level where fishermen operated one of two hoists to launch their boats. He pedaled along a tall concrete splash wall that had been built after the 1984 and 1988 winter storms had wiped out two restaurants and the entire bottom floor of the Porto Fino Hotel.

Ahead he saw the ancient wooden pier from which the Pride of Redondo fishing boat departed twice daily. Directly before him rose the faded sign above Pauly's on the Pier Restaurant and Coffee Shop. He sometimes came here for an early breakfast of eggs and sausage, sitting at one of the outside tables. From each table umbrella hung a plastic encased sign that said "Do Not Feed Birds." The first time he ate breakfast at Pauly's, he paid little heed to the warning and was astounded when a seagull swooped down and snatched his paper cup full of butter and ate it, paper cup and all, from the safety of the greasy wooden guard rail six feet away. Nancy, his waitress, laughed at him and brought him another butter cup.

Nancy had worked at Pauly's for years and moved with a dexterity and good humor that seemed to belie her age. Wrinkled and deeply tanned from years of outdoor exposure to sea and sun, she smiled a toothy smile, with one gold tooth and slight discoloration from years of cigarette breaks. She wore a head scarf wrapped about her gray hair and tied neatly behind her head. He looked for her now and spotted her clearing off a table. She reminded him of his aunt Mary, back home. Way back home.

I haven't thought about Zia Maria in a long time. She never saw California. She came from Italy—Andali, Calabria, to be exact—to upstate New York. That was her life. Now she is gone. How long has she been gone now? At least a couple dozen years. I wonder what she would think about her little great nephew, now in his eighth decade, riding a bike along the California coastline.

She would say, "'Ow is you father, Nicky? 'E is okay? You say 'ello per me. Va piano con la bicicletta. Non cadere."

Go easy with your bicycle. Don't fall.

10

Aunt Mary

We called her Zia Maria, or more commonly, Zi' Mari', referring to our aunt Mary.

As nearly as we can figure, Zi' Mari' was ninety-eight years and eight months old when she died. She was really my father's aunt which, I guess, made her my great aunt. During her teen years, she helped to raise my father through childhood in Southern Italy—a rugged, agricultural place of immense poverty. During the late 1800s and early 1900s, some fourteen million Italians fled the hunger of Southern Italy for the shores of the United States. Zia's family was among them.

After immigrating to the United States, she and her husband, my great-uncle Pete, bought a house on Milgate Street and proceeded to generate a family of four boys and one girl.

Her new home was a chunk of Southern Italy nestled in upstate New York. The house had votive candles on the mantle, crucifixes on the walls, and air continuously perfumed by canning, cooking, and baking. A large backyard boasted apple and pear trees, grapevines—one white, one purple—and many rows of vegetables. They made their own red and white wine in the cellar. One especially potent variety was "dandelion wine" made from fermented dandelion leaves. They purchased pork and casings and made sausage each fall season. Some of it was hung in the cold cellar during the winter to dry out and harden then was bottled in extra virgin olive oil. She mixed flour and yeast and baked fresh bread every few days.

In the early years, the men worked in the local cotton mills. On weekends, they often hunted in the nearby hills and fields and brought home rabbit, woodchuck, squirrel, pheasant, and venison. They picked mushrooms in the woods and fished the local rivers and lakes. I tasted all of their catches at one time or another and remembered an older cousin cautioning me, "Chew that squirrel slow 'cause if Ma missed a BB you could break a tooth!"

The youngest cousin raised guinea pigs in a shed he built in a corner of the garden. It was multistoried inside, with ramps and tunnels for the critters to scamper around. An opening in one wall connected to an elevated tunnel that allowed them to leave the inside of the shed, climb down a ramp, and wander around a screened, outdoor enclosure. There was always something new to capture an inquisitive child's imagination.

Zia always had a full larder. Her cellar held rows of shelves full of goodies that made the long New York State winters cheerful and filling.

During the early autumn harvesting months, Zia and some of her friends arose in the dark hours before dawn, donned head kerchiefs and aprons, and walked to the corner of Milgate and Bleecker Streets where stake-bed trucks stopped to pick them up. They were driven to farms to pick peas or beans or whatever crop was ready. They were paid a few cents per bushel. She stored the money in her apron pocket tied in another kerchief. At home each night, she untied the kerchief and spread the coins on the table where she again counted them out before putting them in the jar in the cupboard. Much of the talk during that time of year was about the events and activities surrounding "going picking." "'Ow many bushels you pick today? I make twen'a t'ree, but Rosina Maniscalci, she make t'irty! She'sa hard worker, 'at Rosina."

Zia had one dog and one cat at all times. They had no money to pay a veterinarian to have them spayed or neutered. No one we knew paid to have that done, anyway. The dog was seldom a problem, but the female cat sometimes wandered, became impregnated, and multiplied. When that happened, it was Zia's job to eliminate the unwanted newborn in a potato sack lowered into a tub full of water. I watched her do it once, tiny bubbles floating to the surface and popping. She caught my stony look of shock and volunteered, "'Ow I can feed them all? Is better they die before the eyes open than starve in the street." When Zia thought the cat was getting too old, she would save one kitten from the next litter and raise it as the heir apparent.

My brother and I often walked the couple miles or so from our house to hers to hang out with our cousins. On the way, we stopped in at the Family Theatre lobby to buy a box of cocoa-butter flavored popcorn. We ate this as we walked, my taller brother controlling the box, tearing off the cardboard on his side of the box as the level of the popcorn dropped, leaving a cardboard wall on my side and holding the box high enough so I had to reach up and over. This limited how much I could take with each handful. He would laugh at my frustration as if it was being done in fun, but he never lowered the wall on my side.

As we turned the corner onto Milgate Street, Zia's family dog recognized us from a block away and came running. Then it leapt up, licking faces and making happy little noises, tail wagging fiercely.

The first dog I remember was Dicky, a small, brown, short-haired mongrel—smart as a whip, lean, fast, and playful enough to keep two young boys busy all day. There were others after that, but Dicky is the one I remember.

Even after our cousins and my big brother were grown and gone and Dicky was a dim memory, I still loved to go there. I could play in the yard with the current dog, pick and eat a fresh pear or some grapes, climb a tree, and ambush imaginary protagonists until Zia called me to dinner or supper or to go to a movie.

Zia went to the Family Theater every Saturday and collected the dishes they sold cheaply as premiums, one per person per visit. She had several complete, matching sets of dishes, cups, and saucers for many place settings. The extra ones and unmatched pieces, she gave away. Now and then she would take me with her so she could buy an extra piece she needed to complete a set.

When Aunt Mary was in her thirties, she had some kind of stomach surgery. Her doctor told the family she would not live long. She had difficulty eating spicy food after that, but occasionally, over the next sixty odd years, she pointed out that she had outlived her doctor by many years.

Aunt Mary's use of the English language was broken. When neighborhood kids did something disturbing outside her house, she would shout at them, in broken English, from her front porch. Her favorite expression of disapproval was to forcefully ask them what was wrong with them, using the little English she knew laced with a smattering of fractured Italian. Something like: "Ay! Whattsa matta pe' you?!"

Uncle Pete, Zia's husband, enjoyed his Italian stogie cigars— black, crooked, ugly-looking things—and his wine. He smoked and drank and stroked his thick, black, brush-like moustache by the hour as the men sat after meals discussing politics or the cotton mills.

I've heard it said that he is lucky who dies doing what he loves best. If so, Uncle Pete died happy. He was drinking wine and smoking a stogie cigar in the nearby Eagle Bar & Grill with his friends when he had a massive stroke and fell off the stool. He never regained consciousness. He lasted several months, in bed, at home, cared for by Zia, and departed in his sleep, apparently unaware of anything that happened after that last sip of wine and puff of smoke.

What had struck me since then, in retrospect, was how the older Italian families kept terminally ill members of the family at home, under family care, until the end. It did not occur to them to place a failing family member in any sort of institution. Such unselfish and caring dedication to loved ones seems rare today.

Family gatherings and feasts over the holidays were legendary. So many relatives and friends were in attendance. These were long, full days with appetizers on the table as we arrived before noon. We sat through several main courses and desserts and then munched on nuts, cheese, and fruits fresh from the garden. The women moved into the kitchen, cleaning and fussing, gossiping and laughing. The men lingered at the table, telling jokes and solving complex world problems until the women joined them. Card games and laughter were accompanied by gradual, drawn-out departures as the wee hours came.

During her last years, when sons, daughters-in-law, and grandchildren did all the household chores, Zia still insisted on helping with cooking and canning, all the while remaining bright and cheerful. Her hearing and eyesight dimmed, but her enthusiasm and fervor for life remained vivid and jovial to the very end.

I have some old photos and a grainy movie from one of my last visits. When I look at them, I remember the smells and sounds and pleasures that titillated a little boy when he visited this person and this place. It was truly a different and magical piece of old world culture.

A place that is gone.

A place I cannot find again.

11

Dockweiler Plateau

He left Pauly's on the Pier and rode without incident past King Harbor in Redondo Beach and on through Hermosa, Manhattan, El Porto, and El Segundo Beaches. As he rounded the point at the end of the El Segundo Oil Refinery, he dropped the bike into lower gear and braced himself for the short, steep climb to the top of the plateau which overlooks Dockweiler Beach. He counted the pedal strokes as he stood up on them to overcome the climb. He counted forty-seven grueling cycles of the pedals, slowly creeping up the demanding grade, breathing openmouthed as he reached the flat at the top. From this elevation he could see the long, sandy coast below and ahead where, in the distance, lay Marina Del Rey.

On his left, a group of instructors and students were gathered for hang gliding lessons. A vapor trail appeared on the horizon behind Point Dume, climbing in an almost vertical arc over the ocean, weaving and dispersing like a smudged chalk line. The sunshine fragmented through the vapor, creating a shimmering rainbow of colors—pinks, yellows, and whites.

That has to be a rocket launch from Vandeburg Air Force Base, he thought.

Probably a satellite launch or a weapon test.

Not like the big ones out of Cape Canaveral when we were reaching for the moon.

Not like the missions I worked on.

What year was that?

1968?

That's when it happened.

What an exciting time that was to be alive!

12

A Kick in the Ass

The Apollo 7 mission was to be an eleven-day, Earth-orbital flight to check out the redesigned command/service module for the first time since the catastrophic fire which killed the Apollo 1 crew in 1967. A short time ago, Apollo 7 had left earth's orbit and was now plunging off into space for the very first time.

But this flight was not intended to go to the moon. It was not equipped to do so. Instead, they would soon turn the Apollo Command Module until the Service Propulsion System (SPS) was pointing into space. The mighty SPS engine would then be fired and act as a retro-rocket, slowing the module's flight and returning it to earth's orbit... if it worked

They had been in orbit for a few days. Vital statistics were being monitored by three teams: the primary Mission Control team in Houston, Texas; our crew in the North American Aviation site in Downey, California; and a third facility in Australia. I was on duty in Downey that afternoon as the Houston team talked the three astronauts through the steps that accelerated the command module out of earth's orbit and sent it hurtling into space. A limited public address system located in the large monitoring room permitted us to hear the conversation between Houston and the flight crew—Commander Wally Schirra, Command Module Pilot Donn Eisele, and Lunar Module Pilot Walter Cunningham.

While Houston Mission Control and the Apollo crew were working, I collected the latest data read outs of the astronaut's vital statistics—body temperature, heart rate, blood pressure— and the command module's environmental measurements— temperature, pressure, humidity—which were being controlled by our equipment. I took these data down to my office to plot them. It was evident from the data that the astronauts were experiencing elevated stress during this maneuver. That was expected.

By the time I returned to the control room, the rotation of Apollo 7 had been completed and preparations were now being made for the SPS burn. This burn was crucial. If it worked, Apollo 7 would stop its space journey and return to earth's orbit. If it failed, Apollo 7 could become another piece of space debris sailing on forever, carrying three doomed astronauts.

The preparatory steps were completed and the final countdown began. Tension in the room was thick. It was silent as death as the count reached zero. We could not hear the SPS and had no way of knowing if it had fired. The silence was longer than we had expected. People began to look at each other. It was sweaty palm time. After the trauma of the 1967 deaths, much of our confidence was damaged. Was this another catastrophe? Was Apollo 7 still heading for outer space at thousands of miles per hour, or had the SPS fired successfully? Anxious seconds passed.

Then a voice shouted over the public address system.

"Wow! What a kick in the ass!"

A roar of laughter and relief filled our room. We all assumed that was Wally Schirra, but later reports credited him with shouting "Yabbadabbadoo!" They also claimed Eisele had described it as "a real boot in the rear." The expletive we actually heard was never broadcast to the general public nor reported in the media. Frankly, the astronauts I met and came to know were not men who used words like "real boot" and "rear."

The North American Aviation facility in Downey, California, manufactured the Apollo Command Module for the Apollo program. My employer provided the environmental control system to North America. There were three of us engineers, representing my employer, working at Downey. We shared an office in a trailer at the site. We kept a complete set of drawings of each component we provided. In the event that a problem occurred with one of our components during assembly, testing, or actual flights, we were on site at Downey to troubleshoot it. Before entering a Module during manufacture, we first emptied all our pockets and removed all our jewelry, including rings, wedding bands, and wristwatches. If we needed to take in tools or parts, these were carefully inventoried and logged before we entered and again when we left to be sure nothing was left behind. A loose screw or tool could wreak havoc in the weightlessness of space. On the way out of the module, we reclaimed our jewelry and pocket contents.

After final assembly, each Module was mounted to an overhead mechanism that slowly rotated the Module in a complex pattern which was supposed to encourage any loose object to fall out of the open hatch. Whatever fell out landed on a very large white sheet lying on the floor below. Despite all the precautions taken during manufacturing and testing, we were always surprised at the number of small items that were found on that sheet after the gyrations: a washer, a screw, a tool, a small piece of wire.

During active mission flights, when astronauts were out in space, like this one, each of us worked overlapping twelve-hour shifts so there were always two of us on duty. We kept a list of all our engineering experts, their phone numbers, and their exact locations at all times during the mission. If, for example, one of our experts left home to visit his mother, he called us first, gave us his mother's phone number, and called us when he arrived. Ditto on his return. This continuous on-call system lasted from pre-launch countdown until the astronauts landed back on Earth and the mission was safely concluded.

I had joined the team at Downey shortly after the 1967 fire and was allowed to visit the burned out Apollo 1 module which was stored at the Downey facility. The charred hulk did not bother me. What gave me chills was the smell. I stuck my head inside and that was a mistake. The hatch door had been bolted shut. The combustion gases built up the internal pressure rapidly and the module had burst. They had no chance to escape. The redesigned module, now being flown and tested as Apollo 7, restored our confidence in the program; and Apollo 8 was scheduled to orbit the moon with another full crew very soon.

On my first day at the Downy facility, I met my teammates Neal and Rollie. I knew Neal from past dealings. He introduced me to Rollie. "This is Rollie Do-piss," Neal said with a straight face. We shook hands. After a familiarization tour of the facility, Neal left to take care of something or other. I was left with Rollie. I looked at the name tag on his desk. It read "Roland Dupois."

"How do you pronounce that?" I asked.

"It depends," he said. "Around here they pronounce it 'Rollie Do-piss.' That's how Neal and everybody else says it. I fought it for years, but now I'm used to it." He was silent for a moment then turned to me and, with a twinkle in his eye, added, "But... if you are introducing me to a pretty girl, please, please try to say... 'Rrroolando Do-Pwah!'"

Our work continued with renewed vigor after Apollo 7 returned and on December 21, 1968, when Apollo 8 was launched. We went on twelve-hour shifts again. Just under three hours after launch, they performed a translunar injection and headed for the moon. They flew two elliptical lunar orbits then eight more circular orbits transmitting the first live television pictures of the lunar surface. About ninety hours later—while they were behind the moon—they entered transearth injection, which means they left moon's orbit and headed home. We read data, plotted charts, and hastened to the monitoring room to listen in on the more interesting events day and night. The most exciting procedures always involved major maneuvers that were critical to their survival, like the trans-injection operations.

Now the program was cooking. All systems were working so well the public began to view the lunar trips as a routine bus ride.

Rollie had a picture on his desk of his attractive wife and new baby boy. He shared with us that his wife had suffered an injury while giving birth to his son and that injury was slow to heal. It prevented them from making love. It had been many months since Rollie and Mrs. Rollie had indulged. The doctor gave them a date, several months hence, when they could safely engage in an "affair of the heart." Rollie had the date circled in red on his calendar. Each morning, with a flourish, he posted the number of days remaining in the upper right-hand corner of our office blackboard. As the time neared, Rollie grew almost feverish with excitement.

The program was winding down. A few more flights of Apollo and our team would be disbanded. Neal and Rollie would be the last to leave. I applied for a transfer to another aerospace department in another city. When it was approved, we celebrated by going into town for a pizza lunch. On my last work day, Neal and Rollie and a few other Apollo engineers insisted on buying me a celebratory drink after work at a scruffy local bar in Downey. We lost track of time and I had consumed a number of free drinks when the party broke up.

Neal said, "I don't think you should be driving right away. You need some coffee."

"I live near here," Rollie volunteered. "You ride home with me, and we'll get you some coffee. I'll bring you back to get your car later."

So that was the plan. I rode to Rollie's home with him. I met his wife. She was very pretty. Rollie was excited. The house smelled of perfume. Several candles were lit, and a glowing fire emitted flickering shadows in the subdued lighting. She prepared coffee while Rollie snuffed the candles and fireplace and turned on more lights. They gave me coffee and a ham sandwich and urged me to eat and drink. They put the baby to sleep, and we sat at the table. She held the coffee pot at the ready, filling my cup almost before I had drained it. Rollie handed me a cookie as soon as the sandwich was gone.

"How are you feeling?" he asked me at regular ninety-second intervals.

I was feeling woozy and hazy. Slowly, like a nearly drowning man who was floating back to the surface, I saw things come back into focus. I looked more closely at her. She was very flushed. Her cheeks were pink, and her eyes darted from me to Rollie to me. Then I looked at Rollie more closely. He was feverish with anticipation. Was his tongue hanging out, or was that my imagination?

It was getting late. The sun had set. The baby was asleep. They stared at me.

Then it hit me. Today was Friday. The red circled Friday. Today was zero in the upper-right hand corner of our office blackboard. It was "D" day as in "Do It" day. And I was in their kitchen, gulping coffee and sandwiches and cookies.

I bolted unsteadily to my feet. "I'm fine now," I said. "I can drive now."

Neither one of them asked, "Are you sure?"

Instead, in unison they chorused, "Okay, then."

Rollie helped me put on my jacket, handed me my car keys, and urged me toward the door while she quickly swept away the coffee cup and pot and cookie crumbs and relit the candles and fireplace while turning off lights.

He drove me to my car and waved good-bye while I struggled to unlock my car door.

A few blocks down the street, I was stopped for driving erratically and eventually paid a fine for reckless driving.

On July 20, 1969, Neil Armstrong stepped off the Lunar Excursion Module from Apollo 11 onto the surface of the moon and uttered his oft misquoted, "That's one small step for man, one giant leap for mankind."

I am sure *Rrroolando Do-Pwah* thought something just as passionate on that red circled Friday night at about the same time that I was explaining myself to an Orange County Deputy Sheriff.

13

Burton Chase Park

He left Dockweiler Plateau and cruised without much thought the next four miles or so. Foot traffic had increased, and his attention focused on avoiding collisions with the multitudes crossing his path. He looked forward to his usual rest stop at Burton Chase Park in Marina Del Rey.

Cutting through the parking lot at the end of Mindanao Way, he threaded the busy sidewalks inside the park. He would stop here, briefly, to rest before turning back.

It was Wednesday. He knew this because the bus that brought old folks from the Brighton Extended Care Facility was parked outside the entrance. They came every Wednesday to enjoy the park. He filled his water bottle. He would drink all of it before leaving. Hydrate, his family doctor had repeatedly told him. Be sure to stay hydrated.

A thirty-six-foot sloop was tied up at the pump-out station dock. The skipper, a bearded young man, was connecting a large hose with the help of a beautiful young lady in a very tiny bikini.

The Old Man propped the bike on its kick stand and sat on one of the concrete benches that faced the harbor, the half-filled water bottle in his hand. Here he could view the marina to his right all the way to where it ended just short of Washington Boulevard and all the way to his left, beyond the Loyola Marymount University boathouse at the main channel. And he could get a close-up look at the two young people when they walked up the ramp from the dock and opened the chain link gate in front of him.

The gate swung open. The bearded young man held it open for his lady friend. She looked vaguely familiar to the Old Man. The reddish blond hair she wore in a wave over her forehead, the slightly turned-up nose, and a charming small black mole just above and to the left of her smile brought back something from deep within his memory.

Like a phantom appearing slowly through a thick, cold fog bank, the Old Man began to recall.

It was so cold that winter.

That Syracuse winter.

14

Syracuse Winter

Syracuse is cold in the winter. Steam radiators rattle and clunk. Ice forms on the inside of windowpanes, down in the lower corners, in graceful arcs. Outdoors, breath forms clouds of condensing vapor. Inside, wet mittens drape radiators and boots stand just inside the entryways, forming little puddles from melting snow.

He looked out the window of his rented room in the Young Men's Christian Association building to the street, six floors below. Snow plows haven't come through yet. It is still too early. Snowfall during the night lies half a foot deep. Double car tracks round the corner, crisscrossing each other, carved by night-shift workers headed for home before dawn. The traffic signals at the corner cast a red glow on the snow that coats the street beneath it. As the light sways gently on its wire supports, it paints the snow with color. It turns yellow, then green, giving permission for traffic to move, except there is no traffic. It mindlessly cycles the lights to a street that remains empty and quiet.

One block away, visible from his room, is the Young Women's Christian Association building, the only other building as tall as his. It, too, is a gray-brown brick structure. It stands silently with hundreds of dark windows looking like the myriad blind eyes of a large insect. Here and there a window at the end of a hallway shows a dim light. He scans the rows of windows on each floor, seeking one which, he knows, will have a light on soon. Then it tripped on and he found it.

It flickered in a room on the fifth floor. Only one lit room in the hundreds of windows. He saw movement and a shadow that swayed back and forth as the overhead lightbulb swung at the end of a long wire hung from the ceiling. He knew who made that shadow. She, like him, had just returned home.

His breath formed a rapidly growing cloud of condensation on the window. With the palm of his hand, he wiped off the glass pane to see more clearly. There she was, in her slip, connecting an iron and preparing to press the wrinkles out of a blouse and skirt by the glow of that bare ceiling light. When she turned out the light and left the room, he turned and went to bed.

They had met on a blind date several weeks ago. She was new to the city, having moved here from one of the small, outlying farm communities, in search of employment. She seemed nice and they agreed to meet again. A week later, her mother came to the city, bringing along a little sister. They went to see the Ice Capades at the Syracuse Veterans' Memorial Auditorium. They ate hotdogs at the show. They stopped briefly at a bowling alley where they bravely tried bowling, a sport with which none of them had any prior experience. His very first toss of the bowling ball nearly ended in disaster. He was unprepared for the massive inertia generated by the heavy weight of the ball as he swung it back. It left his hand, tearing itself free of his fingers, and thumped loudly as it landed on the spectator bench behind him, tucked neatly between her and her mother. That was only a few weeks ago.

Last night, scant hours ago, he had waited for her on the front steps of her building. They walked to dinner at Ringo's Restaurant, just around the block, choosing from a menu that hadn't changed in years. The Diner's Special was always a favorite. For a very reasonable price, it offered a main meat entrée surrounded by mashed potatoes and gravy, creamed corn, green peas, hot buns, butter, and a cup of coffee. On this particular night the entrée was meat loaf. It was always meat loaf on Thursday night. And it was always served on a heavy blue ceramic plate with white filigree trim around the edges. The dish had raised ridges that served to compartmentalize the food—meat in the largest section, mashed and vegetables in each of the two smaller sections.

He had eaten here often, usually accompanied by several male friends, one of which was blind. The waitress knew them and always positioned the blue plate before the blind friend so that the meat was at the lower right-hand side. After dinner, the blind friend smoked a cigarette. Igniting the metal lighter with his left hand, he held the cigarette with his right hand and extended the small finger of his right hand to the far tip of the cigarette. As he drew the flame nearer, he sensed the heat and deftly withdrew the little finger, miraculously escaping the flame as it merged with the tip of the cigarette. He used the same little finger to sense where the fire was as the cigarette burned down. All eyes watched anxiously as the burning tobacco neared his mouth, but this blind friend always seemed to know exactly where it was and when the cigarette was almost entirely consumed and should be put out in the empty dish.

But this night he dined only with her. They lingered over coffee, exchanging more details of their lives. She asked if he had brought some of his poems. He had idly mentioned them on their previous date, and she had asked him to bring them tonight. He read them to her. They dwelt on yearnings, philosophical questioning, and pretentious wisdom. She seemed to enjoy them and fawned, with starstruck adoration, over his simple compositions.

She asked if he would like to hear some that she had written. He said he would. She hesitated, saying that she wasn't a very good writer. He said he was sure they would be very good and cajoled until she brought them out of her purse.

She read them to him. She was right. They were simplistic and predictable but a large cut above "Roses are Red, Violets are Blue..." They spoke of dreams and aspirations, of a young lady's romantic idealism. She read them, pausing now and then, unsure, and then she pushed on.

Her eyes glowed with anticipation as she stopped reading and stared, expectantly, into his eyes for a reaction. He praised her efforts. He expanded his praise with adjectives and editorial phrases. He added more compliments until she seemed to be satisfied, and to his relief, she put her poems back into her purse.

Immersed in the warm feeling of shared interest, they walked, arm in arm, the long way around the block, passed the YMCA entrance, then the YWCA, then circled the block several more times. At several points in their walk, they stopped, alone in the empty streets, and kissed, cold noses against cold cheeks. They held hands until fingertips grew numb in the cold and they had to be pushed into warm pockets.

They did not want to part. It was too cold to remain outdoors. He could not enter her building. She could not enter his.

As they passed the seedy, rundown Hotel Merit for the third time, they stopped. Yellow light from the lobby shone through the wood-framed glass door and cast a luminescence on the snow-covered steps. A lambent haze glowed in the light from the doorway.

He said, half-jokingly, that they could get a room. She replied, softly, that they could. Wordlessly they walked up the steps to the hotel entrance, leaving two sets of footprints.

The sleepy, wizened-faced clerk, key in hand, led them upstairs, unlocked a room door, and swung it open for their inspection. Barely glancing inside, they nodded approval, took the key, and locked the door behind the retreating clerk.

The room was dingy with worn chenille bedspreads. A faded drape covered a view of the brick wall of the building next door. A steam radiator sat beneath the window. It was tepid to the touch and added no heat to the room. The bed squeaked as they sat on it. They talked a while then embraced. They kept warm the best way they could. They fumbled awkwardly.

Afterward they drifted off to sleep in each other's arms.

At 3:00 am, they dressed and left. He walked her home, just around the corner, stopping at the lobby entrance, exchanging runny nosed good morning kisses.

It was 4:00 am when he crawled into his own bed.

He shut off the alarm clock at 5:30 am, got up, walked to the window, and looked, again, to the street below then across to the now-dark window on the fifth floor.

Cars were beginning to move through the streets. Motor sounds broke the silence, punctuated by the louder roar of an occasional truck or bus. Now and then a horn sounded.

It's time to start another day, to shower, shave, dress, scrape the ice off the car windows, drive to the coffee shop, order two eggs sunny side up, wheat toast, coffee, wolf it down, buzz off to work, running late, taking risks on the slippery roads, pull into the parking lot, enter the building, where the steam heat is too high, peel off gloves, coat, scarf, and boots, drop into his office chair.

He would struggle to stay awake all day and, now and then, would think warm thoughts about last night.

The Old Man stood up and placed his empty water bottle back into the rack on his bike frame. He checked his helmet strap, pulled on his riding gloves, and kicked back the stand, lost in thought.

Syracuse, he thought.
It was such a cold winter that year.
We were so young.
What was her name? he wondered, struggling to recall.
What was her name?

15

The Bus Driver

The Brighton Extended Care Facility bus driver sat on a nearby bench reading a copy of the *Los Angeles Times*. He looked up as the Old Man walked up, pushing his bike.

"You must be a new driver," he said. "Don't think I've seen you here before."

"That's a fact," the driver answered, happy to have company to talk to. "I usually work on Friday. I drive them to Santa Monica beach on Friday, but Gracie, the Wednesday regular, called in sick today, so I get to do an extra shift. Have a seat. You wanna read the *Times*?" he asked, pushing a section of the newspaper across the stone bench.

He sat down, picked up the paper, and looked idly through the pages while the driver studied him over his section of the *Times*. "You live around here?"

"No. I rode up from Torrance Beach. This is usually where I turn around and ride back. It's a good place to rest a while. The people are so different."

The driver looked up inquisitively. "How is that?"

"They are so diverse. On Monday, a bunch of old folks and their instructor gather up on that hill and go through exercises to music. Tuesday, a group holds a big barbeque under the sheds. They

75

speak some foreign language. I think maybe Polish or Hungarian. The food always looks and smells good. And of course, your people come here on Wednesday. Another group from some Jewish retirement community meets here on Thursdays, dressed in their finest clothes and carrying parasols. Friday, the place is overrun by a bunch of young housewives with little babies. They seem to be organized—the mothers, I mean. Those are the regulars. And weekends are totally unpredictable. You never know when a special school group or something like the Boy Scouts or Girl Scouts will show up. Once in a while a group of military veterans meet here. They're interesting to listen to. Full of war stories."

The bus driver leaned over, tapped the Old Man's shoulder with the back of his hand, and whispered, "Talk about interesting people, see the old guy with the blue cap over by the water fountain? That's Willy. He's ninety-one years old, fought in World War II, landed in Normandy on D-Day. He still has his medals, keeps them on his dresser in his room back at the home, doesn't like to talk about it much."

Neither did Stanly, the Old Man thought.
They fought in the big war, but they didn't like to talk about it.
Stan was there too. Omaha Beach. He would have been in his nineties now.
Stan was a Ranger.
Stan the man. Stan had stories about Omaha Beach.
When you could get him to talk about it, he would get a faraway look in his eyes and then grin.
He must have told it a hundred times. About the cow.
That crazy French cow.

16

The Ranger

In 1962 our company headquarters building was located on the corner of Sepulveda and Century Boulevards on what is now a parking lot for Los Angeles International Airport. The office building, test laboratories, and manufacturing facilities are gone now. Cars come and go where engineers once designed and developed cutting-edge military and commercial aerospace products.

We shared bullpen offices, each holding two to four desks. Sharing my bullpen was another engineer, Stan Jakubowski, a guy whose Polish parents had immigrated to the United States in the early 1900s. Stan was born in my hometown. He was a first generation American, like me. He was a decade older and much more experienced in engineering and in life.

I liked Stan. Everyone did. He was a solid family man, a good father and husband, a reliable provider and conscientious employee. He had a great sense of humor that was at its best when the laugh was on him. When Polish jokes were popular, the best ones came from Stan. He sometimes told stories about his World War II exploits that were self-effacing, like the one about the shell-shocked French cow.

Stan was inducted into the United States Army shortly after the start of World War II and was assigned to the Rangers, an elite infantry unit of outstanding physical specimens trained in special warfare at the United States Ranger School. It included the type of training we associate, in more recent years, with the Green Berets. Parachute jumps, climbing up, and rappelling down cliff faces were among the physical skills he developed. He learned to use a wide variety of weapons and how to kill an enemy with a knife without making a sound. Stan was prepared for the invasion of Normandy as a highly trained and proficient killer.

He and his assigned fighting buddy formed a Browning Automatic Rifle (BAR) team. The BAR fired .30-06 rounds of ammunition at a fairly fast rate. It was more devastating than a rifle, and while it did not put out as many rounds as a machine gun, it was far more accurate. This light machine gun used twenty-round magazines and is mounted on a bipod stand, although it was not uncommon to fire it from the hip. Because of the heavy weight, one member of the team carried the BAR while the other team member carried the ammunition boxes of twenty-round clips. The smallest member of the team always carried the BAR as he would be harder to hit. Stan was one of the smallest men in his company at five feet two inches, so he had the assignment of carrying the rifle. His taller partner carried the ammunition. All the men in Stan's company had received training in the use of the BAR. If Stan was killed, any one of them could take over and operate it.

On D-Day Stan rode in on a landing craft full of troops. Plunging through the surf with their heavy backpacks and weapons, they reached one of the narrow sand beaches at the base of tall cliffs on the French coast. They were part of nine US Army Ranger Companies whose targets were the chalk cliffs between strong German defense points at the western end of Omaha Beach. Enemy fire from the top of these cliffs was expected to be lighter because this area of beach was not suitable for large landing parties and was thought to be lightly defended by the Germans. There were supposed to be five German artillery pieces which the Rangers were supposed to destroy. Instead, the weapons had been removed and German casements, pill boxes, had been installed.

Stan and his buddies burrowed into the sand while they studied the sheer ninety-foot cliffs directly in front of them. They were receiving unexpected machine gun fire from the pill boxes. At a signal, they proceeded to scale the cliff as planned. Using small rocket launchers, they fired grappling hooks to the cliff top. Stan had the BAR disassembled and strapped to his back. His buddy had secured the ammo containers to his belt and backpack. Straining with ropes and climbing equipment, they reached and topped the cliff. The plan was to meet up with the rest of their company and circle and launch a rear attack on any German fortifications, disabling vital communication and combat control centers.

Ahead lay pasture land. They could hear the sounds of battle at the main beachhead landing site, a short distance up the coast. Overhead, heavy US Naval artillery screamed by and exploded fiercely just ahead of them, close enough to shake the ground and fill the air with smoke and debris.

Stan and his buddy ran through the smoke haze toward a prearranged rendezvous point with the rest of their company. They separated to make smaller targets. Out of sight from his teammate, Stan cut across a fenced field which held several cows.

The cows were restless, terrified by the melee. As he ran, the equipment bouncing against his back and sides, one of the cows, perhaps shell-shocked, wheeled and charged him. Stan heard the hoof beats and turned in time to see the lowered horns thundering toward him. He ran as hard as he could, heavily burdened by his backpack, gas mask, canteen, grenades, and BAR. He saw the far fence and judged he could not make it before the cow reached him. To one side lay a small pond. Stan circled the pond. About halfway around, he looked ahead and saw that the cow had circled the pond in the opposite direction. Stan was running at the charging, angry animal. He spun around and sprinted away, his highly trained muscles exerting themselves to outrun the bovine. The cow wheeled and reversed direction again to head Stan off. After half a dozen of these reversing maneuvers, they stopped and looked at each other across the small pond.

Nearby men of different uniforms struggled to kill or be killed for their country and their beliefs. Stan and a French cow were stalemated. Stan reasoned that the cow, being French, was an ally. He was reluctant to take its life.

Look at me. Look at the uniform! I am one of the good guys! I'm on your side, he thought. The cow would have none of it.

As seconds passed, the choice became imperative. Stan had a war to fight, enemies to kill, a partner waiting somewhere. Stan determined he would have to kill the crazed animal, ally or not.

It would be his first kill of the war. All those months of intensive training, all those hours of instruction on how to take life quickly, efficiently and deliberately, would be brought to bear on a cow on the fabled west coast of Europe. A cow that had him trapped across a small pond in an unknown pasture in France. He untied the BAR components and began to assemble it. Occasionally he had to pick up the pieces and run a short way as the cow made threatening moves in one direction or the other. Finally, he raised the fully assembled weapon of devastation and remembered that his partner had the ammunition. Stan was at an impasse with the cow.

Thus it continued for some time, the two adversaries eyeing each other, starting and stopping short in semi-circular dashes. Stan glanced repeatedly in the direction where he was supposed to rendezvous with his partner.

It was another few moments that seemed like hours before his partner came within hailing distance. Stan shouted a warning and the cow reacted, chasing the partner. His buddy fled back to the fence, clearing it with one leap. Each time Stan or his partner tried to dash to meet the other, the demented cow swerved to cut them off. Finally, while Stan baited the cow by drawing closer to her, his partner successfully made a wild run to join Stan at the pond. The frantic cow pawed the ground, snorted, tossed her head, and stared at this enemy duo.

Breathing heavily, they smoothly and quickly, as trained, united the ammunition with the BAR. Slapping a twenty-round clip home, Stan reluctantly dispatched the insane, four-legged ally with some remorse.

Scrambling now across the pasture with one eye on the other cows, they cleared the fence, found their company, and joined the action against armed men.

Circling eastward, they came up behind a bunker built into the earth on the slope below them. It looked down on the beach head and was pouring machine gun fire on US troops that were pinned down on the sand below. The concrete roof was just slightly raised about the surface of the earth. Stan ran downhill, stooping low, toward the sloping concrete roof. He crouched tightly to the ground and against the wall next to a firing slit on the right-hand side wall. The pounding staccato of the machine guns muted the shouting German soldiers inside the bunker. But he could still hear them, and it sent shivers down his spine. With heart pounding, Stan lay down the BAR and unhooked a grenade from his belt. Holding it in his right hand, he slid down the slight embankment alongside the wall to get closer to the firing slit. He pulled the pin, released the firing lever, counted to three, as he had been taught, leaned quickly forward, tossed in the grenade, and slammed backward and away from the slit. The sound was like two large, flat boards being clapped together next to his ear. Smoke and fragments belched from the slits. The guns fell silent inside the bunker. Stan's ears were ringing, and the war became strangely silent as his damaged ears lost the ability to hear. Then, as he slithered down toward the slit, his hearing began to return. Someone inside was moaning and calling out feebly. He placed a hand on the remaining grenade clipped to his ammo belt. The voice stopped. He waited another moment and heard nothing more from the bunker.

The air around the beach and overhead remained filled with explosions. The occasional bullet or shrapnel screamed nearby. Stan rolled over, scrambled to his feet, and trotted, hunched over, back up the slope. He was up and in a full run, carrying the BAR, alongside his buddy when a stray bullet struck his foot, knocking it out from under him. He stumbled, fell, and as he liked to tell it, "By sunset, I was on a hospital ship heading for England."

Men were killed and men bled on both sides. Stan never spoke of that. But many times he regaled us with the story of the mad French cow and his first brush with death in World War II.

At lunch one day, Stan told us that he had been diagnosed with cancer. He went home for an extended medical leave. I missed him at work and went to visit him. When he announced that he was going to take early retirement, we surmised the diagnosis was terminal. We threw a grand retirement party for Stan at a local restaurant. He told us some of the latest Polish jokes he had recently collected.

I asked him to tell the story, again, of the mad French cow who tried to kill him above the chalk cliffs of Omaha Beach, and he did, word for word, as he had told it for years. Everyone laughed.

I visited him at home one more time after that. We reminisced about the people we worked with and the projects we had worked on. As our conversation wound down, he said, "Come and see me any time. I miss you guys." We said we would, soon.

But he was gone shortly after that.

Sometimes, when those of us who knew Stan get together, we remind each other of the story, and if someone new to the group is there, one of us will tell it. Then we drink a toast or two to Stan the man, a charter member of "the greatest generation."

17

Sweet Spots

The Old Man stood up suddenly. "Do me a favor, will you? Watch my bike while I run over and use the men's room?"

"Sure, I ain't going anywhere for a while," the bus driver said.

He walked over the low hill that separated the waterfront from the barbeque areas and entered the men's restroom. This was another part of his routine: take a leak in Burton Chase Park before starting back down the coast. The urinals were new. They had replaced the old flush urinals with waterless units. Just above each was a small plaque that boasted that each of these new urinals saved over forty thousand gallons of water per year. As he looked down, he was surprised to see a pretty good-sized horsefly sitting inside the dry urinal. It seemed only natural and right to aim for the fly and try to hit it before it escaped. He did. It didn't move. It was a picture printed into the enamel in each of the three urinals in exactly the same location. Whoever had designed the urinals understood that the natural hunting instincts or meanness in every man would lead him to try and pee on the fly. Perhaps that was the "sweet spot" in the urinal which resulted in the least amount of splash back.

He learned about urinal "sweet spots" from Wilhelm, an old German engineer he worked with just after he got out of college. Wilhelm spent his first few years in a German engineering firm designing toilets. His job was to get the shape of the urinal and the mounting height above the floor just right so that the amount of urine splash back would be minimal. The shape and height that worked best would provide a urinal with a large "sweet spot," the area which would minimize splash back onto the user's pants. To test his designs, he provided one pair of pants to each man in the shop. With rigid German discipline, they were required to put on the same pair of pants each time they went in to pee. At the end of each test period, the pants were analyzed to determine how much urine had splashed onto them.

Maybe whoever put the horsefly images in these urinals had determined that this was the "sweet spot" for this design. He supposed that every time he came here from now on, he would be tempted to try and hit the fly even though he now knew it was not real.

The moment felt familiar. There was something about a urinal and aiming for something. Afterward, he stood outside the restroom doorway, trying to recall.

Oh, yeah! That button I saw on my first day on that new job. I never missed that button, either. Well, I mean, when I aimed for it I never missed it.

Until it disappeared.

Then I missed it.

I wonder where it went?

18

The Button

The first day of work on any new job is a tough one. So much to learn, so many people to get to know. You just don't know your way around. And so it was with me. I made it my business to find out what the business hours were, where I was supposed to sit, what the lunch schedule was, and most importantly, where the men's restroom was located. Everything else came later.

When I visited that strange new bathroom early on that first morning, I saw the usual array of booths with doors and wall-mounted urinals, each individually hung with modesty panels on either side. This was a step-up from the last job I had where the urinal was a long ceramic trough with a rusted, dribbling pipe running across the top of it. No modesty panels on that one, and four guys could easily stand shoulder to shoulder. Here I would have privacy—of a sort—that I did not have before. I felt better about this job already. I fell into the habit of visiting the very last urinal at the farthest end from the doorway. I don't know why. Maybe it seemed even more private.

About one week later, I noticed something in the bottom of that urinal. It was one of those small, white shirt buttons, lost, no doubt, during someone's visit. It was made of some kind of plastic or bone, I suppose. It had four small holes in it designed in a square configuration. Thread must have coursed through and around these four holes at one time, holding the little button firmly to the fabric of one of the hundreds of white shirts our male employees wore to work each day. Yet one day, that thread must have failed and the little button sprang away to freedom to its present resting place.

I expected that the janitor would remove it during his nightly cleaning rounds. But he didn't. It was there the next day, and the next, and the next. I soon realized that due to the geometry of the urinal, it was difficult for the janitor to retrieve it without using his fingers, so it would probably lie there until the water flushed it away. But it never moved. Nor did it show signs of deterioration from the frequent exposure to acids and whatnot.

Days passed into weeks. Weeks passed into months. Each day I looked for the button, and there it was, unmoved, shiny and bright, smiling up at me. If that urinal was in use when I came in, I lingered at the sink until it was available. The endurance and tenacity of that little button fascinated me.

I thought, *It doesn't mind where it is. It is impervious to its surroundings, content to be visited so often by so many people.* I wondered how many years it would last.

One year went by, then two, then three. There it was: intact, unfazed. Someday, I thought, when this building changes ownership, the new owner will inherit this little button along with the state-of-the-art computer systems, test laboratories, and manufacturing facilities. It won't be listed on the inventory of sale, but it will be there nevertheless. Why, it might outlast the building. The idea struck me that years, decades, eons from now, archaeologists might find little white shirt buttons as ancient reminders of a civilization long since demised, like Indian arrowheads.

I came to draw comfort from that little button; it's steadfastness an example of how to find contentment in any environment. Each time I visited and looked down, there it was, like an old friend. I wondered if anyone else noticed it and that I looked for it each day.

Did anyone else feel a special, friendly bond with that button, or was our relationship special?

Then it disappeared. I don't know where it went or how. It just vanished between visits.

I felt a sense of loneliness in the restroom after that. A silent friend was gone. Visiting the men's room was just a necessary chore now. Any urinal would do now. It didn't matter anymore.

I've always known that everything that has a beginning must have an ending, but somehow, I thought that button would beat the odds.

Well, maybe it has. Maybe it finally flushed down the pipes and swept through the sewage plant in Hermosa Beach, washing into Santa Monica Bay with the pure, treated water. And maybe it will wash up on the beach, all shiny and bright, waiting for a shell-hunting child to find it, wonder, and proudly take it home.

19

Fisherman's Village

He left Burton Chase Park as he had come, cutting through the Los Angeles County boat storage yard, skirting around the launch ramps, and going up the incline to Fiji Way. Turning southwest on Fiji Way, he was greeted by a stiff wind smack into his face. It was no surprise. Most days, at about this time, the wind shifted around and blew from the southwest, directly on his nose as he headed back home.

Pumping hard against the new headwind, he reached Fisherman's Village where he pulled into the parking lot and out of the wind behind the restaurants and shops. Here he would take another short break, get another drink of water, and perhaps chat with the Thai couple who owned and operated the small fast-food stand at the base of a faux lighthouse that served as the architectural icon of the village.

Every tourist with a camera took a picture of the lighthouse, and many ate hamburgers or hotdogs purchased from the Thai lady. He walked the bike between the bolted down outdoor tables and benches, peeked around the corner, and saw her, arms folded, sitting inside the shop, watching a television set on which little oriental people were chattering in a language he could not understand. Several hotdogs rolled on a small grill, slowly being moved by a motorized set of rollers. The aroma of grilled onions and ground beef wafted toward him. When she saw him standing there, she rose and came to the window.

"Herow! Gu morning," she said in her usual, jovial voice, happy to see him. She was just tall enough to lean her arms on the wide windowsill, her round, shiny face framed by tightly pulled-back hair gathered in a fist-sized bun. "You come wi'out you gran'sons?"

Years ago, he often came with one or more of his grandsons, by car at first, then on bikes when they grew old enough to ride. He usually ordered hamburgers and French fries for them and visited with her. Though the grandchildren had not come with him in several years, she still asked about them.

"They live far away now," he said. "Where is your husband?"

"He rookin' for cans 'n bottles. He sum'prace around."

"Business seems very slow. No people here today?"

"Oh, yes, velly srow now. Many more on weekend, but still no same as befaw. People no spend money now."

She and her husband had struggled in recent years to keep the shop open. Since the economy crashed a few years ago, many of their neighbors had closed down, and the blank storefronts with "For Lease" signs were depressing. The Thai lady said they depended on the money from recycling cans and bottles to pay for the gasoline they burned to drive out here from Orange County.

They had once been prosperous in those early years in California and had sent two children through college. Now they barely subsisted. Some days, in the barren winter months, she simply closed the shop during midweek. The children were grown and gone; the dreams were behind them; the years had slipped through the hourglass of time.

Her husband came around the walkway in front of the ice cream shop on the corner carrying a large black plastic bag full of rescued cans and bottles. His slight frame, sallow complexion, deeply grooved face, and soiled, worn clothes caused people to mistake him for a vagrant instead of the coproprietor, especially when he rummaged through the trash barrels looking for cans and bottles, as he was doing now. He recognized the Old Man and smiled a toothless smile.

The hunched-over husband lugged his black plastic bag of booty to the rear of the lighthouse, the brief smile gone, empty eyes staring out of a skull that looked like it was covered with dry parchment paper.

He has lost the dream, and after all these years, there is no place to go home to.

So many have come here to find the dream and then lost it.

Like Johnny Giancarlo did.

When was that? Christmas. It was a long-ago Christmas.

My kids were still young and living at home. How well I recall that night.

The phone rang and I rushed to get it, thinking it was another Christmas call from a distant relative.

But it wasn't.

20

The Palms

I had been living in Los Angeles about twenty years when the phone call came. Christmas was just around the corner. It was mid-evening here, late for a call from my old east coast hometown. Christmas lights were going up in Los Angeles. Shops were open late. Holiday music filled the air. I could imagine the white snow and bright decorations back there in Utica. It would be colder there, and snow would be covering the ground and adorning trees, lampposts, and power lines. The tableau would appear soft and comforting.

A woman with a slight Italian accent introduced herself to me as Rose Giancarlo. She said her mother was a friend of my mother and that was how they got my phone number.

Rose explained that her younger brother, Johnny, had moved to Los Angeles about ten years earlier to find work in the movies or in aerospace. Johnny played guitar and sang. He had some training as a mechanic too. She said he used to call and write regularly the first couple years. He would tell them about his work, his music gigs and his friends, and how good the future looked. He often talked about going home for a visit, but he was always too busy. He promised his mother that someday he would send them all airline tickets and show them Hollywood and Disneyland, movie studios and beaches, Beverly Hills and Rodeo Drive, and all the places they had heard about and seen on television. He would take them to Graumans Chinese Theatre so they could see the foot- and handprints of famous movie stars and place their feet and hands in the very same imprints just as they had seen in the movie magazines. He would show them the Pacific Ocean, the Malibu beach homes, the famed California surfers that the Beach Boys sang about, and the exact location of the TV series, *77 Sunset Strip*. He would take them to famous restaurants where the waiters knew his name and his favorite foods. They would be proud of their Johnny.

His calls became less frequent over the years and stopped altogether about three months ago. At first they assumed he was just too busy. They waited patiently for him to find time to call or write. But now, with Christmas almost over, they became concerned. Rose said they hoped I could find him. She gave me his last known phone number and address.

The next day, I made several phone calls and eventually traced him to a hotel in central Los Angeles called The Palms. The desk clerk at The Palms said they did have a John Giancarlo who lived there for several years, but he had died a few months ago. He had no particulars about Johnny and knew little else.

I called my parents and asked them to tell his family. I thought it would be less painful coming in person from friends.

A few nights later, Rose called again. She thanked me for my trouble and asked me if I could do one more thing. The family was taking the news hard. Johnny's mother was inconsolable. She needed to know how he died. Did he suffer? Was he alone? They knew so little about his life in California. Would I please inquire and let them know?

I called the desk clerk again. He said he seldom saw Johnny and didn't know much about what happened. He suggested I talk to the night clerk, an old codger named Reggie. Reggie came on at ten p.m. every night and worked the lobby until morning.

I called Reggie later that night and made an appointment to go see him. A few nights later, I drove downtown. I parked in a nearby underground garage and walked two blocks to The Palms. It was an old brick four-story building. The large, double wood-framed glass doors opened into a worn linoleum-floored lobby with dim imitation gas lights on walls covered with peeling paint. The ceiling fan that hadn't turned for years looked down on a small countertop. In its day, The Palms was probably elegant. Now it was little more than a flop house.

I introduced myself to Reggie, the night clerk. We talked.

"Sure," he said. "I knew Johnny. He kept to himself mostly. Slept all day. Used to go out around ten, eleven every night. Get boozed up and come in three, four in the morning. Sometimes he wouldn't come back for two, three nights. If I was here when he come in sometimes, we'd talk a while. Different stuff. His family. His hometown. Sometimes he thought maybe he'd move back home. Back east someplace. He used to drink all night. Come in n' stand around the lobby a while, just him and me. Then he'd go to his room until the next night. He didn't have a job. Not as long as I knew him. Lived on food stamps and welfare so far as I know'd. I dunno, maybe he did some panhandle'n."

"How did he die? Do you know?" I asked.

"Yeah. One night he come down real late. About one o'clock in the morning. He was half-dressed. There was blood on his shirt and hands… bleeding from the nose and mouth. He was scared. So was I. I called the paramedics right away, but it didn't do no good. I think he bled to death before they got here. Right there, on that floor. They said it was because he drank so much. Nobody knew how to reach his family. Took him to the city morgue. You're the first person to ask about him."

When I called Rose the next evening, I was evasive. I said he didn't suffer. I said it was quick. She asked me how he died. She needed more. I held the phone to my ear, trying to figure out what to say to this sister that she could repeat to his family, to his aged mother.

I looked into my living room and saw my Christmas tree. The lights were on. Presents were wrapped and tucked under the low branches. The window shades were up, and I could see Christmas lights on the houses across the street. I pictured the living room in the Giancarlo home. It would be similarly decorated. I imagined Johnnie's mother, brothers and sisters, aunts, uncles, cousins, nieces, and nephews gathering in the next few days to celebrate Christmas. There would be food and drink, children opening presents. They would talk about Johnny. What they said, how they felt, what spirit would visit them on this occasion would come from what I told Rose next.

I heard myself say, "They said he didn't suffer, that it was pretty quick. He had lots of friends. They were all with him at the end. They said he had a good job and it kept him very busy, but he talked about his family all the time. They spoke highly of him. He was a good man. He went peacefully. Tell the family they can be proud of Johnny."

Other members of the family got on the phone with questions. Relief and sorrow filled their conversation. Someone was crying in the background.

That was a long time ago.

I was recently in central Los Angeles. Something compelled me to walk several blocks out of my way to see The Palms again. It stood vacant. A protective wooden wall was erected around the perimeter of the sidewalk. Demolition was underway.

I looked up at fractured windows that had sheltered so many people over the years. A filmy lace curtain drifted out of a broken window below a torn shade.

I thought of Johnny, who had left home with his youth and a bag full of dreams and had spent his last days here, trying to numb the loneliness.

Like many of us, he had left the home of his youth far away in time and distance and circumstances.

Like many of us, he must have known that he could never, ever go home again.

21

The Bike Shop

N ext to the Thai family's faux lighthouse hamburger stand is a long, narrow building with a central hallway running its length. On either side are shops, mostly empty and gated shut with "For Lease" signs. Halfway down the silent hallway is a bicycle rental shop. It is one of the few commercial entities still thriving in Fisherman's Village. The Old Man often stopped here to visit with Lance, one of the employees. On the first day they met and introduced themselves, he had said, "I'm Lance, y'know, like Armstrong? But I don't do drugs!"

The famed Lance Armstrong he referred to had won the prestigious Tour de France bicycle race a record seven consecutive times after surviving testicular cancer and before falling out of grace due to doping charges. This Lance, however, was a stocky black man with very white teeth beneath an inverted V mustache on a shiny black face. It was not the same guy, but who could forget that name? Bike shop... Lance!

Sometimes the Old Man asked technical questions about bike equipment, and Lance enjoyed giving detailed explanations. One day, Lance readjusted the seat and brake system on the Old Man's bike, at no charge, just to demonstrate the right way to do it.

Today, Lance sat in a corner, reading a copy of *The Bikers Almanac*, rocking slowly back and forth on a blonde oak rocker.

"Hi, Lance. Another slow day, huh?"

"Hi, old-timer. Yeah, kinda slow today, but you should of been here last weekend. A bus-load of guys and gals from a Canadian bike club popped in an' rented out most of my stock for the whole weekend! I'm still resting up on my new rocker!"

The rocker didn't have the traditional rocker rails on the bottom. The seat assembly hung from a static base on swinging arms that allowed a rocking motion without the usual tipping backward and forward. It was built more like a porch swing that moved forward and backward in an almost perfectly horizontal position. More like sliding than rocking.

"Yeah, I noticed the rocker. I had one just like it, only smaller. It belonged to daughter number three. She left it behind when she moved away some years ago."

"I like this design," Lance said, "because I can rock it without my toe leaving the floor, and as it don't tip much it's a lot easier for reading without losing my place. Actually, it's a glider. That's what we called 'em in the day. The pendulum arms it swings on describe a longer arc with a longer radius. It glides more than rocks." He described the motion with his hands while he talked.

That was typical of Lance. No explanation went without a detailed analysis.

He is right, it is a glider. That's what they called them when I lived back East. A glider. Usually out on the front porch. Such a soothing motion.

The little Mexican guy who bought mine from me—was it Juan?—liked it because of that soothing motion. It would be easy on his wife and new baby.

I wonder whatever happened to them. I wonder if they remember me.

The Glider

It was fairly late that night when a man named Juan came to my house to look at the little glider chair. I had advertised it in the Penny Saver, a small local sales brochure. "Solid Oak Glider. Like new. $25."

His wife had called me earlier that night after reading my advertisement. In a heavy Mexican accent, she said she had a new baby and had to sit on a box to nurse it and it was uncomfortable. She asked if this glider was something she could sit on comfortably while nursing her new baby. Her husband, Juan, was out driving to other addresses looking at rocking chairs for her. It was early evening, and he was doing this after having worked all day. I suggested to her that he call me when he got home, and if he had not already purchased a rocker and was still interested to see my glider, I would wait up for him. I gave her driving instructions to my house.

Later, Juan called to say he was on his way if it was not too late for me. He showed up soon after. With him was a little boy, around three years old. We said hello, and he introduced himself and his little son. Juan was a distant descendant of the historically famous Segundo family whose ancestors had one time owned huge tracts of land in Southern California, deeded to them by the King of Spain. They operated cattle ranches and rich orchards. Through the vagaries of history and bad fortune, their vast possessions were dissipated over the years. Present generations of this once-wealthy family were now reduced to survival by unskilled manual labor—when it was available.

We spoke briefly. Juan was well-spoken though he also carried an accent. He tried out the glider and said it was perfect for his wife and new baby. He counted out $25, all $1 bills, all tightly folded. It was all he had with him. He held it out to me.

I thought of the time when my wife and I were very young and moving into our first home in the foothills above Glendale. We had one child, a two-year-old, and another on the way. Our few possessions were stacked on the front porch as the sellers, husband and wife, were loading the last of their possessions into a rental moving van. They were an older couple whose children were grown and gone. They were downsizing. The wife looked around at our scant furniture, the smiling two-year-old, and my pregnant wife. She turned to her husband and said, "Leave them the garden tools. They have nothing for the garden. We won't have a garden in the retirement village."

We had little money and shopped hard for every piece of furniture. I bought a small, used single bed with a horsehair mattress from a recently widowed old woman. She asked about my family, and I proudly told her about them. I explained that the bed would be for the two-year-old because the crib would soon be occupied by a newborn. I handed her the $20 asking price, the bills folded tightly in my hand. She watched while I loaded the bed and mattress into the back of my old station wagon. Then, as I was saying good-bye, she took my hand and pressed the money into it. "You know," she said, "I think I would like you to have that bed. I think my John would like that too."

We were struggling then. Now years later, my children were grown and gone. I lived alone. The years of worry and toil were all behind me now. But Juan, like me all those years ago, had little more than his ambition and pride. He didn't even haggle over the price. In that regard, he was more guileless than I. I had expected him to haggle. I would have taken less.

I cannot explain my feelings as I reached for that small packet of folded bills in his calloused hands. I recalled the sweet innocence in his wife's voice in that earlier phone call. I was impressed by his open sincerity as we spoke. I didn't mention any of that. I took the money.

But I simply could not put his money into my pocket. A voice whispered, insistently, "Pay it forward. Now is the time."

I held his money out before me, and calling him by name, I said that, with his permission, I felt moved to give him the glider. I pressed his money into his hand. His dark brown eyes glistened. He spoke softly and almost reverently. He said they had much difficulty paying their bills since the new baby had come. He said this was truly a blessing. I carried the glider as far as the front steps when Juan said, "I will take it now," and he lifted it lightly from my arms.

We were at the top of the brick steps, in the dark, with small step lights on. His son raised his tiny hand up to mine. He reached for me. I took his hand and we walked down the steps, one by one, and continued out to the pickup truck, following his Daddy.

When the chair was loaded, Juan turned toward me, perhaps to gather up his little son who still gripped my fingers tightly.

"Your son resembles you," I said. "What is his name?"

"Juan," he replied. "Like me. Little Juan. He is our miracle child."

He told me this little boy was expected to be born prematurely due to severe physical problems. Little Juan would be born much too early, sickly, and with serious defects, they told Juan and Isabel. The doctors recommended an abortion.

"We pray, Isabella and me. We ask God for guidance. We decide we keep the baby and trust in God. His will be done."

Little Juan weighed three and one-half pounds at birth and quickly shrank to two pounds. Death appeared imminent when, suddenly, all his symptoms disappeared. He grew healthy and normal and now stood there at my feet, still holding my fingers, looking up at me with shining, large brown eyes and a trusting smile.

I asked Juan to call me someday and tell me about his growing family.

"You have my phone number from the newspaper advertisement. Call me and let me know how little Juan and the new baby are doing."

He said he would. He belted Little Juan into his seat. As he climbed into the truck, he turned back to me and said, "I will pray for you. God will bless you."

That night was just another night. Except now there was one more person who would pray for me.

It had been a good night.

23

Blue

L ance held up a cautious hand by way of warning, leaned forward out of his new glider, and reached for something underneath the desk. His hand came slowly out with a handful of peanuts in the shell. His other hand pointed outside the doorway where a black, steel bicycle rack rested against the curb. On top of one rail sat a scrub jay. Most people call them blue jays, but the common variety, seen in Southern California, are scrub jays.

"Watch this guy," he whispered. He placed the peanuts on his desk, leaned back, and called out, "Come on, Blue!" The jay squawked, fluttered his wings, and flew in through the doorway, landing on the corner of the desk. Lance did not move. The jay hopped forward, picked at one of the peanuts, and flew off with it, shell and all.

"He comes almost every day for a handout. I call him 'Blue'. He must've been somebody's pet once. He'll be back."

Sure enough, in about one minute, the jay fluttered back to the desk, picked up another peanut, and departed. This sequence continued until the last peanut was gone.

"He'll be back tomorrow. He's been coming around for the last few weeks."

"Back in the eighties," the Old Man remembered, "when I was remodeling my house, I had a young jay who'd come into the house where the outside wall was torn down. He was pretty tame too. If I sat very still, he would pick at my shoelaces until they were untied. He ate shelled peanuts out of my hand. That went on for a couple months. Then he disappeared. I don't know what happened to him. Maybe it was because the wall was rebuilt and he couldn't get back inside."

"Cat might of got him. 'Specially if he was that tame."

"That's true," said the Old Man.

Like the pair who built a nest in one of my trees, he remembered.
They were not friendly.
Far from it.
It was the summer when our last child got married.
I had time on my hands and spent much of it around the house and yard.
That's how I came to notice what was going on, that time of the scrub jays.

24

The Time of the Scrub Jays

I n 1988, my employer was hit hard by the economic recession. They eliminated some of the managerial positions. Mine was one of them. For the next few months, while waiting to be recalled, I was busily planning the wedding of our youngest child, daughter number four. In between those activities, I worked on the house and in the yard painting, building, and landscaping.

It was spring time in Southern California. April, May, and June of that year our yards were brilliant with colors. Flowers burst from every corner. Bees busily tested each flower. Humming birds flitted in and out of the yard. But what I remember most of all were the scrub jays, beautifully blue-grey, noisy scrub jays.

Eggs had hatched, and the hatchlings were in the nest. I couldn't see them, hidden high in the trees, but Gerry could. He could hear them too. They nested up in the liquid amber tree on the west side of the house. The parent birds were wary of Gerry, and with good reason.

Gerry was our cat. He was a short hair tabby my daughter had found as a kitten wandering the nearby hillsides. He was a lovable kitten but had a knack for doing clumsy things, like leaping up onto a lap, losing his balance, and falling off the other side. One evening as we discussed possible names for him, the History channel was showing a television show about former President Gerald Ford. It showed him descending from the presidential plane, stumbling, and almost falling into the arms of one of his guards. The report showed an additional clip of President Ford on his skis, being interviewed in Vale, Colorado. As they talked, he began to helplessly slide backward down the hill. It was hilarious.

The vote was unanimous. The kitten became Gerald Ford, Gerry for short.

Gerry had caught his share of scrub jays of all sizes over the years. He was eyeing the hatchlings in our tree now. They were comparatively safe at the beginning of that spring, but as the days wore on and they grew larger, the time when they would attempt to leave the nest drew nearer. And that's when Gerry was his most dangerous. He knew the way of things. They would have to try out their wings soon. He would watch and wait. He might be clumsy, but with a little bit of luck, he might catch himself one or two fresh, juicy baby scrub jays.

The adult bird's tactic was simple. They would take turns harassing Gerry to drive him away from the tree. With dangerous, swooping dives and screeching voices, they made him duck and flinch and eventually retreat. When not physically threatening him, the jays would park nearby at a safe distance overhead and repeat a raucous screech at regular five- or six-second intervals to threaten and remind him to stay away.

I had heard the jays making that piercing sound in previous years, but I never got to see the stark pathos of this drama like I did that year.

In the beginning, Gerry would amble away from the tree to avoid the threats and harassment. As he did so, the jays settled down, even desisting for a while. But when Gerry stirred from his nap and began to roam the yard again, the parents resumed their attack. As the days passed and the babies grew, at least one parent always remained in close proximity to Gerry. Their vocal protestations grew more persistent, and they would hassle the cat even when he was at the far end of the yard away from the tree.

Eventually they hounded him incessantly, all day long, no matter where he was or what he was doing.

Gerry became accustomed to the activity and grew uncaring. He learned to ignore them; even napped while they dive-bombed him. They sometimes settled on the ground or a low branch within feet of his sleeping ears, screeching repeatedly.

We could now see the fledglings high in that tree, thrusting their beaks upward each time a parent arrived with food. They would soon have to make their maiden flights. The jays—and we–grew more concerned with each passing day. What to do? We could not lock Gerry inside the house indefinitely. He was an outside cat. We had no litter box and did not want one. Should we board him away for a week or two? But there were other cats in the neighborhood. With Gerry gone, the others might move in. We decided to let nature take its course.

Our daughter's wedding date loomed upon us. Decorations, cake, church date, reception arrangements, invitations, all fell into place. The rehearsal dinner zipped past. And then, it was over. I looked into her bedroom. She was the last child to leave. The nest was empty now, save for her bed and dresser and some of her things. That was all that she left behind. That and silence.

The next morning, we awoke to find Gerry asleep just outside the windows, curled up in the early morning sunlight. He seemed to have no interest in the liquid amber tree.

On that day, the conflict stopped. The threats and squawking of the jays was heard no more. Gerry was uninterested.

I did not see the events on the morning the nestlings left the nest. I don't know if they took wing successfully or met with disaster. I looked around the yard but found no feathers or evidence of a kill. The parents had cleaned out the empty nest. A few egg shell fragments lie in the ivy. That was all they left behind. That and silence.

My phone rang that day, and I returned to work. I had accomplished many tasks that spring. Now I resumed the routine of an office job, no longer aware of the life events that would take place in my yard during the working day.

Whenever I recall that spring, I do not think of it as the spring of unemployment or the spring a daughter got married or as the spring I accomplished so many projects around the house and yard.

No. I think of the drama that took place in the trees above me and how hard those parents worked and fought to protect their progeny and bring them to independence; every bit as committed as I was to do the same with our children that spring of 1988, that time of the Scrub Jays.

Sea Lions

"**G**uess I'll head on back," he told Lance. "Nothing else to see here to compete with that bird-feeding display."

"Well, yeah, there is. Drop by the bait dock on your way out. Lots of sea lion action. It's that time of year. The females are flirting and the males are on display, trying to get lucky. One 'specially big guy, must be about seven hundred pounds. That's worth seeing."

"Thanks. I'll have a look. See you next week, Lance."

He rode carefully along the brick walkway, turned back toward the faux lighthouse, and exchanged waves with the Thai lady as he passed her window again. Turning southwest at the railing, he cruised slowly next to the closed shops and down to the bait dock. Five large tubs held spacious nets that imprisoned bait fish. They sold bait to the several fishing boats that stopped on their way out each day with paying passengers. Fishermen on foot could also walk down the ramp to the office shed and buy bait and fish off the same dock. The presence of so many fish attracted a wide variety of sea birds, which was worth seeing on most days. Often there were as many as five or six species competing for the discarded fish. The pecking order was size-determined. Larger gulls bullied smaller ones—cormorants bullied gulls, pelicans bullied cormorants and egrets, and so on. The boss bully birds were always the blue herons whose rapier beaks and long, snakelike necks frightened off competitors by sight alone.

Just as Lance had said, a dozen sleek female sea lions cavorted on and around the dock. A short distance away, several bulls, identifiable by the bulbous forehead protrusions, posed and postured in their most winning ways. And there was the beach boss, an imposing bull whose ear flaps were larger than the others. All of them sported ear flaps. It was the ear flaps that distinguished sea lions from most seals. The full grown California sea lion was, he knew, a formidable hunter who could eat upward of thirty-five pounds of sea life at each meal.

That's a lot of food for one meal, he thought.

Sea lions! The lions of the sea!

He visualized that scene from many years ago when he watched as twenty-pound hunks of raw meat were being tossed out of the barred windows of a jeep to a group of hungry lions. Their roars caused his car to shiver, sending a terrifying vibrato clear through his body that seemed to terminate in his teeth. They were only a few feet away when the chunks hit the ground. The lions snarled, snatched the beef chunks away, and with ears laid back, crouched defensively, teeth bared, until the others had caught their own chunk or backed away to await leftovers.

That was in Orange County, or was it in San Diego County?

Lion Country Safari.

I think that's gone now. All that open acreage is probably now covered with houses.

Those lions, boy, they were something. And all those other wild animals... walking around the car.

Just a few feet away. No one was ever killed.

But they did have some close calls.

Like that time my friend, Paul, visited Lion Country Safari. What a story!

26

Lion Country Safari

Paul is a tall, well-dressed, good-looking guy with a rugged jaw, good physique, smiling brown eyes, soft voice and mannerism, and a ready sense of humor that thinly hid a no-nonsense set of expectations when it came to business. He had attained a high position in the engineering management of our Arizona division.

I met him when he was transferred to Los Angeles. This was an exciting and busy time for Paul. He began disposing of his Arizona home and making other personal arrangements for his departure. A short time later, he moved into his new office in Los Angeles. During the next few weeks, he lived at his sister's home in L.A. On weekends, he flew to Arizona to take care of final last-minute details.

But one weekend, he decided to remain in Los Angeles, hunt for a home to purchase, and see some of the sights. That Friday evening, he asked his sister what might be of interest other than the usual tourist attractions. Disneyland was old hat. He had been there. Hollywood and Grauman's Chinese Theater were jaded attractions. He had been there many times too. Then, as one, the family blurted out excitedly, "Lion Country Safari!"

Lion Country Safari was a chain of parks comprised of a number of fenced compounds, spread over hundreds of acres, which housed wild animals native to Africa. Each compound held several species of compatible African wildlife. Predators were separated from prey by tall chain link fences topped by razor wire. A narrow road ran through the entire facility, connecting each compound. Visitors drove through the facility in their own cars. A rented tape player described what was to be seen in each enclosure. By starting and stopping the tape player, visitors could take their time enjoying close-up encounters with each species of wildlife.

The paved road that led through the immense compounds was sectioned off by remotely controlled gates that let each car through to the next enclosure. Antelope, cheetahs, giraffes, ostriches, rhinoceros, zebras, lions, and other animals numbered in the hundreds. Most of the fencing was hidden in deep, wide ditches so the visitor had the illusion of driving through an African savanna. Watch towers, located near each gate, housed armed guards who opened the gate for each auto as it approached. They kept in touch by radio with several roving jeeps that patrolled the route. The guard's jeeps were painted a delightful zebra pattern. Windows on the jeeps were barred to protect the guards, whose additional duty was to throw raw meat to the big cats at feeding time.

All of the staff, including the guards, wore appropriate safari garb and hats and the occasional pith helmet, all of which served to maximize the illusion of being in wild Africa.

The first Lion Country Safari was opened in Florida in 1967. Its popularity led to the construction of six more around the United States. In June 1970, one opened in Irvine, California, forty miles from downtown Los Angeles in beautiful Orange County, so named for the miles of orange groves that occupied it during its early years.

But the Irvine facility had an unusual drawing card that none of the others had. In 1970, an old lion named Frasier, who had performed for years with an old Mexican circus act, was donated to the park. Frasier brought with him an uncanny charm that the lionesses found to be irresistible. He had already sired many dozens of offspring and was a favorite of the females. Photos appeared in Los Angeles newspapers of the aged Frasier mating with one lioness while being supported by other females who, standing on either side, helped to hold him upright. All the while, younger males scowled jealously from a distance.

There was a rumor that the other males had been fixed to avoid competition, but no one knew how true this was. In 1971, a movie was released called *Frasier the Sensuous Lion*, which added to the legend. Wristwatches and T-shirts bearing Frasier photos and comments were all the rage. His prowess had been publicized throughout the country. Even Paul from Arizona had heard of Frasier the virile lion.

Paul had not moved his car to Los Angeles yet. His brother-in-law volunteered. "Use my car. I won't need it tomorrow." The new white Ford Pinto, sitting at the curb, was a neat little two-door job that would be perfect for this type of sightseeing. He handed Paul the keys.

Early Saturday morning, Paul set out, map in hand, to see the wonders of the Serengeti up close and personal.

After a drive of several hours, he arrived, bought his ticket, and rented the tape recording. He saw the signs that said "No Convertibles Allowed" and "Remain in your car with windows closed at all times!"

He was greeted at the entrance of the first compound by a large sign bearing the warning "No Trespassing. Violators Will Be Eaten!"

As the first gate closed behind him, he started the tape. The thrill of being in the open with this wildlife was enhanced by frequent signs that urged visitors to remain inside their vehicles with their windows closed.

Paul was about to leave the elephant, hippopotamus, and rhinoceros compound. The tape player informed him that the lion compound was next. He looked forward to the excitement of driving in the midst of Africa's top predators and was especially anxious to see Frasier and the lionesses. Feeding time was fast approaching, and according to the narration tape, the attendants would arrive to feed the lions. In the distance, he could hear the already impatient roars of the hungry cats.

Up ahead he could see the large gate and just beyond that the guard tower. In front of him, in the center of the roadway, strolled a large rhinoceros. Paul stopped and waited for it to complete its slow walk across the road. The rhino stopped, halfway across, turned, and stared directly at him. Paul waited patiently. No movement. Paul edged forward cautiously. The rhino did not move. Paul edged the car closer then stopped again. The rhino stared fixedly at the Pinto. Paul and the rhino stayed thusly for what seemed to be a long time.

Finally, worried about missing the lion feeding time, Paul blew the horn.

As if being called by the sound, the rhino began to trot forward toward the Ford Pinto. A few feet in front of the car, the rhino stopped, tossed its head, and snorted. Paul was filled with apprehension, not knowing what to expect or what to do next. Did the Pinto horn sound like a challenge from another male?

He had just decided not to antagonize it with the horn again when it took several quick steps forward, reared up directly in front of the Pinto, mounted the hood, and proceeded to mate with the front grill.

Perhaps the Pinto horn sounded like an amorous female.

The hood collapsed, the radiator split. Hot water gushed out the bottom of the car. Paul could only stare in shock, his foot pressed rigidly on the brake pedal, as the little car was rocked, backward and forward, by the frenzied sexual encounter. Steam rose from under the crushed hood and enveloped the passionate rhino. As if inspired by the gushing hot water and steam, the rhino increased his efforts.

Paul sat petrified with a mixture of horror and fascination as the rhino sated himself then backed off and, without so much as a "Thank You" or "I'll call you in the morning," ambled away.

There were no cell phones at that time. Paul could not exit the car. It was too dangerous and, in fact, forbidden. All he could do was sit and wait for the watch tower to summon the patrol jeep to rescue him.

Once safely outside the compound, Paul waited in the ticket office. A tow truck entered the compound to extract the violated Pinto. While waiting, he contemplated the embarrassing and awkward task of calling his sister.

After struggling for some time, searching for the right words, he made the phone call and reported that his brother-in-law's shiny, new white Ford Pinto had been raped by a horny but nearsighted wild rhinoceros.

By way of apology, the management offered him free tickets for another visit... perhaps, they suggested, in a slightly larger, darker-colored vehicle.

Then, in a misguided effort at levity, the ticket attendant asked if, since they had provided the sire, Lion Country Safari could have first pick of the litter.

27

Ballona Creek

He rode his bike out of Fisherman's Village and around the traffic circle at the end of Fiji way and headed directly toward Ballona Creek, a freshwater creek that drained into the Pacific Ocean. On his left was a high chain link fence that protected a wild nature preserve where the elegant blue herons built nests. He looked, as he always did, for nesting herons and saw none this day.

The path took a sharp right turn at the creek and continued for a long half-mile due West, directly into the prevailing ocean wind. It often reached ten or fifteen knots, blowing straight into his face, doubling the effort required to pedal up the long, gradual incline leading out of the main channel toward the sea.

As he made the turn, he noticed something he had missed when he came in earlier. Just below him, along the north bank of Ballona Creek, were dozens of stone statues. He pulled over, got off his bike, and strolled closer to where a small crowd was gathering. Columns of rocks and stones, gathered from the thousands that lined the creek banks, were expertly balanced, like stone snowmen, each resembling a different figure of a man or woman or unique geometric figure. No two were exactly alike. One looked like an early Californian Spanish missionary priest with frock and triangular hat who was holding a staff. Closer inspection revealed three stacked rocks, a large trapezoidal-shaped base resembling a friar's frock, a small, round rock with a flat top for the head, and a slightly larger triangular-shaped stone sitting atop the flat spot on the head. The arm was nothing more than a raised ridge on one side of the base rock that supported a piece of bleached driftwood for the staff.

A sign hung from the wire cable that bordered the path. It gave the artist's name and listed his phone number. Lower down the embankment, the artist himself was carefully experimenting with a good-sized rock, seeking to balance it atop a larger boulder.

"How does he do that? How does he keep them from falling?" a red-headed boy with black plastic earrings asked his girlfriend. She turned her partially shaved head of hair, which was dyed a bright green, and answered, "Probably glues them together."

A bike rider in brightly colored bicycle club gear and wearing a Van Dyke goatee smiled and said, "No, he doesn't glue them. They are balanced just so." He pointed to the hanging sign and continued, "Mr. Cuisia is famous for these free-standing rock sculptures. I've seen his work before."

The Old Man looked more closely at the hanging sign and read that Mr. Ernesto Cuisia was born in 1942 in Manila on the island of Luzon in the Philippines.

That would have made him three years old or so when my cousin Dick landed with American troops to drive out the Japanese during World War II. This sculptor could have been one of the starving, frightened little Filipino children that my cousin Dick gave chocolate to when he helped to liberate the Philippines from Japanese occupation. What was it he told me about those awful days in Manila?

Something about a gold chain?

Oh, yes... I remember now...

28

The Gold Chain

Dick Morelli was born in 1917, the child of Italian immigrants. His greatest love, before he met my cousin Liberia "Lil" Giangolini, was to ride his motorcycle which, in the 1930s, was still considered a daredevil activity akin to flying one of those things called an aeroplane. When he decided Lil was "the one," he asked her permission to approach her parents. They approved on one condition: Dick must give up his beloved motorcycle. He did and, in his words, "never regretted the trade."

The United States Army drafted Dick at the start of World War II, trained him at Kings Ranch, Texas, and shipped him to the South Pacific.

Shortly after the Japanese attack on Pearl Harbor, the Japanese invaded the Philippine islands with overwhelming forces that drove back the much smaller United States and Filipino defenses. General McArthur, who was in charge of those forces, fled to Australia, making his famous pledge, "I shall return." On the Bataan peninsula, on the island of Luzon, he left behind— abandoned, some would say—US troops who were instructed to delay the Japanese as long as possible. The horrific details of that human sacrifice were later memorialized in a movie called, aptly, *They Were Expendable*. When American and Filipino armed forces collapsed, the Japanese took seventy-six thousand prisoners. These prisoners of war were force-marched eighty miles inland under brutal conditions that caused many deaths. It became known as the Death March.

Three years later, on January 9, 1945, the US Sixth Army invaded Luzon, landing on the shores of Lingayen Gulf in the northern third of the island and drove south toward Manila, the capital of Luzon. A week later, another landing was made south of Manila. Japanese army general Yamashita ordered all his forces out of Manila in order to concentrate his resistance inland. However, about ten thousand Japanese marines under Vice Admiral Iwabuchi ignored orders and remained behind. Their anger and frustration was vented in what became known as the Manila Massacre. They killed some one hundred thousand Manila residents, looting, burning, executing, decapitating, and otherwise abusing men, women, children, Red Cross personnel, prisoners of war, and hospital patients.

Dick's outfit did the usual island-hopping invasions that slowly but inexorably recaptured them from the Japanese Imperial forces.

The US Eighth Army launched a mop-up phase on the island of Luzon. Cousin Dick was assigned to special ground forces fighting their way through Luzon.

"It was awfully hot. We did a lot of killing. We were knocking out Jap machine gun nests in advance of the army, then we'd radio back that it was clear for them to move forward. When we got to Manila, they ordered us to clear out the town of any remaining Japs. We had to weed them out of the homes where they were hiding."

"What should we do with prisoners?" his men asked. But they had almost no food or water for themselves and no place to hold prisoners.

He gave the tough answer that his superiors had given to him: "We can't take prisoners."

With a platoon of sixty battle-hardened men, he proceeded to work from building to building. They had captured the city in three and a half days but fought on for another two and a half months.

As they moved up one rubble-strewn street, he saw four figures huddled on the front steps of a two-story house. A little boy and an even smaller little girl cried uncontrollably. Squatting behind them were, he assumed, their parents. They were dirty, hungry, and frightened. Dick walked up to them and noticed that the boy, still crying, kept pointing guardedly upward and behind his head. Dick spoke to them using the few native words he had learned, trying to console them. But the boy kept crying, shaking, and pointing upward toward the building behind him. It took a moment for Dick to figure it out. He called together six of his guys.

"Looks like there are Japs upstairs in this one. They've kicked this family out and are hiding up there. Kill 'em, then throw 'em out the back door—not the front." They did.

Dick gave his last K rations—basic hard tack—to the parents and some of his chocolate to the children. The boy stopped crying, but the little girl could not stop sobbing. Dick had a gold chain necklace and medallion hanging around his neck. He removed it and offered it to the little girl. Sniffling, she took it, fingered it, staring at it in awe. Then, very slowly, she looked up at him and smiled. He put it around her tiny neck. It was a touching moment, but only that. They could not linger. The platoon had to keep moving, under pressure to finish clearing out the remaining enemy as soon as possible.

His platoon grew to about ninety men as it absorbed survivors from other platoons which had suffered heavy losses. They were tired, hungry, thirsty, and dirty. They had not bathed or shaved in some time. They received two canteens of water a day, barely enough to slack their thirst in this hellishly hot climate. They had received no food in a couple days and were starving. They sat inside a captured building, taking a twenty-minute break from fighting. Dick was having trouble breathing. The heat, dust, and dehydration were taking their toll on him. He went outdoors thinking he'd feel better if he could sit outside in the shade of a large tree in the yard. As he rounded the tree, he saw General McArthur standing there with a contingent of his minions. McArthur crooked a finger at him to call him over.

"Why do you look so dirty and unshaven?" he asked.

"We have no water to wash up with or to shave. We can't wash our clothes."

"How many men report to you, Sergeant?"

"Ninety, sir."

"Well, you are setting a very poor example for them."

Dick had been living under the shadow of death for months now and no longer feared the pompous foolery of pretentious brass.

"Well, General, if you gave us as much water and food as you have and a fresh new uniform every day like you get, we could look like you, too, sir!"

The General stared for a moment directly at this tough subordinate. Behind him the General's staff grinned and gave Dick thumbs-up signs. McArthur turned on his heel and walked away. The Colonels remained behind, grinning. One leaned forward and said, "Nobody talks to him like that! Good for you, Sergeant!"

Shortly thereafter they were issued extra water, clean clothes, and a three-day rest.

Not long afterward, Dick's Major offered him a promotion to second lieutenant. It was common knowledge that the Japanese targeted anyone wearing Lieutenant's bars. They had a short life expectancy. Dick refused. "I'd get the same pay and be put on the front lines. I don't want it."

During subsequent combat on other islands, he was shot in the leg and lay on the ground for four hours before being rescued. The bullet entered the bone and remains there to this day. His leg, from stomach to toes, was turning blue. They gave him blood and penicillin then loaded him on a twin engine bomber headed to a hospital in Australia.

On final approach over the Pacific Ocean, he saw smoke coming out of the right engine. He looked out the other window and saw the same thing. Both engines smoked and had stopped running. It was terribly quiet.

Turning to the Aussie pilot, he asked, "Did we lose our engines?"

"Yeah, I turned 'em off," he lied. "But no worries. We'll glide in. Hang on, mate. With no power, we've no brakes. It's bound to be a bit rough."

They bounced hard then rattled and banged radically down the runway, coming to a stop just short of the tree line. The landing was so violent; Dick felt nauseous. After landing, he learned the engines had not been turned off—they were burned out.

He was transported to a hospital where an American doctor eventually showed up and asked where Dick was from.

"Utica, New York," he said. The doc said they were neighbors. He was from Ilion, a nearby small town.

When his leg had recovered sufficiently, Dick was asked where he wanted to go for rest and recuperation (R & R). He said he'd like to go home. They laughed and said that wasn't possible, but he could go to a small town in Australia which had been set up for the Yanks to have R & R. He filled up on hamburgers, fries, and other Yank food for the first time in two years. One day, he asked an Aussie if he knew where there might be an Italian restaurant. Yes, he was told, there was one run by an Italian family just a few blocks away. For the first time since he left home, Dick got his fill of spaghetti and meatballs.

After his discharge, he resumed civilian life with his wife, Lil, and met for the first time his now three-year-old daughter, Beverly. Years passed, Dick retired and moved the family to Florida, eventually building a new home on a golf course in Clairmont, Florida, a small town about thirty miles northwest of Orlando. The long, cold winters and high snowbanks of upstate New York became a distant memory.

One day, recently, he developed a bad cough and went to see his physician. The staff checked him in at the desk and assigned him to a small waiting room. He sat there, looking at wall charts and old magazines, waiting for his doctor to appear. Another doctor walked by, looked briefly into the open door and disappeared. A moment later the strange doctor returned, stopped in the doorframe, and stared at Dick, smiling quizzically. Dick recognized him immediately. He remembered that smile. It had been sixty-two years, but it was unchanged.

This new doctor stepped inside the room, took Dick's hand in both of his, and said, "You are the soldier who gave me chocolate on the front steps of my father's home in Manila."

Choking with emotion, he continued, "My sister is still in Manila. She still wears the gold chain necklace you gave her. She has worn it every day since then. It was so worn she had to have it re-plated."

They chatted for a moment more. Then he added, "My sister has made a necklace for you and hopes one day to visit you and give it to you. She wants to thank you in person for what you did for us."

"I will be here, waiting." Dick grinned back. "I'm not going anywhere."

Dick and Lil are now in their mid-nineties. They still live in Florida but have moved to be closer to their children.

One day, perhaps, a Filipino woman, now grown but still smiling shyly, wearing a worn gold chain necklace, will walk into their doorway. She will be carrying a small gift, a handmade necklace, and the chain of memories will be completed.

29

Playa Del Rey

The Filipino sculptor on the bank of Ballona Creek continued to select various pieces of stone, slowly turning and balancing each one, testing for appearance and fit. It was deliberate, tedious work, and the Old Man soon lost interest. He resumed his ride into the stiff westerly wind, dropping his gear ratio several levels, hunching over to reduce wind resistance. At the end of the harbor channel, the path turned left over Ballona Creek Bridge then another right to the beach and a final left heading south, parallel to the shoreline.

A half mile past the creek, at the end of some volleyball nets, was one of the larger rest areas, complete with restrooms and a snack bar. He stopped to take a sip of cold water from the fountain. Several groups occupied the picnic benches, just outside the snack bar. His attention was drawn to a girl who looked familiar to him. He could not tell her age, but there was something distinctly odd about her appearance. She looked to be about twelve years old, with chubby arms and legs on a stocky torso. Her face was full and round with puffed lips and small, slightly bulging, close-set eyes on a head that seemed overly large, out of proportion to her body.

It was when she spoke to her parents, slowly, with a heavy, plodding, lisp that it came to him. She resembled Ellen. Ellen was born with Down Syndrome. He had known her during his years in grammar and high school. She did not attend school, but she did live in his neighborhood, and he saw her often. Ellen was sweet and shy, and she knew his name. Sometimes when he and his little friends were playing outdoors, she would come strolling up the street wearing a clean but plain dress, bobby sox, flat-soled, laced shoes, and straight hair in a Dutch-boy cut with a colorful bow or ribbon which her mother had tied on one side. She would stop in front of him and stare at him until he looked at her eyes. Then she would incline her head to one side and shyly whisper "Hello" and then his name with a slow, thick-tongued lisp. She seldom said anything other than that. She would stay and watch the children play a while then slowly retreat back down the street to her home.

I haven't thought about Ellen since I left high school.

Come to think of it, Ellen was the youngest sister of Mr. Del Buono, my high school teacher of English and Composition.

Everybody in school liked Mr. Del Buono.

Our high school… what were those words over the doors?

…how did that go?

…the reason,

…the skill,

…the observation,

…the spirit…

30

Proctor

Boy! Our first day of high school! Chickie and I, freshly scrubbed and dressed, met at the front of the alley that ran between our apartment building and Flemma's Shoe Store next door. We walked to the corner and made small talk—nervous talk—as we waited, watching down Mohawk Street for Sammy to appear. We were filled with excitement and apprehension. A small figure appeared several blocks away and moved slowly toward us. It soon became recognizable as the shuffling, grinning Sammy.

Together we began our first fourteen-block walk to high school. The usual route was up Albany Street then a right turn over Hilton Street. One warm summer day, we turned right off Albany one block earlier, crossing over Jefferson. We encountered a young woman who seemed mentally challenged. She sat on the very top step of her porch, tapping a small pencil slowly against her lips and staring at us as we walked by. It was not the pencil or the tapping that motivated us to occasionally repeat that route. It was the fact that as she sat on that high step—at our eye level—we noted that she wore no underpants. But alas, it never happened again, and we gradually returned to the Jefferson crossing.

The luxurious long green lawn in front of the school seemed majestic. We had no green lawns where we lived. Two broad sidewalks, one at each end of the building, led up to two cathedral-height double doors. Cast into the white concrete lintels over each door, intaglio style, were four phrases.

Over the left hand entrance, we read:

The Reason
The Skill
The Observation
The Spirit

And over the entrance to the right was:

The Intellect
The Will
The Imagination
The Memory

This would be the first thing we saw, high above our heads, mighty and intimidating, like a stern but benevolent mentor, every school day thereafter. I found it stirring and inspirational. Though I never had it explained to me, I assumed it implied that these were things we must attain in order to succeed in life and that they were available behind these doors.

That first day of attendance was fraught with new feelings. Some of us had older brothers or sisters who had attended before us and had come home with stories of football games, dances, high school sweaters, and sports letters. They brought home notebooks and textbooks held together in stacks with leather belts strapped around them, which the boys carried slung over one shoulder. The girls, of course, held them without belts, bunched under one arm or held close at chest level. No one used backpacks back then. We did not know what a backpack was.

CARMEN

I was assigned to Ms. Mary Nolan's homeroom—number 141. Ms. Nolan was unmarried and wore sensible clothes and shoes with short, Cuban heels. She was the younger sister of Mr. Nolan who taught auto mechanics in the basement of the school. She was a gentle disciplinarian with a softness that she tried to hide behind a stern exterior.

I sat about two-thirds of the way back near the rear of the room, just behind Carmen Del Monico, a senior with beautiful olive-black eyes and hair, amazing eyelashes, lips like tiny roses, a voluptuous figure, and a sensuous way of sliding into her seat each morning. Our desks and chairs were single, one-piece units. The back of her chair butted up against the front of my desk. I could smell her perfume and mentally stroke her long, shimmering, thick, wavy hair just inches in front of me.

Carmen dated our football team quarterback and was far beyond my simple, freshman's reach. But she was sweet to me— kind of motherly, if you will. One day, she turned to me and asked me if I had a girlfriend yet. My heart skipped a beat.

"No," I answered, looking shyly up at her through my eyebrows.

"Don't worry, sweetie," she cooed. "Your time will come!"

I recorded that voice, those words and the promise, and played it over and over in my head.

Most of the boys in the room were smitten with Carmen. Jerry, another senior student who sat to her left, was obsessed with teasing her in order to get her attention. One morning, before she arrived, he placed a thumb tack on her seat. She sat down and, luckily, missed it just enough so that, although she felt a slight pinch, it did not seriously pain her. After that, she was very scrupulous about inspecting the seat before sitting down. Jerry tried a new technique. He waited until she inspected the chair and then, as she lowered herself to sit, he leaned over to slide the tack under her. She was too wary and caught him every time. At lunch one day, Jerry and the boys conceded defeat and said it simply couldn't be done. Carmen was much too cautious. The element of surprise was lost.

I suppose I wanted to be noticed and accepted by the older boys. "I could do it," I foolishly announced. They examined me, a mere freshman, with skepticism.

"Yeah? How? I've tried every which way, and she catches me. It can't be done."

"I can do it," I said.

"Yeah, right," one of the other seniors smirked.

"I can do it," I stubbornly repeated.

In a voice dripping with derision, a third snapped, "Okay, frosh, you do it. Tomorrow morning. We'll be watching."

They exchanged glances of ridicule, got up from the table, and walked away as the warning bell announced that our lunch hour was over.

I worried about it all night. The next morning I made it a point to arrive early. The other senior boys came shuffling in soon after, and finally, as she always did, Carmen came oozing into the room like flowing honey, every move a romantic melody. And as usual, all the boys watched her and exchanged smiles with her. She said good morning to me as she always did, smiling with her eyes in that special way that women all over the world greet a little cute, loveable, innocent baby. She put down her books, inspected the seat of her desk, and slowly lowered her lovely posterior into the seat, carefully looking around her for any extended hands that might attempt to place a thumb tack on the seat. Satisfied, she plopped down the last half inch.

A piercing scream filled the room. Carmen sprang to her feet, both hands clamped over one buttock cheek. Ms. Nolan leapt to her feet, dropping her pencil, and came running down the aisle to her aid. They looked for the offending tack but found none. The subsequent investigation yielded nothing. Carmen told Ms. Nolan of her previous experiences with the seniors and thumb tacks. The boys denied any involvement in this episode. There was no thumb tack, nor any other explanation for the pain Carmen had felt. The senior boys looked in surprise in my direction with little smiles of admiration and curiosity. I had earned their respect.

Ms. Nolan announced that if no one confessed, she would hold the class after school. The bell rang, releasing us to go to our first class. We filed out of the homeroom and scattered in all directions, going to our respective classes. At the end of the day, I returned to the homeroom as quickly as possible before most of the other students, meekly approached Ms. Nolan, and confessed. She ordered me to remain after the others were excused. When the bell rang to release us for the day, no one moved. Ms. Nolan rose and said, "You are excused." They went home. I remained seated. The senior boys looked back at me with newfound respect.

After about fifteen minutes, Ms. Nolan motioned me to the front of the empty room. I stood in front of her desk and awaited my execution.

"What did you do to Carmen?" she asked.

"Put a thumb tack on her chair."

"Why would you do such a terrible thing? That's not like you."

I explained about what the other boys had done, how they said it could not be done again because Carmen was too wary, how I foolishly boasted that I could do it, and how the older boys challenged me in disbelief. Ms. Nolan asked me to promise never to do such a thing again. I promised. She told me to apologize to Carmen in the morning. I said I would. She excused me.

As I turned to leave, she called out my name. I turned. She looked at me for a moment and then said, "How did you do it?"

I approached her desk and asked for a thumb tack and a sheet of paper. I folded the sheet in half, lengthwise, twice so it was about two inches wide, eleven inches long, and four paper thicknesses. I punched the tack through it about half an inch from the far end and explained while I demonstrated. "I held it under my desk, behind her seat, like this, and when her bottom was only half an inch from the seat and she was not looking down, I slid it forward. When she screamed and jumped up, I withdrew it back under the desk. I hid it inside my books when we stood up to go to first hour class."

Ms. Nolan took the paper and tack from me, remained silent, looking intently at me, then without another word she waved me away, her mouth held tightly shut, the little muscles around her lips quivering ever so slightly as she fought to withhold a smile.

I apologized to Carmen in the morning.

Mr. Del Buono

I discovered a love for composition and the proper use of the English language a few years earlier in a grade school class whose teacher had taken the time to show us how to use timing and inflection to bring the written and spoken word to life. It was Mr. Del Buono who inspired us and taught us to create our own compositions. His editorial reviews of the essays I wrote were at once instructive and encouraging.

Mr. Del Buono was always approachable. Somehow he managed to make me feel he was just one of the students, a highly educated and gifted student, but one of us nevertheless.

He was bold with the techniques he used to teach us and in one particular incident not only convinced me that he was "one of us," but the lesson learned has remained with me ever since.

I was reading one of my compositions in front of the class and mispronounced the word "asterisk." I pronounced it as "a-*stare*-isk," with the accent on the second syllable. When I was through, he thanked me, then he addressed the class.

"Several of you have mispronounced this word," he said as he wrote it in large letters on the blackboard. "I know the correct pronunciation is counterintuitive. I'll tell you a story that may help you to remember." He put down the chalk, dusted off his hands, and turned to us, smiling.

"Once upon a time, there was a small village. In this village was a pretty girl who caught the attention of a young man who was new to the village. This new young man approached his friend, who knew her, and asked for an introduction.

"'She looks so sweet and innocent,' he said. 'I think I love her. I want to ask her to marry me.'

"His friend replied, 'You do not want to take this girl to meet your mother. She is extremely promiscuous. She has slept with many of the men in this village. She is neither pure nor innocent. You might say that she has no "*ass*-te-risk."' He placed the accent firmly on the first syllable."

Boys laughed. Some snickered. Girls blushed. Some giggled. But none of us ever mispronounced the word "asterisk" again.

We had a pleasant conversation on one of the last days of school. With my yearbook in hand, I approached him for his autograph. I mentioned that I lived just up the street from him.

"I know," he said. "My sister, Ellen, sometimes talks about you."

"She's really nice but a little strange," I said. "She comes up and watches us hang out and calls me by my name."

"Ellen suffers from Down Syndrome. Some of the kids make fun of her. Kids can be cruel to someone who is different. They don't understand. You've treated her with kindness. Ellen feels safe around you. That is why she remembers your name. Thank you for that."

Ellen lived an unusually long time for someone with that condition. I like to think that my kindness contributed to that.

PHYSICAL EDUCATION

When the bell rang before our physical education class, it meant we had just ten minutes to get to the gymnasium locker room, grab the wire basket that contained our gym clothes, change into gym clothes, and run outside to the field to stand in a straight line, shoulder to shoulder. Our coach conducted roll call before sending us out to run a couple warm-up laps around the quarter-mile track.

If he called out a name and there was no response, he marked the boy absent. The coach would revisit the name if the boy came out later.

One afternoon, two boys failed to answer to their names—Stan Usyk and Sal Vitello. Just as the coach finished roll call, one of the missing boys came running out of the building. The coach knew it had to be one of the two. He took a guess.

As the boy drew close, Mr. Hammes shouted, "Usyk?"

"No, coach," Sal replied, "I ain't sick. I had to pee!"

Drafting Class

Several technical courses were held in the basement of the school—woodworking, machine shop, drafting, and technical toolmaking. Each class lasted two to three hours.

Drafting class was taught by Mr. Pope. In this room, each student had his own high stool, a drafting board with a T square, a couple triangles, and an assortment of drawing tools for creating mechanical designs.

Mr. Pope was an elderly, soft-spoken gentleman with sparse white hair and a pink-cheeked, cherubic face. He wore a three-piece suit and a tie every day. His eyes squinted behind thick wire-rimmed reading glasses perched on the end of a little round nose. Mr. Pope taught us the art of mechanical design by lecture and example. After each class lesson, he gave us a design challenge that would use the principles he had just demonstrated. During the several days it took to complete these assignments, there was very little for Mr. Pope to do. A couple times each afternoon, he walked around looking over shoulders, making comments, or giving help. But during the rest of those long hours, Mr. Pope slept. He didn't mean to fall asleep, but the room was deathly silent with only the whisper of T squares and plastic triangles being slid over drafting paper. It was a recipe for dreaming. The occasional growl of a pencil sharpener and the tick of the large black-numbered clock high on the wall over his desk only added to the lullaby. He often drifted off.

Walter Desmond, a gifted roller skater and cartoonist, who delighted in drawing and coloring pornographic comic strips while the teacher slept, liked to torment Mr. Pope. He waited until Mr. Pope was deep in slumber, his chin resting gently on his tie. Holding the T end of a T square firmly down with his left hand, he bent the long arm sharply upward then released it to slap down on the drafting board with the sharp sound of a rifle shot. Mr. Pope, predictably, jumped in his chair and looked around to see a class of bowed heads studiously working on their drawings.

But what I recall most vividly about Mr. Pope was his log cabin which had been built sometime in the 1700s. It was located in the woods north of the city, in the Deerfield foothills, and was designated as a historical site. To make it habitable, he had been allowed to add gas and electric service. He lived there alone and maintained it for the Oneida County Historical Society.

One day, he asked if anyone in our class would be willing to come and help him to move some heavy furniture which he was no longer able to do by himself. Joe Spano, who owned his own car, volunteered and asked me to join him. The cabin was, indeed, made out of logs. It was very small, with the original mud pitch between the logs replaced by what appeared to be light-gray colored clay. The cabin consisted of one large room that had a kitchen with a stone fireplace at one end and a combination bedroom and sitting area at the other end. Hanging blankets served as room dividers. After we moved the furniture for him, he offered to pay us for our trouble. We declined.

"Well, at least let me give you a treat," he said. He bent over to pull back a large rug from the center of the cabin. There, recessed neatly into the polished half logs of the floor, was a heavy trap door. He opened it and ushered us down a short flight of stairs into a dirt cellar. He turned on a lightbulb that hung from the cellar ceiling. The cellar was very small and held a wooden bench and a large freezer chest. He lifted the lid. "Help yourselves," he said, gesturing inside with his open hand, smiling so hard that it made his elfish eyes squint tightly behind the thick glass orbs of his eyeglasses. We looked inside, expecting to see frozen meats or packaged food.

Instead there were layers and layers of frozen ice cream bars of various flavors. We helped ourselves.

As we climbed back up the stairs, he said, "See the two heavy bolts under the trap door? They lock the door shut from underneath." He explained that the historical society had records showing the cabin had been attacked by Indians at least one time and the residents had taken shelter in this cellar. When we returned upstairs, he showed us the hatchet marks on the top side of the trap door that were allegedly made by the marauding Indians in an attempt to get at the hiding family.

Joe and I talked about the cabin and Mr. Pope on our ride back to town with renewed wonder. This gentle old man was living a child's dream in an old cabin filled with dramatic vestiges of adventurous frontier times. We envied him.

THE FIGHT

Little Hank Maggio was my shortest buddy and one of my staunchest friends. He was determined to overcome his stature by courage and persistence. Because of his size, he was presumed to be an easy target by the campus bullies. They never made the same mistake twice.

One epic event, which set the tone for several others, occurred after school one afternoon. Two kids were bickering out on the rear lawn outside the woodshop windows. It escalated into shoving and then blows. The much larger of the two, a kid we called Big Al, was badly beating his smaller opponent. When the loser attempted to withdraw from the fight, Big Al continued to pummel him. That is when Hank stepped in.

"He quits. Leave him alone, Al!" Hank said.

Hank was even smaller than the loser, so Big Al eagerly attacked Hank. He promptly knocked Hank to the ground with a couple of well-placed blows. As he stood looking proudly around at the ring of onlookers, Hank sprang to his feet and lunged at the big guy. They exchanged punches, and again Hank was knocked off his feet. He rolled over onto his hands and knees and shakily rose. He had a cut lip and a bloody nose. He charged into Big Al, knocking him backward and off his feet. They rolled on the ground. Big Al got up first, and as Hank struggled to his feet, he received two more hard blows. Down Hank went. This time he was slower to rise. Big Al was breathing heavily. Hank steadied himself and then plunged again, head first, at his large protagonist. His fists flailed, giving punches as fast as he received them. He was bleeding profusely from his nose and lips. His eyes were puffy and turning colors. Large red bruises and small lacerations speckled his face. Still he kept coming back. We watched in awe as the bruiser knocked Hank to the ground several more times, but each time with greater effort and less enthusiasm.

We lost count of how many times Hank got back onto his feet and charged, head down, fists flying, spittle and blood flicking off his face. Big Al began to back off, struggling for breath. His blows grew feeble. Hank should have been backing off, too, but he didn't.

Finally, with a look of exhaustion and surrender, Big Al held out both hands, palms facing toward Hank. Little Hank Maggio stopped in mid-charge, puzzled by the palms in his face.

"Okay, okay," Big Al gasped.

Hank was breathing hard and trembling with adrenaline. He wanted to continue—I could see that. I stepped forward, put an arm around his shoulders, and whispered, "You done good, Hank. You done good. Let's go home."

And we did.

The Blonde

I was a junior in high school, and I still had no girlfriend. Then she appeared out of nowhere. Rosalie was beautiful. We nodded in the hallway and, over time, began to speak. Blonde hair and blue eyes accompanied by a very nice figure and pretty smile. Who was she? Where had she come from?

We spoke several times, each time exchanging more information. Rosalie had moved to Utica from Little Falls, a few miles south of the Mohawk Valley. I did not ask why. I had no girlfriend. I did not date. I was a neophyte—a willing, eager, naïve neophyte. Rosalie somehow learned my class schedule and would strangely appear as I got out of my last class before lunch and at the end of the day. We began to go for short walks, talking and holding hands. One afternoon after school, we wandered to a wooded area just off the campus into a lovely cove of ferns and flowers. We made small talk and held hands. Then we rushed back to the school where she strolled home with a couple girlfriends. I caught up with Chickie and Sammy who were just heading out for home.

A couple days passed after that, and I did not see her. Then one morning, I was summoned to the principal's office. When I arrived, I was met by one of the administrative assistants and a stranger, a man of about forty-five years old with bushy eyebrows, a pulpy nose, and a cigarette stained, straw-colored brush moustache. He wore a heavy, red-and-white checkered flannel shirt, faded blue jeans, and high-top, leather work boots. He smelled of tobacco and other unidentifiable fragrances, musty and masculine.

"This is Mr. Polkoski," the administrative assistant said. "He is looking for his daughter, Rosalie. Have you seen her today?"

I had not seen her and I said so. "Are you sure?" Mr. Polkoski said, leaning toward me, breathing a disturbing cloud of aromas.

The assistant added, "She has been missing since last night. Do you have any idea where she is?"

"No. Ma'am. I haven't seen Rosalie for a couple days."

Mr. Polkoski poured a heavy scowl in my direction. I did not know how to respond, so I said nothing further.

"If you hear from Rosalie, would you please contact the office right away?" the assistant asked.

"Yes, Ma'am."

I attended the rest of my classes. The last class was Mr. Reiman's Machine Shop class held in the basement. It always ran one hour later than all of the other classes in the school. When it was over, I walked out of the machine shop and turned right into the empty, shadowy main hallway toward the stairs that led up to our rows of lockers. Just past the turn, Rosalie stepped out of the shadows under the stairs.

"Hi," she said.

"Hi," I responded, surprised and apprehensive. "What are you doing here?"

"Waiting for you."

"Your Dad is looking for you. He had them call me to the principal's office. Where have you been for two days?"

"Oh, nowhere. I just didn't want to go home. Let's go for a walk, okay? I just want to talk for a while."

"Wait here," I said. "I'll be right back."

I knew the principal's office was closed. Fear gripped my heart. If big, bad-smelling Mr. Polkoski caught me with his Rosalie, he would incorrectly assume that I had been with her all night and all day. If he had the temperament that I sensed in that office, he might, with little hesitation, kill or seriously injure me.

I ran upstairs to my locker and, with much relief, ran into Hank.

"Hank, ya gotta walk home with me. Right now!"

I explained to him what had happened, and after he got tired of teasing me and painting horrible pictures of what Mr. Polkoski was about to do to me, he grabbed his books and we walked back downstairs to the waiting Rosalie. We three walked a block along Hilton Avenue before I steered us two blocks out of our normal route, thinking we might avoid a patrolling Mr. Polkoski. I was wrong. A half-ton truck screeched to a halt next to us. Mr. Polkoski came charging out of the cab, spewing some nasty verbiage.

"I knew you was lying. I knew she was with you. Get in the truck!" he spit out as he grabbed her by the arm and pulled her away. He said a few other unprintable things, slammed the door, and sped off.

"He's gonna kill you!" Hank gleefully said, a big grin splitting his face.

I jostled him back and tried to enjoy a bantering exchange, but honestly, I was inwardly terrified. Would Polkoski report me to the principal's office? I had done nothing wrong, but how would I prove that? How do you prove a negative? Would I get into trouble? What would my parents think?

We neither saw nor heard from Rosalie or her father again. She did not come back to school. Perhaps they moved away. I later heard gossip about the troubles she had experienced in the Little Falls school system and that her family had relocated to Utica to give her a fresh start. But where she went from there, we never learned.

But gosh, she was pretty. Rosalie. What a pretty name. What a pretty girl.

MACHINE SHOP

Good old Mr. Reiman, who ran the machine shop classes, was about fifty years old and wore eyeglasses and the perennial blue shop apron. His smile was customized by one gold tooth next to a slightly snagged tooth, both on one side of his mouth. When he spoke, he tended to smile with a twist to his lips that revealed the pair and made him both endearing and mysteriously profound. This master machinist had brought his skills with him when he emigrated from Germany to the U.S. He had already taught several generations of American machinists before I came along.

Mr. Reiman enjoyed the occasional prank or practical joke. If you were squatting in front of a machine making an adjustment to the settings, Mr. Reiman might slip up behind you and pull you off balance, backward, so you flung your arms into the air to maintain equilibrium. His knees broke your fall so that you would not get hurt by landing onto your back. He would laugh, and you, being his student and dependent on his good grades, would laugh with him.

A large room filled with metal-cutting machines—power saws, lathes, drill presses, shapers, milling machines, grinders, and others—was his domain. At one end of this gymnasium-sized room were a dozen or so chairs and one entire wall of blackboard. We sat, watched, and listened as he explained how to hand-sharpen a drill bit or file a square block of steel and dozens of other skills. He accompanied these lectures with beautifully hand-drawn sketches, in chalk, on the blackboard. He was skillful at shading them so that they appeared to have depth and a third dimension. We were required to keep a notebook with our own sketches. I must admit I so admired his drawings that I copied them faithfully and, if anything, improved upon them in my notebook. I got straight As on every review of my notebook.

Mr. Reiman remembered my older brother who had taken this same course nine years earlier and had gone on to become a master machinist. My brother had been one of his prized students. As a consequence, Mr. Reiman was inclined to be more sociable toward me than toward many of the others. And I felt I could confide in him.

Thus it was that on one of our slower afternoons, I spoke with him about a dilemma I was facing. I was a senior and about to graduate. I had taken qualifying tests and was accepted as a sponsored student at an engineering university in Michigan. I would have to somehow save some money to pay for my tuition for the first semester, and after that, I would be able to work part time and make the money to pay for subsequent semesters.

My dilemma was simple. I finally had a girlfriend.

He listened to my story.

"If I accept this opportunity, I won't see much of this girl that I met this summer. If I go away to school, I might lose her. But I've dreamed of getting a college education, and now I have a chance to do that. I may never get another chance like this," I whispered to this machine shop teacher. I could not discuss this with my friends, who would not have the maturity to give me advice based on experience. I had talked to my family. They had very strong, contradictory opinions that left me confused.

"Well," he started. "I don't know what you should do. It's a personal thing. Only you can make that decision." He was quiet for a moment, and then he said, "I had a similar problem a long time ago. I can tell you what I did. I had a chance to go to college. I really and truly wanted to do that—I wanted to become an engineer. I thought I would make a good one, and I had a chance to do that. But I was in love too. She begged me not to go. I was torn, like you. Then, too, there was my *liebe* Mama," he lapsed into his native German. "My father passed away the year before, and Mama was alone. She said I should go. She said my aunt would watch over her for me. But I was tormented, like you, you know? How could I walk away from my Mama? How could I walk away from my sweetheart?" He grew quiet, contemplative. "But this chance might never come again."

Mr. Reiman was silent for a very long moment. I stared into his diverted eyes, waiting to hear how he resolved his dilemma. He looked out of the windows that covered one long wall of the shop facing soft green lawns and trees in the distance. He turned his face to me, his eyes focused again on my face.

"I declined my scholarship. My girlfriend was happy. My *liebe* Mama was disappointed at first, but then she was pleased that she would have her son at her side. For a short time I was happy that I made the right decision."

He nodded his head several times, slowly, and turned to look out the window at the far trees that marked the farthest boundaries of old Proctor Park. I stood looking at his face, waiting to see if this was the end of his story. Was he telling me to stay home, to turn down the scholarship?

Still staring into the distance, he said, "And then *mein geliebte* ran off with another man. Within the next two months, *mein liebe* Mama passed away. A few months and they were both gone. And my scholarship? It was gone too."

He turned his whole body toward me. I could not see his eyes because the setting sun, shining through the shop windows, reflected off his glasses. He placed a hand on my shoulder and said, "I can't give you advice. Who knows what the future holds for you? Who knows if she will stay or go… if she will wait for you or not? Loved ones can be taken away. But an education—an education will never leave you. Never."

For a time we stood there. It was closing time. All the students had left for home. Mr. Reiman was lost in reverie, staring out the windows.

The bell rang, loud and strident. It broke our spell. "Thank you, Mr. Reiman," I said. He nodded at me, his mind still elsewhere.

I went off to college. My girlfriend and I promised to stay in touch and to remain faithful. Life introduced events much beyond our naïve power to control them. We were not equipped to deal with them. Our paths drifted apart. She later became engaged to a fine young man. When I learned of this, I remembered Mr. Reiman's words: "Loved ones can be taken away… but an education will never leave you. Never."

THE RETURN

Thirty years later, I revisited my hometown and drove a rental car along the length of Bleecker Street, slowly looking for familiar landmarks. Mancuso's Hardware Store was gone. So was Markson's Furniture Store and Farina's Meat Market. The Florentine Bakery was still there, and I stopped to buy a pasticioto, just for old time's sake.

When the traffic signal at the corner of Mohawk Street turned green, I crossed then maneuvered the obtuse turn onto Albany Street, turned right on Hilton Street, and pulled into the now expanded parking lot at Proctor High School. I walked around to the walkway in front of the building. There were new buildings next to the original school. The expansion had changed much of what I remembered, but the lintels above the old main doors remained unchanged:

Over the entrances I once again read:

The Reason
The Skill
The Observation
The Spirit

The Intellect
The Will
The Imagination
The Memory

Did I possess any of these attributes? If so, had I learned them here, behind these large doors?

All of the students were inside their classes, so I was limited to walking by closed doors and peeking surreptitiously inside. I visited Ms. Nolan's homeroom 141 then went down to Mr. Pope's drafting class and Mr. Reiman's machine shop. They had retired years ago. The rooms seemed so much smaller. I saw no familiar faces. I stopped at my locker, counting in from the end of the third row and tried the combination: 34 right, 26 left, 20 right, and yanked upward on the handle. It did not yield. Instead a solid, metallic clank reminded me that I no longer belonged here.

I wanted to find my old friend, Joe Spano. I was pretty sure that if he was still alive, he would be running his father's bakery. The name of the bakery escaped me, and after hunting unsuccessfully for a half hour, I drove to the ancient gas station near my old homestead. It hadn't changed much. I told the guys that I was looking for a bakery that used to be located south of Bleecker and east of Mohawk Street. They rattled off some of the bigger bakery names in town, which did not sound familiar.

"It made Italian bread, but it didn't have an Italian name," I offered.

"Oh. Yeah. The Ohio Bakery," the mechanic piped up. Then I recalled Joe telling me that his father wanted his bakery to have an American name, one with a lofty sound. He always liked the sound of Ohio—short and lofty—so that was what he called it. I got directions, drove to the old building, parked, and walked in. The ovens and conveyor belts were running. A young man came out from behind some machinery, wiping flour off his hands onto a big apron.

"Can I help you?"

I introduced myself and said, "I'm visiting from California, and I'm trying to find a guy I went to Proctor with in the late 1940s. A guy named Joe Spano."

He grinned, reached out to shake my hand, and replied, "That's my Dad. He sleeps late nowadays. I run the bakery. He should be here any minute. Come wait in the office."

Joe drove up a short time later. He still wore the familiar horn-rimmed glasses, red ruby pinky ring, and perpetual smile, all of which I remembered so well. We caught each other up on our lives since high school. Many of our classmates had moved away or passed on, he told me. He took me through the bakery on a short tour, just as he had when we were in high school all those years ago.

We talked for a long time, neither one of us willing to end it. As he finally walked me out to the back door, he picked up two loaves of fresh, hot bread off the conveyor belt and stuffed them into my arms.

"Here's something to remember me by. Come and see me again. Don't be such a stranger."

I promised I would try.

I should call Joe one of these days, soon. He'd be eighty years old now too. I've got to do that.

Maybe tomorrow.

Yeah, maybe tomorrow.

31

Playa Del Rey Beach

The Old Man coasted easily along the relatively flat stretch that threaded through the long sand beaches of Playa Del Rey, dotted with the popular concrete fire pits that attracted so many city dwellers on summer nights. Heavy jet aircraft screamed overhead, lifting off from Los Angeles International Airport, leaving vapor trails as they climbed skyward and disappeared above where the ocean meets the sky. Once out of sight, they corrected course to one of countless destinations.

He looked up to see a Lufthansa aircraft ponderously clawing its way upward. Lufthansa? Of course, he recalled, that's the airline he flew to Amsterdam a few years ago. And what airline did he fly to England many years before that? British Airways—back in 1979. It was to be a business trip to England and Sweden. But he had added two weeks of vacation time so he could visit Italy.

He pulled his bike over to the edge of the sand and stood watching the Lufthansa flight turn northward just before it disappeared. *Probably about to take the polar route to Europe*, he thought.

My wife and I arrived at our gate far too early.

We had over three hours to kill, so we walked over to the Theme Building.

That's where we met the Russian…
and all those drinks…
and all those grand memories…

32

European Interlude

It was late June 1979. Our flight to London was not scheduled to leave for another three hours. We got seat assignments, but it was too early to check in our baggage. The clerk told us to come back in two hours. So we toted four bags out of the terminal, across the roadway, and up the elevator of the Theme Building Tower. It was the first time I had been in the tower restaurant. Small tables lined the 360-degree circle of windows in this structure that resembled a flying saucer standing on four arched legs. It was built in 1961 in an architectural style called Mid-Century Modern, also known as Googie or Populuxe.

All the tables and barstools in the small cocktail lounge area were occupied, except for two stools at the very end of the bar itself where the waitresses came to place and pick up drink orders. The bartender motioned my wife and I down to the last two stools. "Good!" he said. "Now I have somebody talk to, yah?"

Eugene, we learned, was an immigrant from Russia. He wore a formal white shirt and bow tie with wide suspenders that disappeared into a black cummerbund around his ample waist. With a thick brush-type moustache and full head of wavy, bushy hair, he looked the part of a muscular, Russian peasant farmer who had been cleaned up. He had arrived in the U.S. less than two months ago, and this was his first job in his new country. He took our order for two margaritas, brought us our drinks, and asked about our travel plans. We said we were going to England and Sweden on business and then taking a two-week vacation to tour Italy. Between drinks, we got to know each other better. He asked many questions about our backgrounds and volunteered much about his own. Each time he filled a waitress's order for a blended drink, he would bring us two empty glasses and pour out his "leavings," which were mostly strawberry, pineapple, or banana margaritas, grasshoppers, and daiquiris.

"Is no charge, okay?" I lost track of how many times Eugene said "Try this one. Maybe you like it, yah?"

Two hours later, we rose shakily from our stools, said woozy good-byes to our very dear and intimate friend Eugene, and rode the elevator back down to the ground floor, still lugging our bags.

We sat on the plane another hour while British Airways waited for additional passengers from a late connecting flight. "We will leave as soon as we are full up," the pilot announced. Such casual scheduling seemed strange to me, but perhaps it explained the good price we paid for this flight.

Finally airborne, with no empty seats, the stewardess came around and took drink orders. I started with coffee to counter the effect of the free samples up in the Googie tower, but after several hours had crawled by, I asked for a martini. As I was telling the stewardess what I wanted, the copilot stopped to listen.

"Look here, chap. These martinis come premixed in a miniature bottle," he said, holding one up by its neck with thumb and index finger and wiggling it. "You'll pay three pounds for this tiny thing when you can buy a liter bottle of gin and another of dry martini wine, duty free, for a total of six pounds. You'll break even after two drinks and have plenty left over for free drinks the rest of our ten-hour flight."

"I can't possibly drink that many martinis," I protested.

"Course not," he agreed and smiled a conspiratorial smile. "Then you can show your appreciation for my advice by leaving the bottles for us to finish!"

And so it was that by the time we reached London, I had indeed "broke even" and left the almost full bottles for the crew to take home and enjoy.

A connecting flight to Manchester—piloted, I am sure, by an ex WWII Spitfire combat pilot—made a "hotdog" takeoff and landing that I shall never forget.

We were met by Paul, an engineer who worked for our company in England. I walked up to the passenger door on the auto and stood there waiting for Paul to get out of my way. After a moment or two, he said, quite seriously, that if I didn't mind he would like to do the driving. It took another awkward moment before I realized that I was standing in front of the driver's door of this very English, right-hand drive automobile. I went around to what is normally the driver's door in the US. Paul drove us to our hotel, The Red Rum Inn, in Southport where our European factory was located.

We checked in to this charming inn that was named after a famous painting—which hung in the lobby—of a horse called Red Rum. Our room was spacious, with a freestanding armoire in place of the built-in closets so common in the US. The toilet with bath was located down the hall, available to all the guests on that floor. A sign on the toilet door encouraged guests to lock the door when in use and to be considerate of others by not monopolizing its use.

The hotel kitchen had closed early, so after unpacking, we took a stroll through town looking for a restaurant. We were beguiled by the aged architecture of the buildings. Most of the plumbing and drain pipes ran up and down the outside walls of the buildings, probably because those buildings had been constructed long before indoor plumbing existed.

Almost all of the buildings had several windows that were bricked in. The bricks were of a different shade and stood out noticeably. At one time, many years ago, property owners were taxed based on the number of windows in their buildings. To reduce their "window tax," many had them bricked in. They remain bricked shut to this day. There were many fire escapes and skylights. The antiquity of the buildings reminded me of scenes from the movie *Oliver Twist*.

STEAK AND A MARTINI

Eventually we spotted a restaurant and went in for dinner. A waitress seated us in the bar area and gave us menus. I asked if we could possibly get a table in the dining area instead. She politely explained that we should order from the menu while having a drink. She would come and fetch us when a table was ready and the order about to be served. I liked the arrangement. It seemed very efficient.

I studied the menu. I was in the mood for a good steak dinner and a very dry martini. The menu featured a special for the evening: Gammon Steak and Egg with Chips. It sounded good to me. I had never heard of a gammon cut but presumed it was a British version of a US cut like New York or T-bone. I ordered that. She looked at me strangely when I specified, "Medium rare, please." Then I turned my attention to the drink menu. I told the barmaid that I would like a martini. She wrote that down. A moment later, our waitress reappeared to take us to our table. As she seated us, I reminded her I had ordered a martini. She excused herself. Shortly, a sommelier came to us wearing a white vest, black bow tie, and a shiny silver Tastevin cup on a black velvet ribbon around his neck. A neatly folded linen napkin was draped smartly over his left arm.

"Good evening, sir. Your martini… would that be dry or sweet?"

"Oh, very dry, please."

"Yes, sir." He turned to my wife. "And you, madam? Will you have a glass of vermouth as well, or something else?"

"Oh, just a minute." I interrupted, realizing now the connection between his attire and what he thought I wanted. "I don't want a glass of vermouth. I want a martini."

"Yes, sir. Martini vermouth. Italian. Fine choice."

"No, I meant a martini cocktail. That's the name of a mixed drink in the US."

"I'm not familiar with it, sir. But if you'll describe the mix to me, I shall have the bartender fix one for you."

Apparently, despite World War II and the thousands of American GIs who lived briefly in England, the American martini had not made its way to Southport.

"Well, it is a mix of gin and vermouth."

"One to one?"

"Oh, heavens, no."

"Ah," he said. "Too much gin, then?"

"Too much vermouth," I answered. "The usual mix is, at the absolute very least, three of gin to one of vermouth on up to eleven or more gin to vermouth. A drop or two of vermouth would make it a dry martini. If the vermouth bottle is only waved over the top of the gin, it becomes a very dry martini."

"How does one decide?" he asked with the usual English desire for precision in all things.

"Well," I answered with an attempt at levity, "it depends on what kind of a day you've had."

His eyes grew very large and he gasped, with a half-smile. "What kind of day have you had, sir?"

"Six to one would be nice," I said, thinking to keep it simple and mild.

"Six-parts gin, one-part vermouth?" He waited, a bit incredulous, for me to confirm. I did. He departed.

A short time later he returned, bowed briefly, and said, "Sir, the bartender advises his bottles are fixed with a device that controls the measurements as one full shot per use. He asks if you truly want six full shots of gin plus one full shot of vermouth. If so, he would have to charge for seven drinks, and the resulting mixed drink would be very large indeed. He suggests that we serve you one full shot of gin and one full shot glass of martini dry vermouth, which would then be charged to your bill as two full drinks?"

I thought a moment and then said, "That will be fine, but please bring an empty glass as well, and I will mix it at the table."

And so I received three glasses, one with a shot of gin, one with a shot of vermouth, and an empty glass into which I poured a tiny fraction of the vermouth and all of the gin, mixed it gently and enjoyed what may well have been the first approximation of an American martini ever mixed and consumed in that particular part of Southport, England. It came with a twist of lemon. There was no olive and no ice. But it was almost an American martini, and I was grateful.

I sat back contentedly, sipped my martini slowly, and awaited the Gammon Steak and Egg, salivating at the thought. And here it came—a thick slab of ham on a plate, a poached egg, and a pile of thickly cut fried potatoes, a roll, and butter. I stopped the waitress and reminded her that I had ordered steak. She checked her order book and confirmed, "Yes, sir. You did. Gammon Steak."

"But this is ham!"

"Yes, sir. Gammon is a breed of pig."

So I ate my ham and egg and fried potatoes and sipped my self-made martini.

During my following trips into various pubs in England, I noted that most had measuring devices that controlled the amounts dispensed to one full shot. Some of the bartenders were not allowed to change the amount dispensed nor had they learned to make an American martini. Thereafter I simply ordered a shot of each and mixed my own. I got used to drinking it warm with a twist of lemon. And I never ordered Gammon Steak again.

Stockholm and Krona

A few days later, I exchanged some US dollars for krona—this was long before the euro was created—and I left for Stockholm, Sweden. I had a one-day meeting scheduled the next day with Volvo's engineering staff. My wife remained with friends in Southport, England.

From the Stockholm airport, I rode a double tandem Volvo bus—two buses, attached nose to tail—with an articulating joint in the middle. It wended its way into downtown Stockholm. I arrived on their Midsummer's Day celebration, June 24, 1979. The streets were filled with celebrating Swedes, walking about, dancing in the streets, drinking heavily, some already passed out and sleeping on grass lawns and park benches.

After dinner, I retired to my room on the seventh floor with views of the rivers, parks, and a marina. The sun finally set around 11:00 pm, and I forced myself to get to bed. I was scheduled to be picked up at 8:00 am by a Volvo company car to be driven to their engineering headquarters building somewhere out in the beautiful hills of Sweden. I had a wake-up call scheduled for 6:00 am.

I awoke with a start to daylight seeping through the thin drapes. There had been no phone call. I panicked, bolted to the window, pulled back the drapes, and looked outside. The sun was sitting just below the horizon, almost peeking over its edge. It was already dawn. The streets were empty save for one drunk sleeping at the base of a statue of some military figure. I checked my watch. It was only 1:15 am. I had forgotten that we were only seven degrees of latitude below the Arctic Circle. In Sweden, at this time of year, total darkness only lasted a couple hours. I had trouble falling back to sleep, awaking to daylight every twenty minutes or so. By two thirty, it was broad daylight. The drunk still slept at the base of the statue. I gave up trying to sleep. I got up, packed, checked out of my room, ate breakfast, and waited in the lobby for my driver to show up.

As 8:00 am approached, I stood and looked steadily outside for a Volvo company car. They all looked alike. Lots of Volvos. Just then I noted a husky, short-haired woman in a chauffer's cap, striped slacks, and jacket walking up the steps. She came in, looked around a moment, and focused on me. She spotted my briefcase, came closer, read my company ID badge, and introduced herself.

"Hallo. I am Helga. I take you to Volvo today." She took my bags before I could object and led me out to the company car. We drove out of Stockholm on a four-lane road, took an exit onto a narrow, two-lane country road, and proceeded for another hour and a half climbing up into the mountains passing thick, green forest on both sides. Helga and I made small talk during the trip. Her English skill was simple but easy to understand and full of humor.

As we approached the massive office building set in a huge, park-like area, I saw an abstract bronze sculpture sitting atop a large stone base. The metal sculpture was a twisted bronze ribbon that turned and curved upon itself and seemed to flow into the center of the spaces in between.

"What does that sculpture represent?" I asked my driver.

"Oh, dot! Dot is man try to get inside a Volkswagen!" she bellowed then laughed gleefully at this practiced joke about a competitor's car.

At the start of our meeting, I was assured that Helga would return me to the Stockholm Airport in plenty of time for my 6:00 pm flight back to London, but we underestimated the agenda and the length of the luncheon they had planned. By four o'clock, I became concerned enough to point out the time to them. They hurriedly summoned Helga who brought the car and my luggage to the front lobby door. Hearty good-byes and well wishes were exchanged. Helga whisked me away, throwing up a cloud of gravel and dust as we turned off the property and onto the narrow, country road.

Things went well until we began to descend the mountain, then traffic slowed and began its crawling pace, frequently stopping for minutes at a time as other, narrow country roads blended into our path.

Suddenly, Helga pulled off into what appeared to be a large truck stop. Gasoline pumps, a garage, restaurants, and shops covered by a circular dome. She threw open the Volvo's doors, pulled my luggage out, and said, "Follow me, please."

"Where are we going, Helga?" I was really getting worried now.

"I cannot drive faster. Taxis go much faster. You vill get dere faster by taxi." She walked me inside, spoke to the person behind the counter, then walked me back outside, pointing to the rooftop. There was a huge red light sitting at the very apex of the curved dome. It was lit now, rotating and blinking.

"Dot vill get taxi for you. Goot luck." She dropped my luggage at my feet, shook my hand, jumped into the Volvo, and tore out of the lot, anxious to get home.

A few minutes later, a taxi did pull up. A large brute of a man stepped out, reached out with hands the size of Easter hams, threw my luggage into the trunk, and said, "Vere you go?"

I looked up at this square-jawed, blue-eyed giant and said, "The airport. My plane leaves at six o'clock."

He looked at his wristwatch, nodded once, and said, "Das okay. Vee go now."

The traffic was now stop-and-go, but there was a center passing lane. He explained that he was allowed, as a commercial vehicle, to use the center passing lane. We passed many cars, and I was beginning to think we would be on time when the center lane disappeared and traffic came to an abrupt halt. The giant looked frantically at his watch then jerked the wheel hard left and proceeded at breakneck speed the wrong way down the opposing lane. Fortunately there was no traffic coming up the mountain, but as we neared the bottom where the tiny two lane road joined the four lane highway to the airport, we came smack up against a Swedish trooper with a natty cap, big badge, polished leather belts, and knee-length, high-top cavalry boots. He held up a hand, walked over, and admonished my giant driver. Words were exchanged that I didn't understand, but the giant explained it to me.

"I break law. Now he make us vait."

I thought the poor driver would receive a citation, maybe even lose his license. Instead we sat there while a couple hundred cars passed us. Finally the trooper decided we were probably back to the spot in line where we started out. He held up one hand to stop the others and motioned us back on the road. It was only fair. Justice had been meted out without the trouble of paperwork and the court system.

We screeched to a halt at the SAS terminal and jumped out together. The giant pulled my luggage from the trunk as I pulled money out of my pocket. It was all US dollars. I had spent all of my Swedish krona. I looked up at the giant. He said, "Is 40 krona."

"I'm sorry, but I have no krona," I mumbled as I flipped through my dollars, hoping to find some krona somewhere. It may have been my imagination, but I swear the giant began to swell up and grew larger all over. I thought his clothes would split. The veins bulged in his thick neck, his hands curled slightly and his arms bowed out from his sides as he bent over me and glowered, "*No krona?*"

I struggled to remember the exchange rate, but my mind went blank. I grabbed a couple twenties and held them out, "Is forty American dollars okay?"

He stared at the money a quick moment, took it, and said, "Yah. Is goot."

He shrank back down to his normal huge size, shoved the money into his pocket, grabbed my luggage in his ham hands, and ran inside with me at his heels. He was smiling as he waved good-bye.

The clerk assured me my plane was running late and I had plenty of time to get to the gate.

"Tell me," I asked the clerk, "I gave the taxi driver US$40 for a forty krona taxi ride. Did I give him enough?"

"I would say so, sir. You gave him a 120 krona tip!"

ITALY

Finally and at last the business portion of the trip was ended, and our vacation began. We departed for Italy from Manchester to Zurich to Rome on Swissair. The landing at Leonardo Da Vinci airport was quiet and uneventful until we walked down the concourse to the central terminal where we were greeted by dozens of Italian police and soldiers carrying machine guns slung over their shoulders, carefully scanning faces among the crowd. I headed straight for a barred window underneath a sign that read "Cambio" and exchanged more US dollars for lire—again, this was pre-euro—at a rate of 824 lire per dollar. I asked the girl behind the barred window why there were so many *polizia* and *soldati* with weapons. She scowled, shook her head, and said, "La Brigata Rosa." Like two linguistic invalids, we exchanged enough broken English and Italian for me to understand that the large presence of police and soldiers carrying weapons was a precaution against a communist organization called the Red Brigade that was attempting a violent overthrow of the republican Italian government. I would learn more about them later that day, much to our dismay.

We took a bus into Rome then a cab to the Lloyd Hotel in an older part of Rome. A hand-operated, one-hundred-year-old, open-cage elevator took us to the second floor. Our spacious room had a solid marble floor, twelve-foot-high ceilings, and a huge bathroom with an oversized, claw-footed bathtub. The bathroom was so large that using the commode gave you the feeling that you were sitting out in a hallway down which someone might stroll at any time.

A beautifully hand-carved heavy wooden wardrobe—or *armadio*—gave testimony to the age of the hotel. The window air-conditioner and small refrigerator gave the room a touch of modernism.

In the evening, we again rode the ancient hand-operated elevator downstairs and walked through the small side streets of Rome, strolling alongside and eventually through an opening in the old Roman wall that once surrounded early Rome. We emerged on the famed Via Veneto. Here was the night life excitement of the city: lights, music, food, sidewalk cafes, shops, tourists, vendors of souvenirs, and the occasional prostitute of either sex.

MEATBALLS

We stopped at a sidewalk café that had a long glass display case full of hot food. I looked over the display, which was all a la carte, then ordered two plates of rigatone, one beer, and one glass of milk. I paid for it and carried the plates to our table. Then on impulse, I returned and ordered meatballs. The clerk asked me, in Italian, how many meatballs I wanted. *"Quatro. Due per piatto,"* I answered. "Four—two per dish."

As he placed the plates on top of the glass case, he quoted me the price, *"Diecimila lire"*—ten thousand lire. I did a quick calculation. That came to over US$12 for four meatballs or a shade over $3 per meatball.

"Caspita!" I said, using an old Italian expletive I remembered from my childhood which meant, roughly translated, "Wow!" I added, "That is a lot of money for meatballs!"

He understood my English and said, in Italian, dripping with sarcasm, that he supposed it was cheaper in America. *"Si, e vero,"* I replied. "Yes, that is true!"

Then in the philosophical manner that typifies the old Italians, he totally disarmed me by saying, *"Sentire. Siete venuti in questo mondo con niente. Lasciare questo mondo senza niente. Godetevi il vostro polpette!"*

I paid him and carried the plates back to our sidewalk table, smiling as I did. My wife, who spoke no Italian, asked me what he had said. I replied, still grinning, "He said, 'Listen. You came into this world with nothing. You will leave this world with nothing. Enjoy your meatballs!'"

He was right, of course. So we did.

La Brigata Rosa

After dinner, we strolled through side streets and found a *Gelatoria*—an ice cream parlor—where I found, for the first time since my childhood, genuine *granita de lemone* or Italian lemon ice. It tasted better than the lemon ice I had tasted in Los Angeles perhaps because this one, like the one I had as a child, was made by old Italians. I made a mental note of its location then wandered down more small streets in the general direction of our hotel. We passed other small eateries, the families dining at tables brought out onto the sidewalk. People stood about, smoking, nodding, and saying *"Buona sera. Buona sera,"* with the men tipping their hats to my wife. The streetlights were dim in this part of Rome. A full moon shone overhead, throwing shadows of trees and telephone poles across our path. We turned toward our hotel and wandered down an empty streeet lined with closed commercial buildings. We were walking alongside what appeared to be a very large bank building.

As we turned another corner, two canvas-covered trucks pulled up in a hurry, one on each side of the street. Soldiers jumped out carrying machine guns that looked like Uzis. They deployed along both sides of the street, weapons held ready for use. We froze then backed slowly the way we came and went around the far side of the block. Clearly they knew something that we did not know, and the air was filled with tension. For the rest of our walk home, the shadows that a moment before seemed so romantic now filled us with ominous apprehension.

Once safely inside the lobby, I told the desk clerk what we had just seen. "*Ah, si. La Brigata Rosa.* The *soldati* are guarding the National Treasury Building from the Red Brigade. They must have had an alert, or they are expecting a money shipment. It is good that you moved away from there quickly. *Molto bene.* Very good."

Over the next week, we learned much more about this arm of communist activity which involved robberies, kidnappings for ransom, and murders in an attempt to overthrow the government. Many of the founders of the Red Brigade were originally members of the Communist Youth movement who were expelled for their extremist views. The most painful evidence of their presence was the ubiquitous red spray-painted communist graffiti on many of the most precious antiquities in Rome, including statues, columns, and buildings that date back to the time of the Caesars.

THE NUN AND THE SABOTEUR

The following day, we took a bus tour that included St. Peter's Basilica and Vatican City. We were dropped off, of course, in front of a souvenir shop which our guide deftly led us into. Once out of the souvenir shop, we stood with others at the curb, awaiting a break in traffic so we could cross to Saint Peter's Basilica. There was no traffic light, so we were at the mercy of the Roman drivers, each aggressively competing with every car on the road as if this were a Formula One race course. The cars moved endlessly and at high rates of speed. Our corner was soon filled with waiting pedestrians from curb to store front and back up the walk about thirty feet with no break in traffic.

Suddenly, next to me, I felt the push of someone very short, rotund, and solid. It was a Catholic nun working her way to the curbstone, her Flying Nun white hat brushing people aside. Once at the curb she muttered a prayer, fingering her beads, and then, without looking to either side, she stepped off the curb, her arms extended out sideways, palms facing the traffic from either direction, and began walking resolutely, her eyes fixed at the pavement before her with complete faith in Mary, Joseph, and Jesus.

Brakes engaged, tires squealed, and traffic stopped inches from her flowing black habit. All hundred or so of the gathered tourists followed her like ducklings, secure in the knowledge that no right-thinking Italian would dare bump into a nun lest they be struck by lightening, or worse.

I looked for a street called Via Licata to the right of the walls of Vatican City. It was on this street that my mother lived as a little girl before she immigrated to America. It was in vain.

I stopped to buy more film from a small photography shop and struck up a conversation with the proprietor. He asked many questions about the United States and confided that he was a Fascist saboteur during World War II. He was taken prisoner by the US and was held in a prison camp in Texas. He loved the US. He took me to the backroom of the shop where he proudly displayed photos of himself in his youth and a large framed photo of President John F. Kennedy, whom he admired.

A GELATO WITH DRAMA

We made another attempt to find Via Licata to no avail. The Vatican property had grown over the years and now enclosed that street behind its walls.

Toward evening we stopped, one more time, at the *Gelatoria* for a lemon ice. Sitting at a sidewalk table, the sun setting slowly, we noted two robust Italian women walking side by side, each pushing a carriage with a child in it. As they approached us, their conversation became heated. I understood from the bits and pieces I could pick up that they were sisters and one of them had somehow enraged the other. I understood the swear words better than the others. Soon the angriest sister had corraled the other against the windows of a recessed storefront. Carriages became entangled, voices grew louder, and blows were soon exchanged.

A few minutes later I heard the *eeeee-aawwwwww-eeeeeee-aawwwwww* of a police car. It came careening around the corner, a compact two-door Fiat with flashing blue dome light. Two *polizia* jumped out of the front seat wearing two-tone, light blue uniforms with wide white belts and sashes, caps jauntily perched on thick black hair. They interceded as best they could, trying to calm the sisters down. What happened then left us openmouthed. They stuffed the two portly sisters into the very small rear seat. Once crammed inside, the police handed the babies to their respective mothers. Then they proceeded to fold up the two carriages and strapped them to the top of the tiny Fiat. Finally they climbed in themselves, shut the doors, turned on the siren, and drove away. It was like an old black-and-white Mack Sennett movie, the ridiculous image of this tiny two-door overloaded Fiat, dangerously top-heavy, carriages swaying wildly on top, and the flashing blue dome light careening away to the sound of *eeeeeeee-awwwwwwww-eeeeeeeeeee-awwwwwwww!* We looked at each other then burst into laughter. A last night in Rome, Italy, to remember.

Lunch in Valmontano

We rented a Fiat 127 and headed out of town on Autostrada A1, heading south toward Sorrento. As noon approached, we looked for restaurant signs, like those visible from every highway in the US. But none appeared here in Italy. After some distance, I decided to follow the next large truck that pulled off the Autostrada. It was close to noon, and they would surely lead us to a truck stop where we would find food. At the end of the off-ramp was a narrow blacktop road leading into heavily forested hills. A roadside sign read "Valmontano" and pointed up into the hills. The truck turned in that direction. I followed him up the winding road further into the mountains until we encounterd a gas station. I stopped and told the attendant we were looking for someplace to eat. He showed me a small display case with prefabricated, wrapped sandwiches. I asked if there was a restaurant nearby. He pointed up the road and said there was a small place a short distance further, but he cautioned that they might be closed for *Il pranzo di famiglia*, the family's own lunchtime. We drove on, and sure enough, a few houses appeared ahead. And I saw a sign over a door: "Tattoria."

I parked at the curb in front of what looked like a small store. The front door stood open with long strings of beads hanging in the doorway to keep out flies. Inside was a small assortment of picnic-style tables and benches, no two alike. Just beyond was a glass display case containing a few food trays. They were mostly empty now. I saw a family back in the kitchen pulling several hot trays of food out of an oven. A young girl, perhaps fifteen years of age, came to wait on me. She was frowning and asked if she could help me. We conversed in Italian, and it went something like this:

"We would like to order lunch," I said.

"We are closed for our lunch now. This is all we have left," she said, pointing to the almost empty trays in the case.

"What about the food I see coming out of the oven now?"

"That is our lunch. We are closed now," she repeated, her forehead pinched, her face unsmiling. Perhaps the town people knew better than to disturb them at lunch, and we were showing a lack of respect for the local customs.

There appeared to be enough *mannicotti* in the display case for about two decent platefuls, so I ordered two plates of the *manicotti* and two drinks.

She came to one of the picnic tables with a roll of wrapping paper, spread it over the table, and tore it off the roll. That was our table linen. She brought dishes laden with *manicotti*, forks, spoons, and drinks to us; and we proceeded to eat, sitting alone at that large picnic table.

Meanwhile, the family, consisting of our teenage waitress, a man, and three more women of various ages, came out carrying steaming trays of delicious-smelling stuffed peppers, sausage, rigatoni, a small tray of lasagna, another of roasted chicken, and a large bowl of garden salad. They set out dishes and silverware and sat across from us at another picnic table with a similar wrapping paper tablecloth and began to eat. Our teenage waitress sat with them, still scowling. I listened to their conversation and heard the mother ask the teenager how she was feeling. She said the cramps still hurt badly. As they exchanged information, I gathered that the poor girl was not upset with us but, instead, was having her period and suffering from severe cramps.

About the time we were finishing our meal, she arose, came over, tried to force a smile, and asked if we would like another drink. I said yes then added, "You have a pretty smile."

At that she grinned openly and asked if we were Americans, and we began to converse. I used the best Italian I could muster. I thought I was doing a pretty good job of communicating until she asked me if we had been to Rome. I answered that we had just spent a week there and added that I had tried to find the house where my mother was raised as a child, but I could not find it because it is now behind the Vatican walls.

Her beautiful dark brown eyes flew wide open. She placed both hands on the sides of her face and said, "Oh, Dio mio!" She turned, rushed over to her family, and, gesturing with wild flings of her arms, said, "Questo povero uomo venuto dalla lontana America a trovare sua madre a Roma, ma lui non riesce a trovarla!"

I was shocked as she uttered those words in Italian, which translated to "This poor man has come all the way from America to find his mother in Rome, and he can't find her!"

They arose as one, each person grabbing a tray or dish full of food and rushed to our table, all talking at once. Here was an Italian boy separated from his mother. He had lost her. He could not find her. Nothing could be more heartbreaking. They began giving me advice.

"Chiama il municipio e chiedere al sindaco!"

"Call the city hall and ask for the mayor!"

"Devi andare all'ambasciata e dire loro!"

"You must go to the embassy and tell them!"

"La polizia dovrebbe essere in grado di aiutarti!"

"The police should be able to help you!"

"Insistere sul fatto che ti aiutano a trovare il suo!"

"Insist that they help you to find her!"

All of this excited chatter while they sat or stood around us, patted my shoulders, pushed food into our plates, and took turns saying, *"Mangia, mangia!"* "Eat, eat!"

My wife understood none of what was being said. She looked in amazement at all the coddling and attention we were getting, all the magnificent food being thrust upon us. We did the best we could to eat another meal, nodding and chewing and sipping on the drinks they kept bringing. When we had eaten all we could force down and everyone had exhausted conversation, I rose and said we must move on. It was getting late, and we had to get to Sorrento before dark.

I had already paid for the *manicotti* and the first round of drinks, but everything else was on the house. I insisted on paying more, but they responded with equal firmness, *"No, no. Per l'amour di dio. Non pensati neppure di essa."* "No, no, for the love of God. Don't even think of it."

They walked us out to our car, giving more instructions and advice, wishing us well. I started the engine and waved good-bye as we slowly turned around and headed back down the mountain to the Autostrada. The entire family stood in the middle of the road, waving and shouting.

"Arrivederci. Arrivederci." "Good-bye! Good-bye!"

"Vai con Dio." "Go with God!"

"Guidare con prudenza." "Drive carefully!"

I looked back as we turned the last corner at the bottom of the hill. They were still in the middle of the street, waving.

Once we were back on the Autostrada, my wife turned to me and asked, "What in the world was all that about?"

I explained about the misunderstanding which was due, no doubt, to my poor command of the Italian language.

"Why didn't you explain to them that your mother lives in America?"

"Are you kidding? This is the most exciting thing to happen in this little village in years. They loved the pathos of what they understood, the heartbreak of a boy who could not find his mother. To an Italian, the relationship between a boy and his mother is without equal. And they have helped me to find her. This will be a topic of conversation for months to come. They will speculate, 'Did that poor man ever find his mother?' I would have robbed them of something very special. Besides, wasn't that food great!?"

POMPEII

We drove down the Amalfi coast to Sorrento, then the Island of Capri, and to the cliffs looking down on the beaches of Salerno. Now I understood why the German military was so well prepared to resist the Allied invasion at Salerno during WWII. The Amalfi coast is almost continuous cliffs—beautiful, steep cliffs down to the blue Mediterranean. But Salerno was blessed with broad, smooth beaches, perfect for an invasion landing force launched from the island of Sicily. The Germans knew this was where the US invasion would come. They were waiting.

We turned inland and stopped overnight in the new city of Pompeii. Early the next morning, which was Monday, we arose, excited and anxious to see the ruins.

"Ah, not today, Signore. Pompeii is closed," the hotel desk clerk said.

"How can you close a city?" I asked.

"Signore, the old Pompei, the one that was buried by Mount Vesuvius, it is fenced. It is a museum. All museums in Italy are closed on Monday,"

So we had to be content to stare through the bars of the gates and fences while I entertained thoughts of killing our travel agent when I returned home.

Florence and Century Way

Driving north toward Florence, I saw the ancient Abbey of Monte Cassino, high on a hilltop overlooking the approach valleys. The German and Italian armies had dug in on the slopes of the mountain below the abbey and rained deadly fire down on the Allies, stalling the Allied advance toward Rome for five months. Bombed-out stone farmhouses were still visible in the countryside.

Our hotel in Florence was blessed with a desk clerk who proved to be full of helpful advice. Learning we were US tourists, he suggested a restaurant we might enjoy. We went and were surrounded by beer-drinking American college students singing American songs, raising hell while away from the oversight of their parents. We beat a hasty retreat and in my best, though faulty, Italian told him we really wanted to be with Italian people in the resturants the Italians frequented. "Ah," he said in fairly clear English, "you must try Centanni Ristorante. Catch bus no. 33 out in front. Go to the end of the line to Bagni de Ripoli. Walk up the dirt road. Look for a yellow house. Buon Appetito!"

Following his instructionsm we took bus 33 to the end of the line. The paved road ended in a small traffic circle with a sheltered bus stop bench. We were now in a farm village called Bagni de Ripoli which consisted of a few farms separated by four-foot-high stone walls.

A dirt road continued off to our right. It had a sign that read "Via Centanni."

Let's see. In English, that is "One Hundred Year Way. Century Way. Century Boulevard." Gosh. Just like we have in Los Angeles, I realized.

We walked up Via Centanni, passing small farms on both sides of the road. Eventually we came to a yellow farmhouse. The sign over the door read "Centanni Ristorante." The waiter greeted us at the door and, at our request, seated us in the outdoor garden beneath the largest grapevine trellis I had ever seen. We were the only couple in the garden. There was no printed menu. The waiter recited it to us in Italian. It all sounded so good. I understood exactly each dish as he described it in delicious terms, but as soon as he described each next dish, I lost the one before. After a second repeat performance, we asked him to choose for us. He seemed pleased, gave us a pearly white smile, and said, *"Ti porterò i miei favoriti."* "I will bring you my favorites."

An immense antipasto was followed by ravioli stuffed with spinach and cheese, zucchini stuffed with meat, homemade bread hot from the oven, and a hearty red wine—probably a Chianti Classico of the region.

We lingered in the beautiful surroundings, eating and drinking under the stars, until our waiter cautioned us that the last bus no. 33 would soon be leaving. We hurried back to the bench in the circle and found the bus waiting. The same bus driver opened the door for us. "Don't worry," he said, "I remember you. I wait for you."

Venice and Grace

In the Piazza San Marco, I was accosted by a dozen vendors selling everything from clothes to postcards. One persistant vendor gave me a lot of practice in saying "No, thank you" to him. Each time I did, he scowled and finally said, in disgust, *"Grazia se trova in Chiesa!"* I thought about what he had said and slowly realized that during the whole trip I had been saying *"No, Grazia"* instead of *"No, Grazie."* That ever so slight difference in pronounciation of the last letter meant I had been saying "No, grace" instead of "No, thank you." He was right. If I had no grace, I could find it in church!

On our next to the last day, we toured the glass factories on the island of Murano. Our guide spoke excellent English. She walked us through the room where glass blowers were busily making product while we watched. She explained the virtues of each style and color and the unique skills needed to create them. Holding up a beautiful vase of stunning cobalt blue glass, for which Murano is famous, she expounded on the special difficulty in attaining that color then pointed to a hunched-over old fellow sitting in a far-off corner of the room. His back was to us, his head laced with long, sparse white hair moving rhytmically as he worked the glass. "That man is the only artisan in Murano who can create such a masterful piece of art," she said. "No other glass blower on this island can match his skill. He is eighty years old and one of the last of the great glass blowers. When he dies, the art dies with him." Her implication seemed obvious: that we had better buy his wares while we could, before he died.

A woman at the back of our group stepped forward, looked skeptically at the old man, then, as if to mock the absurdity of such a claim, said, *"Dovete pregare ogni giorno che lui rimarrà in buona salute."* "You must pray every day that he will remain in good health." The tourists laughed, and that laughter broke the guide's enthusiasim; and for the rest of the tour, the young lady refrained from using excessive hyperbole.

Words to Live By

The flight from Venice to London to Los Angeles was uneventful. As our luggage came sliding down the chute from the carousel, I noted that our newest piece of leather luggage was unlocked. The lock had been picked. The contents were disturbed and the inside lining was slit open in several places. The handle had been wrenched off a gold-plated hand mirror as if someone thought it might be hollow and contain valuables. Nothing was missing, but I was outraged.

I thought about filing a complaint at the airport baggage counter. I could write a nasty letter to the carrier. I would threaten legal action against someone. I might demand some kind of restitution for haveing been violated. I could...

Then I remembered: I came into this world with nothing, and will leave with nothing. I decided to go home, mix a good old American martini, fix dinner, and enjoy my meatballs.

33

Dockweiler Rest Area

T he Old Man pushed thoughts of Italy out of his mind and got back on the bike. It was a short distance from Playa Del Rey Beach to the recently remodeled Dockweiler Beach recreational vehicle parking area located at the foot of the long steep climb back up to the Dockweiler Plateau. He had climbed it from the other side earlier today, heading north. Now heading south, he wanted a short rest before tackling that grade again. The Dockweiler rest area contained restrooms, showers, and laundry facilities that catered to the people whose idea of an ocean vacation was to park their coach in a twelve-foot-wide slot between two other coaches for one or two weeks each summer. He used the restroom, enjoyed another swig of cool water from the fountain, and sat quietly on a pink concrete bench.

A bevy of bicyclers wearing matching outfits pulled into the area for a few minutes, nodded to him, and continued on. Shortly two more riders pulled up, used the restroom, and came to sit on the matching concrete bench across from his. They were younger men who appeared to be in good physical condition. One wore a white T-shirt from the American Youth Soccer Organization. It read "plAYSOuth soccer" across the front. The Old Man recognized the triple play on the words that implied the message: play AYSO soccer in the South Bay.

"I haven't seen one of those T-shirts in a few years," he said. "Where did you get it?"

"I just registered my five-year-old son for his first season. When I signed up as a volunteer, they gave me this T-shirt."

"You're lucky to get it. I thought they were all gone by now. I helped to design that logo. AYSO National Headquarters objected to the design. We had to stop ordering them. Some of the older volunteers consider them collector items. I still have mine at home."

The young man looked down at his T-shirt with renewed respect. "Are you one of the coaches?" he asked.

"I was the Regional Director of Referee Instruction in South Torrance at one time. Are you going to coach a team?"

"No. They asked me to, and I'd like to, but I can't spend two nights a week on practices and attend games on weekends too. So I volunteered to be a referee on weekends. That's when they gave me this T-shirt."

"Great. You will like that."

"I don't know that much about the game."

"They'll teach you, just like they taught me. And I knew nothing when I started."

"I don't know. Seems like a lot of pressure. They say those parents can be pretty tough."

"Take the referee course anyway. You won't be forced to referee games if you don't want to, but you'll understand your son's games better."

"Yeah, I guess so."

"Being a referee was one of the most rewarding things I have ever done in my life," the Old Man said.

The young man chuckled and said, "You don't mean financially, right? 'Cause I understand none of those volunteers get paid."

"Not in money, they don't. But in ways that are priceless, they do. I like to think that I might have helped to change the lives of some kids for the better."

The young man looked pensive. "What is it like to be out there with so much responsibility?"

"It's frightening at first, until the children give you their trust. Then it becomes fun," the Old Man said, warming up to the topic.

That's been a few years ago now, but I recall it as if it were yesterday.

I didn't know much about soccer when I registered my grandson, and I hadn't planned to get too involved...

until that day when my phone rang.

I think it was a Sunday...

and we were having dinner...

34

Soccer Saga

I answered the phone thinking it was another annoying salesman calling to offer me a once in a lifetime chance to get my furnace air ducts cleaned for half the price, or a political pitch for a local contender for the office of Property Tax Assessor. I was surprised to hear a stranger say, "Hi! My name is Tom Young, and I'm a coach with AYSO. Your son is going to play on my team."

I had forgotten. Last Saturday I had taken my five-year-old grandson to join the under-six group of soccer teams in the South Bay Region of AYSO.

"Well, I guess you ought to talk to me. He is my grandson, but I'll be taking him to practice and to his games. How can I help you?"

I had no idea this would be the start of a seventeen-year involvement. The voice on the other end of the phone went on to tell me that each team was responsible for providing at least one parent who would volunteer to be a soccer referee. I assumed a couple things: first, he had probably asked a number of parents already and been turned down; and second, he had no idea that I was fifty-seven years old.

"Would you be willing to be our team referee?"

"Sure," I volunteered, "but you'll have to teach me how." I had played a little soccer some fifty years earlier, as a child, when an assistant gym teacher visiting from Italy taught us how to dribble a ball with our feet, of all things. That was all I knew how to do. When that teacher moved on, I neither saw nor heard much about soccer again. Until now.

My AYSO referee instructor was a cheerful but serious-minded young man named Eric. The classes ran for three consecutive nights. At the end of night three, Eric gave us a one-hour test. We all passed. He gave us each a thin black plastic wallet holding one red "send-off" card and one yellow "caution" card and a packet of blank referee report forms. Then he handed us a whistle and a referee patch. I felt suddenly empowered. I had watched soccer games. The referee was the all-powerful arbiter on the field. Now I was a referee. I had much authority with limited responsibility—a combination not usually found outside the military establishment.

"We will give you a traditional referee uniform consisting of a shirt, shorts, and long stockings all in black with white trim," said Eric. "They should be here in a couple weeks. Meanwhile, you can wear whatever shirt and shorts you may already have at home. Try to pick a color that will be easy to see. You will need to buy your own gym or soccer shoes. They should be black to match your uniform. Look for soles that will not slip on grass, but don't buy a pair with raised cleats. Most of our school fields are dry and hard. The cleats won't sink into the soil. Instead they'll poke into the soles of your feet. After refereeing several games in one afternoon, your feet will be very uncomfortable."

A couple days later, I received a call telling me that I was to referee my first game that next Saturday, just before my grandson's first game. I shopped with enthusiasm for a pair of black gym shoes with rippled soles that might work. The soles felt stiff and unyielding, so I bought a pair that was two sizes too large and inserted two sets of soft inner liners.

I pictured the rolling green grass of the field and decided that my clothes should be a bright yellow. After all, some golfer friends of mine used yellow golf balls because it was easy to see them against the green grass. So I picked out a yellow shirt, yellow shorts, and yellow socks to wear. I wanted to be sure the children, and especially the parents, would have no trouble spotting me on the field. I stayed up late two nights before the game, reading my notes and trying to memorize the rules. Early the next morning, I woke the grandson. We ate breakfast and dressed. My grandson looked sharp in his little team uniform. I looked very yellow with oversized black feet. The kids and parents would think they were being refereed by a cross between Big Bird of *Sesame Street* and Goofy the Walt Disney dog.

My First Day

Arriving at the appointed field, I was dismayed to note that the ground was, indeed, hard and dry and the grass was yellow for lack of water. I would blend in so well the parents and children would only see my gigantic black gym shoes stomping around the field.

I faced two teams of seven kids each and some forty or so excited parents, grandparents, aunts, uncles, cousins, and siblings. I checked out the field for hazards, the nets for holes, and the children's uniforms and shoes and the soccer ball for compliance and safety as I had been carefully taught by Eric. We did the coin toss ceremony. The captain of the team that won the toss took possession of the ball for the kickoff. The other captain was supposed to pick which side of the field he would defend. He shrugged his shoulders, so I told them where to stand.

One goalkeeper stood in each net at opposite sides of the field where they would invariably look up at birds or at airplanes, pick at the grass, or stand staring down at an insect, sometimes waving at their parents while the other players fought over the ball. With heart pounding, I blew the whistle for the start of the game.

One little boy kicked the ball forward. It rolled about three feet and disappeared. It was engulfed by a crowd of bouncing, flailing feet, raising a cloud of dust from the yellow grass. Children yelled while parents screamed "Kick it! Kick it!" over and over again.

As the gang of dancing feet and crowded bodies shifted around the field, I had to assume that somewhere inside that cloud was a soccer ball. I pictured it being kicked simultaneously from several opposing directions at one time so that instead of moving in any direction, it simply winced and uttered silent expletives like "Oof!" and "Ouch!" and pleas like "Lemme outta here!" Occasionally the ball would attempt an escape, spurting out of the cluster of body parts and dust. But its freedom was always short-lived. The kid cluster pursued and pounced upon it in seconds, hiding it from view. I tried to stay close to the action to spot fouls or injuries. In my mind I went over the proper calls to make in the event of either occurrence. The parents continued screaming "Kick it! Kick it!"

Out of the corner of one eye, I noticed one little boy standing alone in the middle of the field. He was the smallest and possibly the cutest of them all, with thick, curly blond hair, deep blue eyes, and pink round cheeks. He stood stock-still, his head bowed, his arms hanging at his sides. We referees had been taught to stop the game immediately in the event of an injury and to call out the team coach to care for the injured player. But this little boy did not appear to be injured.

Without taking my eyes off the other players, I drifted in his direction. When I got close enough, I bent slightly to see his face. Very large tears were rolling down his peach-sized cheeks.

"Are you okay, son?"

Still looking at the ground, he slowly shook his blond curly head from side to side and said in a tear-choked little voice, "I'm so confused…"

So I blew the whistle to stop my first game for the very first time. I motioned for his coach to come onto the field and informed him in my loud, officious referee voice, "We have a very confused player here."

After some counseling and a hug from his coach, the little boy was ready to resume play. I pompously restarted the game, knowing that I had handled my first crisis with professionalism.

Dissent

Showing disagreement with a referee's decision either by word or action is a punishable foul. It isn't tolerated from the spectators either. On that first day, the children, without exception, treated me with complete respect. My authority was not challenged. Most parents and relatives did the same. There was, however, one relative—perhaps an uncle—who openly complained about some of my officiating. I explained the law to him, and he did comply. Nevertheless, I was surprised at such behavior knowing that I, as a spectator, would never ever create such a display of open defiance of a referee's decision. Not me.

My grandson's game was scheduled to start in the next field over, just across from the paved area that housed basketball hoops. I donned a jacket over my yellow shirt and referee patch, set up my field chair, and sat near the midfield to watch him play. Another referee would run his game. My grandson and I exchanged knowing glances of acknowledgment. The whistle blew, and he joined the dust cloud of players. The referee made a call against my grandson's team. I bolted up from my chair and shouted an objection. I, of all people, dissented.

Three things happened at once—the referee shot me a stern look, I sat down and shut up, and I thought to myself, *My God! So that's what caused that uncle to dissent. The instinctive need to protect a loved one is overpowering.* I resolved to be more understanding of spectator's behavior, or misbehavior, in the future.

Ten Minutes per Goal

I refereed two or three games every Saturday after that, usually just before and after my grandson's game. I came to know and recognize the children and many of the parents.

One morning, I arrived at the field just as the previous game ended. I walked through the gate and past parents and children filing off the field. One little boy walked past me rubbing knuckles in his eyes as he cried inconsolably. His mother trailed behind carrying a folding chair and his water bottle. "Hi, Phyllis. What happened to Jerry? Is he hurt?"

"Naw," she answered. "He's okay. He plays goalkeeper. Every time we lose, he cries. He cries about ten minutes for every goal that got past him. Today we lost 3 to 1. He'll cry for thirty minutes today, and then he'll be okay." She smiled and walked on out to their car, hurrying to catch up to little Jerry whose wailing trailed behind him.

Girls Are Different

Each subsequent year, I refereed increasingly older boys until I had qualified to referee games at all ages in the organization. But I had not yet done a girl's game.

In November, I volunteered to work the Turkey Tournament, a series of all-star games played over the Thanksgiving weekend. One afternoon, I was asked if I would mind doing a game between twelve-year-old girls. The scheduled referee had failed to show up. I had never worked with girls before but did not expect it to be any different. I stepped out on the field and went through all the usual pregame rituals and then started the game. A few minutes later, one girl was fouled by another. I blew the whistle and awarded her a free kick. She stopped, looked up into my eyes, and sweetly said, "Thank you." I was astounded. Any twelve-year-old boy in the same situation would scowl and offer me a look that said "It's about time, ref'!" The rest of that game was an eye-opener. Whereas twelve-year-old boys were already highly competitive and confrontational, the girls were polite even to their adversaries. It was not uncommon to hear them apologizing to an opponent after a collision. It was a sweet, refreshing game, and I came away from it feeling rather fatherly toward them.

The following day I officiated another girl's game. These were fourteen-year-olds. Near the end of regulation time, the Blue and Red teams were still tied, one to one. With seconds left, the Red team fired a vicious shot on goal straight at the defending goalkeeper, a pretty little blonde. She could easily have blocked the shot, without moving, just by raising her hands. Instead she doubled over and ducked under the ball, which flew over her head and into the net for the win. The teams walked past one another, offering high-five hand slaps and "Good game!" expressions. I stood close by—at the end of the line, as we had been taught—to assure that no untoward behavior occurred. As the petite blonde goalkeeper of the Blue Team reached me to say "Good game, ref," I asked her, "Why didn't you stop the ball?" She grinned, held up both hands for my inspection, and answered, "'Cause I just had my nails done for a party tonight! I didn't want to break one!"

That sweet, innocent behavior among the girls changes rapidly as they approach sixteen years of age. The girls became as competitive as the boys and sometimes exhibited a more vicious style. But they are still manageable. Boys at that age are loaded with a wild, testosterone streak that makes controlling them on the field a challenge. One of my referees, after handling his first few games with sixteen-year-old boys, came to me at the end of the day, visibly exhausted, and put it succinctly. "Ya know, their problem at this age is they're always stepping on their dicks!"

THE UNIFORM

As Regional Director of Referee Instruction, I trained twenty to thirty new referees each season. I often attended their first few games, running along the sideline, giving them pointers, and answering questions during breaks. I sometimes had to remind them to tuck in their shirts and to wear the proper uniform. But it was sometimes a hard sell.

A few refused to buy new black shoes when they already had perfectly good white or silver or red or orange gym shoes. One young lady told me there was no way she would wear the long, black stockings that were part of the approved referee uniform.

"Do you realize how that will look on me with my coloring? It's grotesque!" I gave her the lecture about the power of implied authority that goes with the full uniform and how important it was for the children to see a properly uniformed referee conducting their games. I failed to convince her but was relieved when, at her first game that next Saturday, she showed up wearing her long, black referee stockings. When she caught me looking at them and smiling approvingly, she nailed me with a death-look scowl. "I only wore them because I can't find any color that doesn't look worse with this damned, black outfit," she said.

The power of the uniform was demonstrated to me during half time on one Saturday afternoon. I was approached by a young, attractive, divorced mother of one of the kids. She told me how much she admired me. "You look so great out there in that uniform." She gushed flattery while my head swelled and my ego flirted with the thought that I hadn't lost it after all. Until she paused, looked me dead in the eye, and breathlessly said, "I hope, someday, when I am your age, I can still get around so well!" I could almost hear the air whistling out of my popped egotistic balloon.

My last admonition to every graduate referee student was to call me anytime with any questions they might have in the future. On Saturday and Sunday nights, after full days of soccer games, my phone often rang with questions from new referees regarding things that had happened that day.

But some took it a step further. One Saturday afternoon, I received a phone call from the very same young lady who objected so strenuously to the black stockings.

"What is the proper restart when an attacker takes a penalty kick, misses the net, and the ball goes out of the field over the goal line?" she asked.

"When the ball leaves the field and crosses over the goal line out of play and was last touched by an attacker, the proper restart is a goal kick by the defending team." I paused and asked, "Did that happen during a game earlier today?"

"No," she replied, "It just happened in the game I'm refereeing now. I'm standing in the middle of the field. I stopped the game and called you on my cell phone to find out. I may call you again. The game isn't over yet. Thanks. And damn these stockings!" She hung up.

The Volunteer's Paycheck

On the final day of each class group, after they had passed the test and were holding their new uniforms, wallets, patches, and whistles, I recited one last little speech just before they walked out the door.

"People will tell you that what you are about to do is an unpaid volunteer job. Don't you believe it. You will be paid, and paid well, but not by AYSO. You will be paid by the children.

"A few years ago I attended the annual Tri-Region breakfast meeting. Our guest speaker talked about the last VIP awards banquet. As you know, the AYSO VIP program is designed for children who are physically or mentally challenged. They play on special teams and in special tournaments. After each tournament, an awards banquet is held, just as we do after all other tournaments. At this VIP awards banquet, the master of ceremonies called each player to the stage to receive a small trophy. One little boy walked across the stage with a wide smile on his face, took the award, looked up into the MC's eyes and said 'Thank you,' and continued to walk back to the open arms of his parents in the audience. After the ceremony, the boy's parents approached the MC, their eyes filled with tears, and thanked him again for what he and the program had done for their son. He said, 'Oh, no need to thank me. He earned that award. And your son already thanked me.'

"'You don't understand,' said his mother with trembling lips. 'We heard him say "thank you." But you see, those are the very first words he has ever spoken in his life.'

"That will be your pay," I'd tell them. "When that child looks up at you at the end of a game and says, 'Thanks, ref,' that is your reward... and it is priceless."

There was seldom a dry eye in the place.

My grandson outgrew soccer and went on to other things. I remained with AYSO for just a little over seventeen years and finally retired when I felt I could no longer keep up with the oldest boys on the field. Anyway, my classroom techniques, using chalk boards and handouts, were outclassed by computer-projected presentations using PowerPoint and by younger, more energetic teachers who could still stand in front of a classroom for hours at a time.

I have a drawer full of pins and paraphernalia from AYSO and half a dozen coffee cups with their logo.

Stop by and see them some time...

35

Whale Barf

The Old Man scribbled a phone number on the back of an old business card and handed it to the man with the plAYSOuth soccer T-shirt. "That's the number of the current Director of Referee Instruction for South Bay. Give him a call, and he'll set you up with referee classes."

"Thanks. My son will be thrilled." The group rode off, heading north toward Marina Del Rey.

He turned south again and rode toward the plateau. At the foot of the long steep ramp, he dropped the gear ratio and started the long, slow grind to the plateau. His heart rate was pretty high as, with a final effort, he topped the crest onto a level path again. He pulled over to the water fountain which was mounted on the rear wall of Kevaccino's On The Beach, a fast-food snack bar. Filling his water bottle, he pushed the bike around the corner and found a bench seat in front of the snack bar, facing the ocean. He sat a while, gulping water and looking down at the rolling surf that nibbled at the edge of the sprawling sand beach. Anchored further out was an oil tanker tied off to several buoys. It was feeding crude oil to the El Segundo refinery just a half mile further down the coast. His eyes were drawn to a broad expanse of grimy-white foam floating in the surf and spreading over the wet sand at the edge of the water. The ocean breeze had scattered bits and pieces of it over the beach. Two couples wearing bicycle riding gear sat at one of the nearby picnic tables eating sandwiches and staring at the phenomenon.

"What is that stuff?" the small blonde girl asked of no one in particular.

"Just scum from that oil tanker, probably," said the boy sitting across from her.

"I doubt it," the Old Man ventured, surprising them. "It's not from oil."

The four diners turned to him. "Do you know what it is?"

He had seen similar foam scum out on the ocean many times during his many years of recreational sailing. He used to tell his kids that it was whale barf. Why not?

"It's whale barf," he said. "The gray whales are migrating. Sometimes they get seasick!"

The blonde looked wide-eyed, for just a moment, but then she noted his smile. "Aw, go on! What is it, really?"

"Would you believe me if I told you it comes from decomposing algae?"

"No!"

"Yes!"

"Really?"

"Really," he replied. "When algae breaks down and the water and the wind cause a lot of turbulence, like today, it sometimes whips up a lot of foam. Sea foam, like what you see out there now."

They turned as one and stared at the huge field of foam with renewed interest.

"It looks like snow," said the blonde. "A big field of snow. In the middle of summer."

"Dirty snow," one boy added.

"Whipped cream," chirped the other girl.

"Dirty whipped cream," the other boy added, and they all laughed.

"Cotton dross. It resembles a field of cotton dross," said the Old Man.

"What's cotton dross?" one of them asked.

"It's the stuff they throw away after they process fresh picked cotton through the gin. There are places in California and Arizona with fields of dross that look just like this beach."

They returned to their food and chattered noisily, no longer interested in sea foam.

He looked down at the foam coating the surf and sand, lost now in thought. He would like to have told them how the fields, hundreds of acres in places like Tonopah, Arizona, were once covered with dross that looked like foam or snow from a distance. He would like to have explained why most of that cotton dross was gone now.

I'd like to tell them about the cotton gin.
And that Indian. What was his name?
It was an Indian name... Silverheels?
No... it was Lightfoot... or... Golightly... That's what it was.

And kicking stones... I'd like to tell them about that...

36

Kicking a Few Stones

There was only one good motel in Tonopah, Arizona, in 1983. It was a one-story Spanish style adobe building with twelve arched entryways that shaded a walkway along the front doors of the dozen rooms. Cactus plants sprouted in the groomed, railed spaces between the arched entryways. Out front, in the middle of a hard-packed cinder parking lot stood a large sign that read "MOTEL" in red letters and a neon arrow pointing to the building. The arrow was lit and flashing. A smaller neon sign below read "NO VACANCY." The "vacancy" was painted in red and backlit so you could read it. The "no" was made of clear glass neon tubing so you'd only see it if the tubing was lit. It wasn't lit when I got there, so I turned in and parked, the tires of my rented car crunching on the cinder surface.

I entered a door labeled "OFFICE." A bell sat on the counter with a sign that said "Ring for Service." After the second ring, a short round man came out through a pair of hanging curtains, gave me a smile, and squinted through thick glasses that sat on a fishhook nose.

"Evenin'. Need a room?"

"Yessir," I nodded.

"Just you?"

"Yep."

"How many nights?"

"Three oughta do it."

After settling in, I went next door to a small bar and grill. There were several tables and a bar countertop with half a dozen stools. A TV set hung on one wall and was on with the sound muted. A guitar-playing singer stood before a microphone on the silent TV, silently mouthing words as he strummed. I found an empty stool and ordered a beer. I was the only guy in the place who wasn't wearing boots and jeans. Just to my right was a tall, lean guy in fitted shirt and jeans, well-worn boots, a sweat-stained western hat, and a tooled leather belt that sported a big silver buckle studded with pieces of blue turquoise.

He stuck his hand out and said, "Name's Wes. Where ya from?"

I shook his hand and introduced myself. "Pleased to meet you. Los Angeles."

"Ya' here to see Mr. Golightly?"

"Yes. How did you know?"

"Ya' look like you're dressed fer business. About the only real business here in Tonopah is the cotton gin. You ever met J. L. before?

"J. L.?"

"John L. Golightly. Everybody calls him J. L."

"Oh, yeah. No, I've never met him. We've only talked on the phone a few times. I'll meet him tomorrow morning for the first time."

"What time's he expectin' you?"

"Nine o'clock."

We sipped our beers for a while. Then he turned sideways to face me, grinned a little, and said, "Lemme tell ya what's gonna happen."

He began gesturing with his hands. "You get there about eight thirty and park right next to the ranch house. Don't go to that door. That's not where his office is. Just west o' that is a house trailer. The office is in there. But he won't be there yet. He lives in

Scottsdale. Then long about quarter ta nine, you'll see a spot in the sky. It'll be a single engine plane comin' out a' the east. It'll land somewheres outta sight beyond his cotton fields. He's got a landin' strip out there. After a while, you'll see a cloud a dust, and it'll get closer and closer and here will come a beat up jeep. J. L. will climb out, dressed kinda like me. He's Indian, y'know, so you're gonna hafta kick a few stones with him."

"Kick a few stones? What do you mean?"

"Well now, J. L. will get outta that jeep with his leather satchel sittin' next to him, a beat-up ol' thing that's tied together with a piece a wire. He'll come up and shake your hand. He's gonna talk about your flight out or the weather. As he does, he'll give a little nudge with his boot to some a the gravel and small stones on the ground."

At this point, Wes got off his stool. He demonstrated the technique, hooking his thumbs on his jeans pockets, looking down at his feet, standing on one foot, and giving little kicks at imaginary stones with the toe of his boot as he talked. He shifted his weight to the other foot and kicked a little with his other foot.

"Then you should answer back and kick a few pieces a stone with your toe. Then he'll make some more small talk with you and you'll take turns like that, chattin' and kickin' stones. It's kinda like smokin' the peace pipe before a serious powwow."

He climbed back on his stool, grinned a grin full of slightly off-white teeth, and said, "When J. L. feels the two a you've kicked enough stones, he'll pick up his satchel and say something like, 'Well, let's go on inside.' Once you're inside the office, he'll talk business—but not 'til you've kicked a few stones together."

At the time, I worked for a young company in greater Los Angeles. We made a variety of unusual products including waste heat recovery and cogeneration systems. We had designed and built a system for the Tonopah Cotton Gin. It was installed and working.

The Cotton Gin was located on a fifty-five-acre parcel of property owned by the Golightly family. They raised cotton and watermelons for years. The gin was built in 1977 and was now able to process both long staple (Pima) and short staple cotton and handled J. L.'s crops and those of many of his neighbors. The cotton came in large open trailers, was sucked by vacuum up into the building, and sent through a dryer to remove the moisture. Then it fed into the cotton gin that removed the seeds and separated the staple from the dross—lint, sticks, leaves, thorns, and tiny bits of clinging cotton lint. The seed was used and sold for planting or to produce cotton seed oil. The remaining dross was dumped on undeveloped acreage, making some of the Maricopa county countryside look like it was covered in dirty snow. When they ran out of room, they paid someone to dispose of it.

J. L. was venturesome and open to new technology. His fields were leveled with laser equipment to minimize water runoff. Any new ideas were welcomed long before many of his skeptical fellow farmers would do so. That's why, when we proposed a unique waste recovery system to him, he was immediately receptive. Our system collected the dross, fed it into a fluidized combustion bed, and burned it. The heat it generated was captured by running a Dow Corning heat transfer fluid through a closed-loop system of heat exchangers. That heat was then used to dry the damp cotton coming into the factory.

This would save J. L. a minimum of $24,000 annually in propane fuel cost. It would also save him the cost of dross disposal. The new system would pay for itself in a few years. After that it was like free money. Now the system was installed, up and running, and saving J. L. money every day.

On that February day in 1983, I had flown 370 miles west to Phoenix, rented a car at Sky Harbor airport, and driven back over fifty miles west to the small town of Tonopah to find the Tonopah Cotton Gin. I did so for one reason alone: J. L. owed us money. I had spoken with him by phone reminding him that his last payment was delinquent. He invited me to visit him to discuss the matter. Here I was.

The next morning, I drove up 411th Avenue, turned right on West Indian School Road, turned left on 395th Avenue, then right on West Camelback Road—and there it was. I got there early, parked near the house, and walked to the large, corrugated sheet metal building. On the west end stood a large overhanging roof which shielded two trailers full of cotton. Another trailer sat waiting to one side. The side doors of the building stood open. Just inside was a bale press. The crew had just processed a trailer full of cotton, and the lead foreman was operating the bale press. From the middle of each bale, he took a sample of the staples, sealed them in a small brown bag, and placed an identification stamp on it. This he attached to the finished bale which was strapped tightly in a yellow plastic jacket. He introduced himself to me as Bobbie, the shift foreman.

Bobbie had been working the gin for about five years now and had lost a finger to one of the machines. Over the next few days, I would come to know him and his very pretty, very young bride about twenty years his junior. She brought his lunch every day and fawned over this fatherly cotton gin foreman.

Bobbie took me on a tour of the plant, showing me the large cotton dryer, the Hardwicketter rollers and saw stands, the auger drives that carried the seed to storage bins, and the dross to a holding bin outside the rear of the building. He walked me outside the rear of the building and pointed to the machinery my company had built and installed. He had some questions about it, and I answered them as well as I could.

About eight thirty I walked back to the house trailer and tried the door, but it was still locked, so I waited. Just as Wes the barroom cowboy had predicted, a plane appeared about eight forty-five and slid slowly down behind the extensive cotton fields and disappeared. Shortly, a dust cloud rose and grew steadily closer until a dust-covered open jeep pulled up and stopped in front of me. J. L. stepped out wearing jeans, boots, leather belt, silver buckle, flowered western shirt, and a sand-colored cowboy hat. He reached back inside and lifted out a battered leather satchel with a small twist of wire holding it shut in place of the torn flap. He set it on the front seat a moment. We shook hands.

"How was your flight out from LA?" he asked, hooking his thumbs on his jean pockets, staring down at the gravel and stones, nudging a few pieces around with the silver-tipped toe of his boot.

"Not bad. Did you have a good flight from Scottsdale?" I dutifully, awkwardly, pushed some stones around with my toe. I hoped I was doing it right.

It went on like that for about five minutes. We agreed that it was unseasonably hot for that time of year. He asked where I was staying the night and how long I planned to be there. We made small talk, slow and easy, nothing important. Then abruptly, J. L. lifted his head, unhooked his thumbs, picked up his beat leather satchel, and said, "Well, let's get out of this sun." He unlocked the house trailer door and we walked in. Someone had set up a fresh pot of coffee on a timer before we got there. The aroma filled the trailer. We filled mugs and sat down facing each other across his desk.

J. L. took off his hat, tossed it on a hook, and leaned back in his chair.

"You're wondering when you're going to get the last $25,000 payment. I'm wondering if your system will keep on working. You know, it failed a couple times. You folks were good enough to come out and fix it both times, but how do I know it won't happen again?"

"Mr. Golightly—" he stopped me, palm up.

"Call me J. L. Everybody else does."

I started over. "J. L., every new system has to be debugged. We've done that. It's fixed. You've now got heavier gauge tubular heat exchangers downstream of the fluidized combustion bed. Our tests tell us we've got a safety factor of at least ten now. We've replaced the failed temperature sensors with new and better ones. I've brought three spares with me, just in case you need them. We've no reason to think anything else will go wrong."

J. L. looked thoughtful, weighing what I had said.

"Y'see, friend, here's the thing." He hesitated for a moment as if weighing how much to tell me. Then he said, "I'm the first guy in our cotton growers association who's bought one of these recovery systems. You can't imagine the kidding I take from the other farmers for buying this thing. They say it'll never pay for itself. They gloat every time they hear that it broke down."

"Look, J. L. The unit is up and running. It has a warranty. If anything fails under warranty, we'll make it good under terms of the contract. I'll even stay here for a few days and teach your guys how to operate and make minor repairs to it. I'll show them how to replace the sensors, just in case. But we should be paid. The job is completed and is under warranty."

He thought about this a while, sipping on his coffee. A clock on the desk ticked. The muffled sounds of the cotton gin drifted into the silence. After a while he leaned forward, arms on the desk, hands folded as if in prayer.

"Here's what I'll do. You stay here a couple more days. Teach my boys everything they need to know about running that contraption and how to make minor fixes and adjustments. In about three months, if it's still running okay, I'm gonna invite all those cotton farmers to the house for a big barbeque. I want them to spend a whole day eating, drinking, and watching that thing do its job without a hitch. I want you here to answer their questions and to make sure nothing goes wrong starting with the day before they get here, all day of the BBQ and until the last of 'em goes home. You do that and the system works the whole time, and I'll give you a check for $25,000 to take home with you. Plus, you'll get a real fine BBQ."

We both leaned back in our chairs. He was asking for something above and beyond what was required by our contract. Still, I could understand his strong desire to rub his doubting fellow farmer's collective noses in a successful demonstration.

"You've got a deal, J. L."

We rose and shook hands. We visited a while longer. He went into the big ranch house for a while then left the way he had come, driving the jeep away in a cloud of trailing dust, disappearing beyond the cotton fields. A short time later, his plane rose from the cotton and dwindled to a tiny dot.

I spent the rest of that day and the next two in the cotton mill, tweaking our equipment, giving individual instructions to several of the more able workers. At lunchtime, Bobbie introduced me to Dawn, his young wife. She gushed, blushed, and smiled, and all the young men in the gin gawked, risking fingers and hands around the machinery until she got back into her car and drove off.

I ran into Wes at the bar a couple times in the evenings. I told him J. L. and I kicked a few stones. It helped pass the time to talk to him and to soak up the local flavors.

By the time I left Tonopah, I had a reasonably good understanding of how a cotton gin worked, and they had a reasonably good understanding of how our waste recycling system worked.

Almost three months later to the day J. L. called and I returned to Tonopah. Nothing had changed. The drive west from Phoenix on Interstate 10 looked more familiar. I recognized the dog racing track to the south and saw the familiar warning signs along the freeway near the penitentiary that warned against picking up hitchhikers because they might be escaped prisoners. When I got to Tonopah, the motel sign was lit, its neon arrow busily pointing toward the front door. Some of the guests J. L. had invited planned on staying at the motel in town, and many of the rooms were reserved for the next night.

I spent the next day inspecting the waste heat recovery system and reviewing the operating instructions with Bobbie, the foreman. Everything looked good. J. L. asked me to be there early the next morning.

I went to bed early and set an alarm. Before dawn I was up, cleaned up, ate an early breakfast, and went to the gin. Bobbie was already there. The cotton gin and the heat recovery system were running. I checked the dross bin to be sure it was full. If we ran out of dross, the fluidized bed fire would go out and shut down the system. Then we'd have to turn on the propane burners and all hell would break loose with J. L. and his visitors. The dross bin was full to overflowing. The fluidized combustion bed was burning perfectly, and the closed loop heat transfer system was taking heat from the burning dross and bringing it indoors to the cotton dryer. Everything looked good.

Out in the yard, between the ranch house and the trailer, cooks were busily preparing the food. Barbeques were heating up. Beautiful cuts of meats, beans, corn on the cob, salads, breads, and rolls were in abundance. Lots of drinks were being iced down. For J. L. and the town of Tonopah, it was reminiscent of the original opening day celebration which had been held on October 21, 1977, when the brand new Tonopah Cotton Gin officially opened for business. This time we were celebrating the newest wrinkle in cotton gin technology.

The first guests showed up about nine o'clock. I mingled with them, slipping away now and then to check on the system. The conversations touched on many things but kept coming back to crops and techniques, yield per acre, irrigation systems and costs, and other fairly technical subjects related to what had become a very advanced body of scientific farming knowledge. I was impressed with the sophistication of these farmers and understood even more how important it was to J. L. not to be embarrassed by any kind of malfunction of the equipment on this day.

J. L. made an announcement that I would conduct a tour of the installation and answer questions. It was a sweaty palms experience. These were not uneducated farmers. They were astute businessmen, knowledgeable and full of penetrating questions. Adding to my fear of being unable to answer a question was the dread that something might malfunction in the middle of the tour. It was a very long one-hour stroll, but everything went smoothly. The rest of the day was spent eating, drinking, and good-natured bantering by this unique band of agricultural experts.

Toward late afternoon, the guests began leaving, some to catch a plane out of Phoenix, others to fly a personal plane out of the nearby landing strip, still others to the motel in town. Around 9:00 pm, I stood with J. L. and some of his local friends and crew watching the last car head down Camelback Road to 395th Avenue on its way back to the hotel. As the car turned the farthest corner, J. L. turned to me and said, "Be here around nine tomorrow morning. I'll have something for you."

I met him outside the trailer the next morning. He had the dusty jeep sitting there with his old leather satchel sitting on the front seat. We shook hands. He hooked his thumbs on his pockets.

"Good morning," he said. "Get a good night's sleep?" He looked down at his foot and poked a few small stones around with the silver-tipped toe of his boot as he talked.

"Good morning, J. L. I sure did. You?" I nudged a small stone or two with the point of my shoe during the exchange. I felt confident that I was doing it right by now.

"I thought things went pretty well yesterday," he said, moving a few more stones with his toe. "They seemed favorably impressed. Of course they won't say so to me, but I suspect a couple of those cotton ginners might be thinking about buying one of these things themselves."

"That'd be nice," I said. "I'm glad things worked out so well."

Then abruptly he turned, twisted loose the wire on his satchel, reached inside, and pulled out a check for $25,000 made out to my company.

"Thanks for the help. Have a safe trip home, my friend."

"Thanks, J. L. Call us anytime if you have any problems with the system."

We shook hands one last time. He tossed the satchel into the passenger seat and hopped into the jeep.

I watched him drive away. When the airplane became a barely visible dot in the morning sky, I drove back to the motel, packed, and checked out.

I guess things went well because we never heard from the Tonopah Cotton Gin or J. L. again.

In 2011, I was speeding down Interstate 10 heading west from Los Angeles. I was on my way to the Loop 101 around Phoenix then up to Sedona to spend Easter weekend with children and grandchildren. We were about fifty or sixty miles short of Phoenix when I spotted a road sign that said "TONOPAH" and pointed to an off-ramp to my right.

"Wow, there it is! Tonopah! God, I haven't been there in, what, twenty-five or thirty years. Do you mind if we take a few minutes to see the place?"

My travel companion nodded. "Sure, let's go. What's there to see?"

"A cotton gin," I answered.

I pulled off Interstate 10 onto the off-ramp and tried to explain what was in Tonopah as I watched for signs. I wasn't sure how to find the cotton gin. I remembered something about an Indian School Road, but that was all. I drove to the crossroad that represented downtown Tonopah. Nothing looked familiar. I drove a little further and saw a motel on my left. I pulled into the parking lot and recognized it, vaguely. This was where I stayed. There was the old building next door that had been a bar and grill. I took a photo and drove slowly further down the road until I saw a small building with a variety of odds and ends for sale in the yard. I pulled over and approached the guy and gal who seemed to be in charge.

"I'm looking for the Tonopah Cotton Gin. It used to be somewhere out around Indian School Road. Can you tell how to get there?"

"Never heard of it," the man said. "You sure you've got the right town?"

"Absolutely. It was about twenty-five, maybe thirty, years ago. I stayed at the old motel down the road and drove out each day past Indian School road."

The gal said, "I don't know about a cotton gin, but there's a bean factory out West Camelback Road." She described the route as well as she could.

Armed with those rough instructions, I headed north on 411th Avenue, past Interstate 10 to West Indian School Road. Following hazy recollections, I turned east and found Route 395. I headed north to West Camelback Road and saw something off to my right that resembled the old cotton gin building. If that was the same old corrugated building, it must have been resurfaced and been painted. The overhang that used to shelter trailers full of cotton was still there. Not much else was the same. The old ranch house and house trailer were gone. The old bunk house where the cotton gin crew lived was still there, far to the left, windows broken out, tattered pieces of curtains blowing in and out of the window frames. Could this be the place? I stared, unsure.

I was standing outside the car taking pictures when I saw the dust cloud of a small vehicle moving across barren fields toward me. I watched, fascinated, as the machine came on. It was eerily like watching the jeep coming from the airstrip all those years ago. As it drew close, I saw the driver, a little man with a scruffy beard stubble, chewing on an unlit, saliva-soaked cigar stub. He remained seated in the forklift.

"Can I help you, folks?" he asked, the stub shoved off to one corner of his mouth, wiggling up and down as he talked.

"I'm trying to find the old Tonopah Cotton Gin. Seems like it used to be right here, but most of it seems to be gone. And those tall steel towers don't look familiar at all."

"Oh, well, this is a bean processing factory now. Used to be a cotton gin around here somewhere's. Maybe right here. Why'n't ya check the town paper. I think I remember readin' somethin' about an old cotton gin in the Tonopah Tribune."

"Where can I find a copy of the town paper?"

"They publish it out at the big trailer park back down 411th. Just keep going down that way and you'll see it."

I thanked him and drove in the direction he had motioned. I saw no trailer park. I passed Interstate 10 again and drove back into town, past the roadside stand where I had stopped before. I saw signs ahead that said "Palo Verde Nuclear Power Plant" and remembered driving out to see it all those years ago. I was sure I had gone too far. I was about to give up.

I made a U-turn into an open lot and realized I was facing a trailer park where the snow birds come to escape harsh winters back home. Ahead was a building with a huge "OFFICE" sign above the entry. We went inside and inquired about the Tonopah Tribune. A very helpful young lady named Shirley said it was published right here. She actually found a copy of the September 2010 issue of the paper and gave it to me.

The headline read "BEAN FACTORY COMES TO TONOPAH." The article covered the entire front page and half of page three. It announced a new bean processing plant which had just opened on the site of the old Tonopah Cotton Gin.

The article recapped the history of the gin and reported that John L. Golightly passed away in October 1988, just five years after I had met him. The cotton gin shut down permanently somewhere around 1993.

I wanted to go back to the bean factory. I wanted to stand about where I think I stood thirty years ago, where J. L. and I stood that morning we first met. It would be nice to hook my thumbs on my pockets, stare down at my toes, and kick a few stones with him one more time.

We were running late. The sun would set soon. The kids in Sedona would be worried. I passed West Old Indian School Road and West Camelback Road. I whipped onto Interstate 10. We passed warning signs that said "Do Not Pick Up Hitchhikers" and the old greyhound racing track. We turned up the Loop 101 around Phoenix and headed for Sedona.

The former Tonopah Cotton Gin.

The old bunk house.

37

El Segundo

The Old Man looked up from his reverie about Tonopah and was surprised to see that the young couples had gone and that he stood, alone, straddling his bike, staring out at the sand and the grey foam that looked like cotton dross.

From here on back to his starting point would be easy. He coasted downhill, at high speed, from the elevated Dockweiler Plateau back to beach level. At the bottom, he curved around a fenced industrial outcropping next to the path and found easy pedaling as he passed the parking lot just before the El Segundo Refinery. He recognized this particular parking lot as the filming location of a murder scene in a movie about a grandfather who had been a professional killer and who had taught his own son how to murder for money. It was a powerful movie

As he turned to look for the exact spot where the murder scene was staged, he saw shiny, expensive motorcycles lined up neatly. Several dozen motorcyclists, all wearing matching leather outfits, wandered about admiring each other's equipment and exchanging motorcycle chat. He pulled off into the lot to get a closer look. They were all Suzukis, highly polished and generously outfitted with luggage carriers. He spoke to the nearest biker, a heavily tattooed man with a yellowed bar-handle mustache and blue bandana around his head.

"Nice bikes! Suzuki club?"

"Yeah. We're outta Ontario. You a biker?" he asked. He grinned, showing several gold-rimmed teeth

"Well, not anymore. I used to be, though. I had a Honda. Sold it about four years ago. I'm too old to be riding a motorcycle. Now I stick to this kind of bike," he said, gesturing down at his bicycle.

"Nah! We got some fellas older'n you still ridin'! Ya shouldn't a sold it," he said through his gilded teeth.

"Well, I think my reaction time was getting a little too slow, and I figured if I kept it in the garage, I'd for sure ride it one time too many."

"Do ya miss it?

"Sure do. Especially on nice days like today."

"Must've been hard to give it up for good after ridin' all a' your life," he ventured.

"Actually, I didn't start riding 'til I was over fifty years old. In fact, I never meant to ride even then. I was sort of backed into it."

"What do ya mean 'backed into it'?"

The old guy smiled as he remembered what happened...

Yeah, it just sort of happened... that one day when she called me on the phone...

"Hey Dad," she said...

38

The Motorcycle

"Hey, Dad, I've got a favor to ask you." I had heard that many times from this particular daughter. It was code for "I need money." She was living on her own, so to speak, with a four-year-old son. She found jobs for minimum wage and was struggling to get by. In the last three months, she could not pay her rent, so she borrowed it from me. The first month she paid half of it back. The second month and third months were still owed to me.

Her ex-husband had moved to another state and stopped paying child support some time ago. During the last few months before he ran away, he gave her some of his belongings, mostly of little value, in lieu of child support.

One of those bartered child support payments consisted of a motorcycle, a 1979 Honda 400 CM Hondamatic. She was a tomboy all her life—excelled in athletics, always up for danger and excitement. She would be delighted to get a motorcycle instead of child support money. Money could only be used for dull stuff like food, clothes, or rent. But a motorcycle? I imagine the conversation went something like this:

Her: "Where is the child support? You are three months behind."

Him: "How about I give you my motorcycle and we call it even?"

Her: "Oh, boy!"

Him: "Uh, it isn't registered. I couldn't pay it this year. You'll have to pay that."

Her: "Oh, boy!"

Him: "Uh, the insurance expired. There's no insurance on it. You have to buy that."

Her: "Oh, boy!"

Him: "It's about out of gas. Probably has just enough to get it over to your place."

Her: "Oh, boy!"

Him: "Sometimes it's hard to start. I don't know what's wrong with it."

Her: "Oh, boy!"

It was a pretty little thing with a deep maroon gas tank, black and gold trim, and chrome décor. She loved to ride it, much to my consternation. I implored her to get rid of it, with speeches about her responsibility as a single mom. She ignored me. Nothing worked until the day I heard, one more time, those code words: "Hey, Dad, I've got a favor to ask you." I had been waiting to hear that.

"Tell you what," I said slowly. "You haven't been able to repay the last couple loans. I'll loan you the rent one more time on one condition."

"What's that?"

"You give me the motorcycle. I'll give it back once you have caught up on what you owe me." I was pretty sure she would be a long time paying anything back to me, if ever.

"Sure, okay. I'll give you the pink slip to hold."

"No, what I want is for you to bring the bike to my garage and sign over the pink slip to me. I'll sign it back to you when you've paid the loans off."

She thought about that for a day or two. Then she called with a proposition of her own. "I'll give you the pink slip to hold. I'll keep the bike here, and I promise I won't ride it until I pay you back. Then you can give me back the pink slip. That way it won't take up room in your garage, and you'll save the cost of registering it in your name and then back into mine."

I thought about that proposition for almost three seconds and responded.

"Well, I know your word is as good as gold," I said with just a little sarcasm. "And I appreciate that you want to save me the cost of registering it in my name. And I admire your concern about cluttering my garage. Not for nothing, but I like my proposal better. You think it over."

She thought about it for another day or two. Her rent was now almost two weeks late, and the landlord, who was a very reasonable man, had called her several times. Finally, I got the call.

"I'm on my way up to the house with the bike and the pink slip. Can you give me a ride back home with your car?"

She parked it in my garage, right in front of my workbench. I got the signed pink slip. She got the rent money and told me she would be back in a month or two to pay me back and retrieve the bike. I drove her home.

And that is how I came into possession of a completely foreign device that I had no use for. I regarded motorcycles as a dangerous pastime associated with people like the Hell's Angels. If God wanted us to ride motorcycles, he would have created extra wheels, doors, windows, fenders, bumpers, air bags, and sheet metal to go around it. Right? Wait, that's a car.

My plan was to keep it in my garage for a year or so and then sell it out from under her—an overly protective, fatherly deception.

Because it was parked directly in front of my workbench, I had to reach around it to get at my tools. Running out of patience one day, I attempted to move it. I almost dropped it. It was so heavy and awkward. I felt intimidated. It was annoying that I should feel this way. I was being challenged! I was fifty years old. I had learned to sail, ice skate, roller skate, snow ski, water ski, backpack, ride bicycles, ride and train horses, but I'd never driven a motorcycle.

How hard could it be? I determined to find out. Then I could move it away from my workbench.

I signed up for a motorcycle training class that was approved by the State of California and showed up for the six weekly classes. The first few lessons were in the classroom where we first learned how to dress protectively.

"If there is any part of your body that you like and you don't want to change it, cover it!"

"It is not a question of 'if you will fall' but 'when you will fall.'"

We learned a lot of good riding tips, legal aspects, and rules of the road. It was fascinating, and I thought, "I still have no desire to ride, but this is good to know." Then we moved outdoors.

They supplied helmets and motorcycles for us, but we had to come dressed properly for the actual riding classes. If we showed up with improper protective clothing, we would forfeit our tuition and be sent home. We had signed an agreement to that affect. On our first outdoor class, they sent two people home permanently with no refunds because they were not dressed properly. I was impressed.

By the end of the classes, I was getting enthused. Riding the motorcycle was exciting even though we had driven only in the large parking lot behind the local community college. I was getting just enough information and skill to become dangerous to myself and others. I finished the course, passed the final test, and got a certificate and a decal to put on the back of my helmet if and when I eventually got my own helmet. Shortly later I bought a very nice full face helmet and two pairs of riding gloves. I also bought a pair of high-top riding boots and a heavy leather motorcycle jacket with lots of zippers and metal buttons. I was ready to rumble.

But I couldn't start her up. Now that I had a license to ride, I could call the bike a "her." That's what we bikers do. I called a motorcycle shop. They came with a trailer and took her away.

They called me when it was ready. I hitched a ride to the shop with a friend. I started her up and rode all the way to the foot of the steep hill below where I lived. Now the thought of stopping this five-hundred–pound bike at a stop sign halfway up a steep hill terrified me. What if I couldn't handle it? What if it started to roll backward before I could pop the clutch (see the motorcycle lingo?) and take off at the stop sign?

I called my stepbrother, Frank. Frank owned an insurance agency, but on weekends he put on a faux troopers uniform with high-top leather boots and rode escort for funerals and weddings. He drove out to me. I drove his car up the hill to my house. He followed on my bike.

"It's got plenty of torque," he said. "You can take it up that hill with no problem."

Thus assured, I decided it was time for me to take her on a real ride next Sunday. On the chosen day, I set the alarm to wake me because I wanted to be on the road before there was much traffic. It was cold outside. Heeding my senses and my instructors, I wore heavy levis, ankle-high leather boots, heavy leather jacket with all pockets and compartments zipped shut, long leather gloves with thick palms (in case I slid if I fell), and my brand new, full-face, white Shoei RF-200 helmet. I had made a special trip to the Orange County swap meet the week before and negotiated a terrific price for the brand new RF-200. He also sold me a pair of long-wristed winter gloves. He threw in, for free, a pair of spring-summer gloves, shorter-wristed with webbed backs to let the summer breezes cool my feverish biker hands.

Sunday morning I donned all the equipment, backed the bike out of my garage, and rolled to a stop in the middle of my quiet street. No one was out yet. Newspapers still lie in the driveways. The neighbors were still asleep. Putting it in gear, I roared down the street and headed for Palos Verdes Drive. This road makes a very long circle around the Peninsula cliffs overlooking the Pacific Ocean. I encountered very few cars. No one was up yet. The early morning wind was cold and damp. I had every inch of my body covered, yet I could feel the cold penetrating my neckline around the high leather zipped-up collar.

I zoomed around Malaga Cove, thundered through Lunada Bay, skirted the cliffs along San Pedro, and rumbled to a stop just below the Korean Peace Bell at Point Fermin. I looked around at the unfamiliar surroundings. Well, I had been there many times before by car. But I discovered that the same locations, seen from the back of a motorcycle, revealed new details and features that had escaped me before. I puttered slowly down a small street next to the public park at Point Fermin and spotted a weathered coffee shop. The faded blue-and-white sign read "Stroller's Café." The thought of a hot cup of coffee sounded pretty good to me. I would pull up to this strange new venue and walk in seeking new and exciting adventures. (That's what we bikers do.) I nosed the bike into the curb right in front of the café, turned off the ignition, popped down the kick stand, swung a leg off the bike, turned the front wheel away from the lean, and walked into Stroller's Café.

I approached the counter where a woman had stopped what she was doing and was staring directly at me. As I drew close, she leaned toward me and said, "What'll ya have?"

I was still very cold, so I only lifted my face piece, pulled off my gloves, and answered, "I'd like a hot cup of decaf coffee, please."

She raised back, placed a fist on each hip, and bellowed, "We don't serve decaf in here!" The tone of voice and clearly confrontational facial expression were as shocking as a slap in the face. Was it my imagination, or did I see tattoos on muscular arms, a butch haircut, and steel studs in ears and one nostril? I sensed rather than heard a rustle from behind and from both sides of me. I looked around and noticed, for the first time, several dozen bikers—tattooed, wearing chains, spiked hairdos, and, without exception, Harley Davidson logos. Every table bore a full pitcher of beer, and every biker had a mug of beer in front of him. And every face was scowling and staring at this full-face helmeted stranger who had ridden up on a Honda. And it was only 8:00 am.

If they see that I am a harmless old man, they won't do anything foolish, I thought. I unbuckled my helmet and pulled it off my head, revealing my white hair and age-weathered countenance, which I hoped would remind them of their fathers. The scowls deepened, and a murmur became audible. It occurred to me that some of them might hate their fathers, and others might not even know who their father was. Meanwhile, she stood with fists on hips, looking taller and thicker than before. I said something lame like, "Oh, uh, never mind then."

I pulled on my gloves, my white Shoei RF-200 full-face helmet, pulled down the visor, turned to the door, and walked—calmly, I hoped—toward the bike waiting outside. That's when I noticed (how had I missed it when I drove up?) the curb on both sides of my Japanese Honda lined with Harley Davidson bikes and, clearly labeled by tattoos and logos, Harley Davidson bikers. They were sitting on the curbstone, each holding a breakfast beer mug.

I slung one leg over the Honda, hiked up the kickstand, inserted the key, and mentally whispered a prayer to the gods of old men, "Please let the motor start!"

It did. And as I backed out from the curb and shifted gears, a number of them rose to their feet. I felt every eye boring into the back of my black leather, zipper-decorated jacket as I sped off.

That was my first Sunday drive. On Monday morning, I went to work and told my adventure to a couple of my coworkers who were motorcycle enthusiasts. When I described the café, they said in unison, "You went into Stroller's Café?!" Charlie explained to me, "That's a Harley Davidson club hangout. You're lucky they let you walk away. They hate Japanese bikes, call them rice burners. Every year they have a fund-raiser for their club. They confiscate a Jap bike, like yours, chain it to the hydrant in front, and for a dollar a whack people can hit the Jap bike with a sledge hammer."

I described the Amazonian lady who bellowed at me. "Yeah, that's Bella. The place is owned by her and her girlfriend. You only met the one. Maybe the other was in the back opening another keg. You're lucky she wasn't out there. She'd have thrown you out!" I don't know if he was pulling my leg or not, but I never had the temerity to try visiting Stroller's Café again.

As I gained confidence, I went out with "my bike" (more biker jargon) more often. I did drop it a few times but only when I was moving very slowly. Like the time in a parking lot when I brought it to a stop and put my left foot down, only to find that a repair crew had dug a one-foot-deep hole right where my foot wanted to go. I learned to be more observant.

One day, I rode the bike up to Green Hills Cemetery to visit my father's grave. I knew he'd be impressed. After the visit, as I started to get back on, I lost my balance and the motorcycle began to fall. To keep it from falling, I pressed hard against the side with my hip and leg. That stopped it from falling but tore the gasoline line and filter away from the fuel tank. The line broke, fuel began dribbling out, and I was stuck. I used the telephone in the flower shop to call a friend, but no one was home. I called a cab to come and get me. The driver, an Indian from India, insisted that he could get the bike into his trunk. But after nearly rupturing himself, he agreed to simply drive me home. I went back the next day with several new parts for the fuel filter and line, repaired it, and drove it home.

I had a few close calls too. Friends and I rode out to the Rock Store in Agoura in the canyons above Malibu. I drove out there a couple times alone. On a particularly sharp series of turns, I hit a wet, sandy spot. The bike began to slide, and I had to take the turn so wide to avoid falling that I was in the opposite lane. The blind curve hid oncoming traffic, so I could not tell if I was about to be killed. By the time I stopped the bike and regained the safe side of the road, I could taste every filling in my teeth—an electric, metallic taste created by fear. When I called my riding partner to tell him about it, he said, "Better check the leather seat cover for pucker marks." And I knew exactly what he was talking about.

Palos Verdes Drive East is a popular stretch of road on the Peninsula. It is steep and snaky, full of tight curves going to the top of the mountain on the land side then down to the sea on the ocean side. I was tearing up this road and leaning into the curves and having a wonderful time when a car full of teenagers came careening toward me on the other side of the road. As they whipped into view, the driver lost control, swerved into my path then overcorrected and slashed back across, tore through a fence, and smashed into the hillside. His skid marks were only twenty or so feet in front of me. Again, I checked the seat for pucker marks.

Each time I went to popular venues, like the Rock Store, I was impressed with the beautiful bikes that showed up. The clothing alone was often worth more than the bikes. Some of them were made of Kevlar with built-in heaters and helmets with built-in electronics for music and communication. I'd been told that Jay Leno sometimes showed up with one of his bikes, although I never saw him.

One morning I arrived early, went inside, had breakfast, and walked outside to find that my poor 1979 Honda 400 was surrounded by fancy, expensive motorcycles whose headlights were worth more than my bike. Riders were milling around admiring each other's equipment. I was embarrassed to climb on my modest bike, so I killed time looking around too. I was waiting for all the attention to drift away so I could slip away unnoticed. Just as I swung a leg over my bike, one of the guys said, "Hey, is that your CM400A Hondamatic?" His voice drew attention, and a group turned to look.

"Yep, I'm afraid it is," I replied almost apologetically.

"Wow, I haven't seen one of these in years," he said as he and a growing group drew closer.

Then he proceeded to tell me that the bike was very popular in its day. The simple two-speed, semi-automatic transmission was used throughout Europe by messenger and delivery services because it was easy to operate in heavy traffic. In the United States, it was especially popular among women. Due to popular demand over the years, Honda had considered resurrecting the model but just hadn't done so. As a consequence, he said, the bike has become a collector's item. An admiring crowd formed around me. I had planned to slink away unnoticed before I was discovered by this man. Now I answered questions and rode off with a curious, if not admiring, audience. That was the highlight of my times with her.

In recent years, I noticed little things that suggested my reaction time was getting slower. I parked her in my garage and told myself that I was probably too old to keep taking risks. The pull was always there, however, and I realized I must sell her or ride her. I took photos, ran ads, and sold her to a young man who wanted a bike for his wife to ride. I gave him all the maintenance records, the owner's manual, the shop manual, and some spare parts. We loaded it in his pickup truck, and I stood in the middle of my street and watched as she turned the corner out of sight.

Sometimes, when the sun shines brightly on an early Sunday morning, I still yearn to get her out and take one more ride to San Pedro, park her outside Annie's Bakery in Ports of Call, order a cup of coffee and a hot, fresh cinnamon bun, and listen to the Portuguese and Italian fishermen dressed in their Sunday clothes, debating world politics or telling fishing tales while they drink strong coffee and smoke black cigars.

Just one more time.

The Iron Horse: Sometimes, when the sun shines brightly on an early Sunday morning, I still yearn to take her out… Just one more time.

37

Iron Horse

A small group of the Suzuki Club motorcyclists had gathered around to listen. As he finished his story, they slowly drifted away, except for one young man who lingered, leaning with his backside against a motorcycle. He lit a cigarette, took a long drag, and let the smoke out in small puffs as he spoke.

"You talk about that old motorcycle like it was an old girlfriend."

"Y'know, that's a good way to describe her. She was pretty and she was exciting. Riding that motorcycle gave me the same thrills I used to feel with my horses. She took me places cars could not go. I felt the adrenaline rush that comes from moving at high speeds, totally exposed to the wind, just like a galloping horse. She was my iron horse."

"I like that," he said. "Iron horse. Got a nice sound to it."

"Well, the motorcycle is a lot like a horse. Riding mine brought back feelings of long ago when the San Fernando Valley was less developed and horse trails crisscrossed the land. It brought back my youth for a time."

"You owned horses?"

"I used to. When I lived in the valley"

The young man leaned back, took another drag of his cigarette, and said, "I tried to ride a horse once. Scared the hell out of me. Didn't bother you, though, huh?

"Oh, it did scare me—just enough to keep me careful. A lot like riding a motorcycle."

"Did ya take riding lessons like you did with the motorcycle?"

"Yeah, I had a few. Matter of fact, my little girls were the ones who wanted riding lessons, and I just went along." He smiled, recalling his little girls.

Little Tammy, our firstborn, was just eleven years old, and her little sister, Matty, barely nine.

They were so bright, so ambitious, and so full of questions.

That was half a century ago...

But it seems like yesterday...

I can still hear their voices...

"Daddy, how do birds fly?"

"Daddy, what makes it rain?"

"Daddy, where do butterflies come from?"

The Horse Years

"Daddy, what's a period?" Tammy stood there, her younger sister, Matty, standing by her side. Two sets of big brown innocent eyes staring up at me; long, rich brunette hair hanging down around two upturned faces.

"A period? You mean like at the end of a sentence?"

"No. I mean what Cousin Becky is having. She said she isn't feeling good because she's having a period. And she said all girls have periods, and someday I will too. But she wouldn't tell us what it was."

"Oh," I said.

"So what's a period?"

Her cousin Becky was a teenager who had come to visit us for a few weeks that summer.

"Ah. Ask your Mom. She'll explain it to you."

"We did. She said to ask you," chimed in little Matty.

I had just come in from cleaning the swimming pool, my soaked sleeves dripping cold pool water. I grabbed a towel and started wiping down, stalling for time. Then I walked to the front living room and sat slowly onto the couch, fussing a little with the pillows. They came over and sat on foot stools in front of me and waited. There was no escape.

I had read several books written by a famous children's doctor shortly after Tammy was born. I think it may have been Dr. Spock. The author said one thing that made a lot of sense. Tell them just enough to stop the questions and no more. Children will not push for more information than they are ready to hear. I began to answer their question, tentatively, feeling for that moment when they would be satisfied.

"Well," I started out, "you know how when Mommy is expecting company to come visit, she buys food and puts it in the fridge and on the shelves in the cupboard and then cooks up meals in the kitchen?"

"Uh huh."

"Well, there is a little room like that in ladies for a baby to come and visit. And every month, that room gets stocked with baby food just in case. So if a baby comes to stay, it will have plenty to eat." I stopped talking and waited.

"Oh. But what's a period?"

"Well, you know how if all the food Mommy cooks doesn't get eaten, it will eventually spoil and sometimes she has to throw it away?"

"Uh huh."

"Well, if a baby doesn't come to visit, all that baby food will spoil, so the room gets swept out and the old food gets thrown away." I stopped again.

"Oh. So, but what's a period?"

"Well, when the old baby food is thrown away, that is called a period."

"Oh! So that's what is happening to Cousin Becky?"

"Yes, it is." I stop and wait. Will they stop asking?

Little Tammy and Matty said "Oooh!" in unison. They slipped off the footstools and trotted to the kitchen where I heard them chirp excitedly to their mother, "Mom! You're not going to believe this!" and proceeded to explain it to Mommy, who deliberately confirmed their assumption that she did not know by reacting with "Oh, really? How interesting. Imagine that."

Riding Lessons

Each day brought new questions about dance classes and bicycles and one day: "Daddy, can we take riding lessons?" And so it was that I drove Tammy and Matty out to the Thunder Head Ranch in the west end of the San Fernando Valley to sign us up for horseback riding classes. The Thunder Head Ranch rented stables out to horse owners, gave riding classes, and held Gymkhanas every Friday evening with barrel races, steer wrestling, team roping, calf roping, and, for the youngsters, goat tying. A highlight of every Friday night Gymkhana was when Bob Eubanks, of television fame, appeared to compete in the team roping events. All the girls waited anxiously in the stands, excited and impatient for him to appear.

We signed up for riding classes, all three of us. On that first Saturday morning, we joined half a dozen other new students and went for a short trail ride around the perimeter of the ranch. I was the only male and the only adult student in that class. Even the instructor was a young lady. She gave me the largest horse, a grey gelding, and we started out, nose to tail, with the teacher out front and me right behind her; Tammy, Matty, and six more teenage girls trailing behind. We began with a slow walk. The horses were totally disinterested and shuffling forward, eyes half-closed, in a dreamy state. Our instructor half-turned in her saddle and said, "Okay. Now we will move into a trot. Gently nudge your horses with your heels and lean a little forward. Watch me."

She snapped her heels firmly into the animal's flanks, leaned forward, and her horse broke into a trot. I emulated what I just saw; I used my heels to encourage the horse and was pleasantly surprised when he broke into a full trot. We strung out as Tammy, Matty, and the rest did the same. I was feeling great. The uncomfortable pounding of a trot was exciting. Everyone was happily bouncing down the trail. We were moving right along, smiles mixed with apprehension on every face.

Then it happened. It happened to me.

In the next few minutes, I got a fundamental lesson about horses. Afterward, our instructor explained what had happened. Horses are prey animals. In the wild, predators eat horses, if they can catch them. So like many prey animals, horses' eyes are set toward the sides of their heads so they can see predators approaching from or hiding on either side. But there is a narrow blind spot between the eyes, for a short distance directly in front of them. When they see something to one side with one eye that startles them, they will turn their heads to see it with the other eye as well. If it is close to them, the object will appear to jump as the image shifts from one eye to the other. This will spook most horses. They assume that anything which moves suddenly and unexpectedly is about to eat them.

Someone had placed a bright red bucket by the left-hand side of the trail just behind a bush. It came into view as we started to pass. My horse was in full trot when his left eye spotted the red bucket lurking behind the bush. He turned his head to get a better look at it. As the image of the little red bucket shifted from his left to his right eye, it appeared to jump forward.

That's when he "swallowed his head." He decided to go into full reverse. To do that, he planted one forward foot firmly into the ground to stop forward motion, swerved his head downward and back to reverse direction, and sent me flying forward through the air in a somersault that ended when I landed flat on my back onto the rock-solid dirt track, several feet ahead of where his nose had been just a split second before. I looked upward and saw a ring of horses and little girls staring down at me. Some looked worried. Others were giggling. I was embarrassed and in pain. My horse had stopped a short distance behind us. The instructor came trotting back to me.

"Are you okay?" she asked.

"I think so. Gimme a minute." I wheezed, not moving a muscle.

"Get up and go get your horse and get back on."

"I don't think he wants me on him," I replied, still lying flat on my back, my arms stretched out like a criminal on a crucifix.

"You've got to show him who's boss."

"He knows who is boss. He is the boss," I moaned from my dirt bed.

"No, seriously, you've got to get back on."

When she explained about a horse's eyes and how all that worked, I began to believe that the nag had nothing against me personally. He just didn't want to be caught and eaten by a red bucket. I did get back on the gelding, and the rest of the day went better.

MELISSA

It wasn't long before Tammy and Matty began begging for a horse of their very own. We agreed that if they earned the money to buy a horse, I'd build a corral for it in our big backyard. I figured that would be the end of that. How could they earn enough money to pay for a horse? I should have known better. They were bright young girls and not afraid to tackle anything. They had no concept of money or how long it would take to earn the price of a horse. But this lack of knowledge worked to their advantage because they didn't know enough to give up the idea. They assumed success.

They hand-printed small sheets of paper offering their services mowing lawns and washing cars, then set out through the neighborhood handing them out. That first week, they made $4. They weren't at all discouraged, even when we drove out to some of the small ranches in the valley to price horses and discovered they would need several hundred dollars—just for a run of the mill riding horse—plus the cost of a bridle and saddle.

I admired their spunk and decided I would make up the difference if we found the right horse. The second weekend, with $7 in hand, we drove out to Chatsworth, checking out horses that were advertised in the local paper. They were big animals and intimidating to these two little girls. We spent Saturday and most of Sunday without finding the right horse.

As we were driving home over Devonshire Avenue just about dusk, they yelled in unison, "Look, Daddy, they're selling horses!"

Up ahead, on our left, a hand-printed sign was nailed to a board hanging out from a leaning fence post. "HORSES FOR SALE!" it said. I turned into a dirt driveway that lead a long way back, past a wood shingle house with peeling paint and sagging wooden fences. As I pulled around behind the house, we saw more fences, small corrals, and a ramshackle barn.

A beefy looking woman with straight brown hair hanging down to her shoulders, wearing a lacy white blouse with lots of cleavage, brown leather skirt, and boots, sat in a plastic lawn chair. She was holding a drink in one hand and a cigarette in the other. Next to her sat a lanky black man with a black felt cowboy hat that had a band of silver medallions around the rim, a black shirt, blue jean pants, and dusty boots. He also held a drink and a cigarette and sat in a twin plastic lawn chair. Between them was an upside-down trash can on which was balanced a half-empty pack of cigarettes, a pack of matches, a half-gallon bottle of cheap vodka, and half a dozen plastic glasses. Two girls, about ten and twelve years old, of uncertain breed, were tossing darts at an old dart board hanging on the front door of the barn. They wore little summer dresses and walked without tenderness despite being barefoot. They stopped to watch us as we pulled up. Neither adult moved when we got out of our car.

"Hi. We'd like to see the horses you've got for sale," I said, holding out my hand to the woman because she was closest. She set her drink down on the upside-down trash can, stood up, and shook my hand.

"Howdy. Names' Beth," she said. "This's Dirk." She gestured to the black man who rose slowly to his feet and ambled over to shake hands, wearing a mile-wide smile full of bright white teeth.

"Howdy," Dirk grinned.

"Dirk, bring Princeton around." Dirk spun around on his heels and disappeared behind the barn.

"Care for a drink?" she asked. Her breath, laden with vodka fumes, washed over my face. She reached for a clean plastic glass and the half-gallon bottle of vodka and held the glass out to me.

"No, thanks."

"Ya sure? It's gonna take Dirk a couple minutes to get Prince saddled up."

"No, thanks."

"You'll like Prince. He's a black gelding, sixteen hands and well broke. Have a drink!"

After the fourth time she had offered and I had refused a glass of warm vodka, Dirk came around the edge of the barn riding a huge, black horse that stood seventeen hands if he was an inch. He was broad of chest with powerful long legs that pranced nervously as if he'd just as soon burst out of a starting gate. This horse was a handful, even for Dirk, who sat easily in the saddle but was clearly on alert.

"Beautiful animal. He'll make a fine ride for you. He's part Tennesee Walker and got a smooth stride. He can carry you and both your girls if you've a mind. I can let you have him for $750, and we'll deliver him free if you live in the valley." She meant the San Fernando Valley, of course.

Tammy and Matty shrank back, close against my legs. Princeton towered above them.

"He's a little too much horse for us," I said. "I need an animal that these two little ones can ride alone. Something gentle and easily managed." The sun had set, and it was getting hard to see. I started to shepherd my girls toward the car when Beth held out a restraining hand to my chest.

"No, wait! I've got just the horse you're lookin' for." She turned to her little girls. "Casey, honey, go get Melissa. Darby, turn on the yard lights, honey."

The smaller of her two girls ran excitedly into the darkness behind the barn while the other reached behind the barn door and flipped on a switch that lit up the barnyard with floodlights.

"We should get going. My girls haven't had dinner yet, and tomorrow is a school day. We'll come back next weekend."

"No, wait. You've gotta see Melissa! It'll only take a few minutes. Just take a look." She took a long swig of her vodka with the same hand that was holding her cigarette. With her free hand, she firmly held on to my arm.

When Melissa came trotting around the corner and into the light, I could hear my girls "Ooohhh" in unison. Little Casey was sitting comfortably, bareback and barefoot, on a pretty little palomino mare who stood just a shade over fourteen hands. Her shiny coat was the color of a brand new copper penny. A pure white forelock, white mane, and white tail gave her the appearance of a Walt Disney cartoon pony. She wore a simple rope bridle. Under the bright floodlights, she could have been part of a circus parade.

"This is Melissa. She is a full quarter horse. Great conformation. We call her Missy. Casey, honey, show them how easy she is to handle."

Casey gently neck-reined Melissa around the barnyard and alternately trotted and walked her, still with no saddle and still barefoot. Softly moving the rope reins against either side of Missy's neck and using light pressure from her bare feet, she performed circles and figure eights. Finally, after several tours of the yard, she walked Missy slowly and deliberately up to us and stopped her directly in front of my girls. With all the skill and salesmanship of a gypsy hustler, she slid on her belly off the horse and handed Tammy and Matty the rope reins. They looked up at me, holding the reins tightly. It was all over after that.

Beth and I did a little negotiating over a finger or two of warm vodka—straight, no ice—and I paid her $250 plus an extra $50 for a bridle and a small saddle. Beth and Dirk delivered Missy to our backyard the next weekend. The girls gave me the $7 they had earned. I paid the difference. We were now horse people.

I built a corral with a lean-to for shelter and a shed to store hay, all in our extra-large backyard. We learned how to ride Missy through the streets of Van Nuys down to the Sepulveda Dam Recreation Center where there were a few miles of trails we could take turns riding. Our riding lessons progressed well, and when we went riding at the Thunderhead Ranch, I rented extra horses so the three of us could ride together.

I spent more time with Missy than anyone else did in the family. I did the feeding, cleaning, bathing, and most of the riding. Often, at night, after dinner and after the children had gone to bed, I walked back to the corral and sat on the top rail. Missy walked over to me and nuzzled my hanging legs. Sometimes, when the weight of the world sat heavily on my shoulders, I sat on that rail for a long time, scratching the back of her ear and speaking softly to her, her head leaning on my leg. The moon and stars shone overhead and it was so silent and peaceful that she and I would drift off into a kind of dreamy state. We comforted each other.

I became aware of the attachment she was developing when, one day, while I was lunging her inside a training ring at the ranch, little Tammy came inside and took my hand. Missy turned to look at her, bared her teeth, and began trotting across the ring, clearly intent on driving Tammy away from me. Tammy turned, ran, and dove under the lower rail to escape. Strangely, Missy would be tender and affectionate to both girls as long as they did not touch me while we were inside the ring. Apparently she regarded our time in the ring as our personal time.

Penesance

Horse ownership, like boat or motorcycle ownership, follows a predictable cycle. You start small. Then you realize that bigger and more is better, and you buy bigger and more. You do that until you've had enough. Then you get rid of the big boats or motorcycles or horses. So it was that we soon determined that we needed more than one horse and that we needed a bigger horse for me to ride.

We drove to White Star Ranch, a sprawling spread in Chatsworth, and looked over the horses running loose in a fenced field. One in particular caught my eye. He was an orange and white Pinto gelding. His beautiful coloring was complimented by white mane and tail and a long, thick, white forelock over his eyes. Broad chest and powerful haunches rippled when he ran. He was a big Quarter Horse, about sixteen hands at the withers, with a barrel chest, well-developed and muscular rear quarter and legs, and a lovable nervous energy in his elastic tight muscles. What a grand animal he was.

"What about that one?" I asked, pointing at the Pinto.

"That's Penesance. He's gelded. He's a working cutting horse from a cattle ranch up north. He needs a lot of use, or he'll get barn sour soon, but he's a pleasure to ride if you keep him busy—$450," the young man said. "And of course, bridle and saddle are extra."

Penesance. What a noble name. It was a name befitting a medieval war horse. I pictured Penesance, bearing Sir Lancelot into battle, his saddle blankets covered with the colors of the family shield.

They chased him for twenty minutes before they were able to corner him and get a halter on his head. I paid the $450 for him plus another $100 for a used bridle and saddle. We signed the papers, and I got a bill of sale that said "As Is." That should have warned me.

When we got back home, the girls informed me that our new horse would be called "Penny." They were fond of the diminutive versions of names: Mommy, Daddy, Tammy, Matty, Missy, and now the humiliating Penny.

"That is a girl's name," I objected. "He is a male, a big, strong male... a fit horse for a man!" I lost the vote. Henceforth my noble steed was called Penny, which, I imagined, embarrassed him as much as it did me.

"When we are alone," I assured him, "you will be known as Penesance the Powerful." He was happy with that.

They delivered Penesance to our backyard. I had not owned a real, working cutting horse before. All I knew was what I had read about cutting horses, and I did not understand fully until one weekend when we took Missy and Penesance down to the Sepulveda Dam Recreation Area. This two-thousand-acre basin contained a small lake, a two-hundred-twenty-five-acre wildlife reserve, golf courses, walkways, bike paths, and a horse trail around the perimeter and along the Los Angeles River that crossed the park diagonally. This basin was built with a dam across the river to act as a catch basin in the event of cataclysmic failure of any of the upstream dams nestled in the foothills at the north end of the San Fernando Valley.

Our teenage niece, Becky, was with us as we rode the two horses down through the streets of Van Nuys. At the recreation area, we all dismounted. We were discussing who would ride which horse next when I noticed that Missy was trotting off down the trail. Cousin Becky had seen me drop Penesance's reins to the ground. She did the same with Missy's reins. Penesance had been trained to "ground tie" during his years as a working horse. You could drop his reins to the ground and he would not move—as if he were tied to the ground. But Missy was not so trained, and she considered herself dismissed to find her way back to our home corral.

I yelled to Becky to catch her, but it was too late. Missy began to disappear into the distance. I leapt into Penesance's saddle and rode off after her. Missy was trotting down the trail alongside the Los Angeles River bed toward the Balboa Boulevard overpass. She knew that Balboa Boulevard led back home. She stopped to graze now and then, but each time Penesance and I drew closer, she would trot off again. Whenever Missy started to veer to her right, away from the river bed, Penesance moved quickly around her to cut her off without any instruction from me. I remembered the young cowboy who sold him to me saying, "He's a trained cutting horse," and realized Penesance was doing just that.

I relaxed my grip on the reins and let him do his thing. He moved around Missy, moving slightly ahead of her and between her and the embankment. At the Balboa Boulevard overpass, Missy stopped. She knew this was where she must climb the embankment to get back home. The two horses faced each other warily. Every time Missy made a move to go around Penesance, he swung his front feet quickly left or right to cut her off, holding his hind quarters steady as if they were pinned to the ground. After some time, Missy stopped dead in her tracks. She was stymied. We stood that way until Becky arrived on foot and took Missy's reins in hand again. Penesance had done what he had been trained to do.

PROUD CUT AND PUMPKINS

Penesance was headstrong and sometimes hard to handle, especially around mares. When I consulted a veterinarian, he examined Penesance more closely and told me, "Yeah, he's gelded all right, but he's got what's called a Proud Cut. He's still got some testicular tissue that's generating testosterone but no sperm. He can't impregnate a mare, but he doesn't know that, and his behavior is as excitable as an uncut Stallion. You've got yourself a spirited animal here. Don't underestimate him. Be careful."

The first time I tried to keep both horses in one corral overnight, Penesance tried to mount Missy. She kicked him and cut his forelegs up pretty badly. I kept them penned separately after that.

At Halloween, we carved pumpkins and placed lit candles into their grotesque heads at night. A week later, as the pumpkin shells began to rot, we carried them back to the corrals. We reasoned that these were vegetables, like hay and wheat grain, and the horses would enjoy them. And they sure did. The next morning we were mesmerized as we watched them burping and staggering around the backyard, bumping into each other and leaning drunkenly against corral posts and trees. They were obviously inebriated from the fermenting pumpkin shells in their stomachs.

RAIN AND GRAIN

Just before Christmas, the rains came, and for weeks it poured to make up for the long drought we had experienced over the last two years. Since I could not put both horses into the corral with its lean-to shelter, I alternated them every other day. Meanwhile, I feed both animals extra grain to generate more body heat. I could see them shivering during their turns without rain shelter, so I doubled the grain ration for whichever one was out in the open each day.

The ground became soggy, and eventually they were sinking knee-deep into the mud. On Christmas Day, the rain stopped.

"We've got to give them a workout," I announced, "to work off the grain and the inactivity." I was dressed in a new blue jean riding outfit which I had received for Christmas. Matching blue jean jacket and pants were adorned with faux pearl buttons and decorative orange stitching throughout. Both daughters had new two-wheeled girls bicycles with very pretty white woven baskets adorned with small bells and plastic flowers.

So we saddled them up. Tammy and Matty rode their lovely new bicycles. I rode Penny, and the wife rode Missy down through the city streets to the dam recreation area. Cousin Becky walked along next to us. Halfway to the recreation area, Becky began to complain about being the only one on foot. Certain of my horsemanship and ignoring the veterinarian's warnings, I invited her to climb up behind me onto Penesance's back.

We knew he did not like anyone sitting on his back behind the saddle. He would rear or buck as soon as a second rider lowered their weight on his back. Perhaps it bothered his kidneys. But I thought I could control him. I had attached a tie-down strap from his bridle chin strap to his chest strap to prevent him from throwing his head up into a dangerous rear-back prelude to bucking.

I gave Becky my right stirrup to use to climb up behind me. She sat just behind the saddle. I felt Penesance tense up and begin to lift his head to rear. The tie-down snapped tight. Then he hunched and tried to throw his head down and arch his back so he could flip his rear quarters and legs into the air in a nasty buck. I pulled his head up tight against the tie-down strap so he could not lower it. We fought each other for just a minute. He began to hop sideways.

I had developed a pretty good saddle seat and thought I could outride his behavior. But as he hopped side to side, Cousin Becky lost her balance. With no stirrups to control her position, she had no way to stay on. She grabbed my shirt and pulled me off with her. I reached out and grabbed the chain link fence to our right, falling with Becky while the horse hopped quickly to his left. When my right boot finally slipped out of the stirrup, the leg dropped and landed on the edge of the curbstone which, we learned later, fractured the right tibia—like an egg struck on the edge of a frying pan.

Penesance took off running down the street. We caught up with him a block later and proceeded to the recreation area, Becky again walking behind us. All the while I was receiving alarming signals of pain from that fractured tibia

The Chase

We rode calmly for a while, following the trail that ran alongside the Los Angeles River bed; I on Penesance followed by the wife on Missy, then Tammy and Matty on their pretty flower-basketed little bikes. Cousin Becky walked patiently behind, awaiting her turn on Penesance or Missy. Both horses were very excitable from all the grain alcohol in their systems and pranced excitedly. Penesance began to sweat, and as white foam broke out on his hide, his body girth shrank just a little, making the saddle slide wetly from side to side. We reached the Balboa Boulevard overpass. I decided we had gone far enough for one day and should turn up the embankment to the trail that paralleled Balboa Boulevard and headed northward toward home. It was along this stretch that things got even more interesting.

A little boy and his dad had received small motor scooters for Christmas and had decided to take them out for a trial ride along the horse trail. I heard the noisy rattle-banging of the motors long before they reached us from behind. Penesance began his nervous hopping, and as the motor scooters shot past us on our left, he made a tremendous side leap to the right. The sweaty, loose saddle spun around his body, dumping me headfirst onto the ground. I lost control of the reins, and as I rolled sideways to my feet, I saw him take off in a mad gallop—the saddle hanging upside-down beneath his belly, the stirrups drumming madly against his legs and stomach as he ran. He must have thought the devil had him by the belly.

He ran wildly into the distance, crossing streets full of traffic, horns blaring, tires screeching. I turned to Tammy and said, "I need to catch up to him. Lend me your bike." I picked up the lariat which had fallen off the saddle horn and hooked it over the little bell on Tammy's bicycle. I hopped on and, with my knees pumping higher than my ears, took off along the adjacent sidewalk as fast as my legs could pump, my blue jean outfit with pearl buttons and orange stitching flashing in the afternoon sun, white lariat swinging to and fro, my cowboy hat and boots emphasizing the absurdity of my appearance.

At each intersection, people stood openmouthed, laughing, pointing, and saying helpful things like "He went that way!" and "Ride 'em, cowboy!" with obvious glee over the ridiculous image I was creating. But I didn't care. I just wanted to catch that crazed horse before he killed someone or was killed himself. A dozen blocks later, I caught up with Penesance. He had run into a cul de sac and up a driveway at the end. A car was sitting across the entrance to the driveway being washed by a couple teenagers. Penesance had jumped over the hood and now stood, wild-eyed, trapped inside the narrow driveway, blocked in by the car he had leapt over. The saddle and stirrups hung like a dead octopus from his belly.

After making sure no one and nothing was hurt, I took control of Penesance. When the family caught up with us, I straightened out the saddle and walked him up the streets with the family entourage. Penesance was too emotionally disturbed to be ridden, so I did my best to walk alongside him, trying to keep my feet from under his erratic, prancing hooves. It was good to be back home that day.

Parting With Penesance

My fractured tibia took a long time to heal. My wounded pride took even longer. Eventually, changes in my job required us to move to another home. We no longer had room for horses. I called a self-proclaimed horse dealer to come make me an offer for Penesance. He offered to give me less than I had paid but suggested that he could get me more money if I would allow him to take Penesance on consignment and sell him at auction in the next county. So I let him take Penesance.

A month later, I chased down the shyster at a small ranch house in the west end of the valley. He told me Penesance had thrown a rider during the auction so he could not be sold that day, but another auction was coming up soon. I heard variations of that excuse from him every time I inquired. After a couple more months and unreturned phone calls, I drove out to the small ranch house where this guy lived. The house was vacant, and no one in the neighborhood seemed to know where the horse trader had gone. No more was heard of Penesance or my money. Penesance the Powerful, my noble steed, was gone.

Thunderhead Ranch

I moved Missy to the Thunderhead Ranch in Chatsworth. On Friday nights, the girls and I went to watch the Gymkhana; and on weekends, we spent time grooming, lunging, and riding Missy. As the girls grew older and their interests changed, I found myself spending more and more time alone with Missy. She and I took long rides out of Thunderhead Ranch along the railroad tracks to a fenced-off area called Devil's Canyon. This private land is many thousands of acres in size and contains beautiful rock formations, hills, streams, and much wildlife. The property was often used in past years as a site for filming western movies. Old movie sets can still be found back in those rocky hills. I found a breach in the fence and often took Missy back into Devil's Canyon.

We rode for hours, picking our way over old trails and blazing new ones of our own. Heading home at the end of the day was easy. I simply gave Missy her head and she headed for home. No matter how far we had traveled or how tortuous the path we took going out, she always knew her way home. I might be a little lost, but she never was.

Our path along the railroad tracks was easy even when a rare train came along. Missy had grown used to them. I worried about stray dogs, though, until one day, a nasty mongrel came out of some underbrush in a menacing, aggressive manner. I was terrified until the dog went after Missy's rear legs and Missy planted a solid hoof into the hound's chest, sending it flying and howling. It disappeared at a dead run.

On our way to Devil's Canyon, we had to pass a small ranch that was completely surrounded by a high chain link fence. Inside the fence, a huge black-and-white dog patrolled. It was nearly half the size of Missy. This beast began to growl the minute we reached the corner of the little ranch and followed us along the fence—he on the inside, us on the outside. All the while he snarled viciously, exposing deadly teeth. This continued until we passed beyond the property fence. I often worried about what would happen if the dog ever got out.

THE OPEN GATE

One bright, sunny day, we approached the corner of the property as usual. Our adversary was waiting for us and began his usual spitting, snarling growls, baring his massive teeth. He followed us step by step. I looked up and saw something I had never seen before. The wide, double gates were swung open inwardly, leaving an opening two lanes wide. My stomach knotted up, and fear crawled up my spine as I envisioned what was about to happen. I told myself that I could trust Missy to defend us.

But this dog was so big and so fierce I had some doubts. I felt the sweat trickle down my sides from my armpits and forced myself to concentrate on staying in the saddle no matter what happened.

As we approached the open gates, Missy remained calm, almost as if she did not comprehend what was about to happen. The dog grew more fiercely agitated with each step. We reached the open gates. The dog, intent on glaring and growling at Missy, ran smack into the first half of the open gate, fell backward, got up, and shook his head to clear it. When he resumed the chase, he did not come out through the open gates. Instead he ran around both halves of the open gates to the far side of the driveway. He stood still inside the fence, at the corner of the second half gate, and waited for us to catch up. Then, as if nothing had happened, he followed us all the rest of the way; he on the inside, us on the outside, spitting and growling and snarling at us until we were out of sight. Now I understood the game. He was happy. He had kept us out of his property.

THE AMBUSH

On a hot September day, Missy and I rode for over four hours heading out into Devil's Canyon, further than we had ever gone before. We were a very long way from home. We turned around and started back. Sometimes I could hear an insect buzzing or a bird chirp. Otherwise it was peaceful and quiet. The sun burned steadily down, and I began to drift into a sleepy haze. Missy was on autopilot, dreamily ambling back home. I had lowered the reins over the saddle horn and sat slouched in my western saddle, my chin on my chest. Missy plodded steadily, her head hanging down, her nose a foot above the ground, her eyes almost closed.

A couple of sleepy hours passed like that. We were approaching a familiar stretch where the trail split. The right fork led another four miles toward the opening in the fence and back to the ranch. The left fork led down into a hollow with a shallow creek at the bottom, a sweet water spot where we often stopped to drink. Missy and I were both pretty much asleep. I was slumped in the saddle, eyes closed, and my chin still resting on my chest. She was putting one foot in front of the other with her head hanging low, eyes glazed, and her mind blank. Then it happened.

Missy passed gas. But it was more than that. She farted a mighty fart. It was long and resonant. The sound and the fluttering flesh of her buttocks had a traumatic effect on Missy. She, being a horse—which is to say, a little bit stupid at times—thought a vicious carnivore had grabbed her by the butt. She leapt forward and bolted blindly, throwing me backward. If I had not instinctively grabbed the saddle horn, I would have flipped backward off her rump and onto the ground.

In her blind panic, she took the left fork, still unaware of what had attacked her butt and unaware of where exactly she was. In half a dozen huge downhill leaps, she reached the creek bed. Unable to stop, she leapt over the creek, a feat she had never accomplished before. She landed and planted all four feet on the other side and stopped, throwing me forward so hard I hit the back of her neck with my face. She stood shaking and looking around, bewildered by what had just happened. I sat laughing and holding my bruised nose.

After much coaxing, I managed to get her to walk back across the creek and up the trail. We took the right fork toward home. Though I continued to drift off now and then, poor, frightened Missy remained very much awake, her ears turned to listen behind her, on the alert for another ambush by the mysterious, noisy, vibrating predator that she was sure lurked somewhere back there.

Farewell to Missy

As life's circumstances changed, it became difficult to devote enough time to Missy. I eventually sold her to a friend of a friend who owned a property with a small barn and corral. The new owners had no horse knowledge, so I undertook to teach them horse grooming and care. Missy was settled in a nice country area with pleasant surroundings, and I took my leave. A week or so later, the man called and said Missy could not be handled. I drove out and found she had gone barn sour. That is, she would not allow them to bridle or saddle her, and she would not leave the barn area. Again I instructed them on how important it was to handle her every day. I insisted that the whole family watch as I approached her calmly, talking softly, slipped a halter over her head after letting her smell it first, slowly introduced her to the trimming shears, brush and hoof pick, one at a time, before trimming her beard and hair, brushing her, picking up each hoof and picking them clean. I showed them again how to stand while working each foot, how I slid a hand over her body as I moved around her so she knew where I was at every moment. We took turns putting on the bridle and saddle and taking short rides around their yard. Everyone seemed happy.

I whispered a farewell in Missy's ear.

Our horse ownership days were over.

41

El Porto Beach

The roar of starting motorcycle engines interrupted their conversation. "Well, looks like we're gonna head on out. Nice talking to ya. I gotta go ride my iron horse!" The biker hopped onto his Suzuki, kick started it, and flipped the accelerator a few times to add to the cacophony of two dozen machines. They peeled out of the parking lot up the exit ramp to the street above in a long, glittering file.

Once the bikers were gone, the Old Man resumed his bicycle ride south from the El Segundo parking lot. The path hugged a mile-long chain link fence topped with razor wire that separated the El Segundo Oil Refinery from the broad sand beach.

He stood up with his full weight bearing down on the pedals to regain speed against a growing head wind. Near the end of the fence, the beach broadened and the surf built into a series of well-timed, rising waves that attracted surfers from near and far. This was the famed El Porto Beach—a Mecca for devoted surfers. When he had the time and inclination, this was a favorite place to stop and admire the young, supple, and talented surfers skittering along in crisscrossing patterns on the front faces of the waves like so many practiced water spiders.

Today he did stop, not so much to watch the surfers as to do a double take when a middle-aged surfer came walking up from the wet sand. Tall, broad-shouldered, heavily tanned, he strode purposefully, carrying his surfboard under one muscular arm. His most unique feature, however, was a highly developed set of neck and shoulder muscles. The bulging, powerful-looking neck stretched tightly against the material of his black wet suit.

He reminds me of Moose.

If Moose were still alive, I'd swear that was him. He could pass for his twin.

I still recall the day I met him. Maybe thirty years ago.

He came walking toward us from that airport tunnel like he owned the place…

Moose

The airport was crowded that morning. He came walking down that airport tunnel and seemed to fill it with his broad shoulders and narrow waist. He was my father-in-law at that time. He had left my mother-in-law many years earlier to marry a coworker, which, I guess, made the coworker my stepmother-in-law. She was with him. I didn't think of her as a relative of mine. I suppose that was because she and my wife barely knew each other and we seldom spoke of her.

Nobody called him by his given name. Everybody called him Moose, the nickname given to him the first time he stepped out on his high school athletic field in shorts and an undershirt that revealed his oversized, muscular, powerful neck and shoulders. One of his coaches turned to the other and said, "God, he's built like a moose!" And the name stuck. He was flattered and pleased by the name and responded to it for the rest of his life.

I had met him and his second wife at a family reunion in Virginia a few years earlier. He was a skilled hunter and fisherman, full of colorful banter. He was also the chief of maintenance at Langley Air Force Base, one of the country's major military air fields. So he was knowledgeable about a lot of things.

The stepmother-in-law, on the other hand, said little, chain-smoked incessantly, and lit each new cigarette from the glowing stub of the previous one just before it burned out. It was difficult to look at her prematurely aged face only because your eyes would be drawn to her tobacco-stained lips and yellowish-brown teeth. She must have been very attractive a long time ago.

Now they had come to visit us in California for the first time and were going to stay with us for two weeks. I wondered how we would deal with the ever-present cloud of stale cigarette smoke for that long. Fortunately, she spent much of her time in our spare bedroom with the door closed or outdoors on lawn furniture in the backyard. It took months to get the sour stench out of the bedroom.

The first few days were awkward. Moose had given us a weather vane which he had made in the little tool shed he built outside his trailer. The weather vane was a wooden roadrunner which he called the Arizona Buzzard. It had two sets of large, curved yellow feet that spun rapidly when the wind blew and turned it to face into the wind. With its tufted crown feathers streaming back, its long brown-and-white speckled body, tail trailing behind, and its yellow feet spinning in the wind, it looked like the Road Runner of cartoon fame. I stuck it on a tall steel rod on the ivy embankment in our backyard where it sits to this day.

The Fishing Trip

"Do you like to fish?" he asked me one day.

"I've done it some, but the only time I ever caught anything was when I fished in a small lake as a kid. I caught small sunfish that I threw back in if I could remove the hook without killing them."

I knew how fond he was of fishing and sensed that he was leading up to a fishing trip out of Redondo Beach, so I volunteered, "I can take you down to the charter fishing boats if you and the wife want to go out one day."

"Sure," he said eagerly, "but I'd like you two to go with us."

My wife, his daughter, demurred. I reached for a truce by agreeing to go out with him if he'd show me how to use the gear.

The next morning, we set out—Moose, the cigarette lady, and me. We parked just short of the old pier, walked all the way to the end, and paid for three setups. A setup was one fully rigged ocean fishing pole and two burlap bags. The bags were folded tightly and wrapped with rubber bands. Soon the Redondo Special pulled alongside the pier and nudged against the pilings, causing the pier to sway alarmingly. We filed aboard along with about twenty or so other fishermen. I followed Moose's example and found a marked space at the railing alongside him and his wife.

The boat moved out of the harbor and into the channel, rolling more than I expected. I was okay with it until the boat stopped. The skipper announced the kind of fish we could expect in this spot and how to set our lines. Moose knew exactly what he was doing; he helped himself to bait fish for himself and his wife and baited both hooks. I followed suit, imitating him as closely as I could. He cast his wife's line out then his own. I cast my line, but not knowing how to stop the reel properly, I soon had a large ball of gnarled line. I focused my eyes closely on the mess and tried to untangle it. I only made it worse. Soon, because I was staring at my hands and not at the horizon, my stomach registered its first and persistent rebellion. I struggled to hold down the bile I felt rising in my throat. Moose saw my dilemma, set his pole in a holder, and came to my aid to unsnarl the line and reset the bait. We repeated this procedure at least five times.

After four hours of thus struggling, the boat started its return journey to the pier. In our four hours of fishing, Moose had caught only one decent-sized Bonita because he'd only had a few minutes to fish between helping me and his wife. She burned a lot of cigarettes but caught nothing. I caught one tiny sunfish which I wanted to throw back because that was something I knew how to do. Moose looked into the huge burlap bag with its hapless haul of one and one-fourth fish. He handed the bag to me and pointed to the two families to my right. Two fathers and two sons had been hauling fish in as fast as they could bait and cast. They had three bags full of good-sized fish.

"This isn't enough to feed all of us at home," Moose said to me. "It isn't worth the trouble of cleaning and cooking it. Give it to those guys and let them take it home."

I took the huge burlap bag with one and one-fourth fish and dragged it behind me over to the foursome, its tiny bulge bouncing along the deck.

"Here, you guys can have these," I said, holding the bag out to one of the fathers. He took it, opened it, and looked in.

"Don't you want these?" he asked. "They're good eatin'." He closed the bag and tried to hand it back to me.

"My father-in-law says there isn't enough to bother cleaning 'cause there's too many of us to feed," I said.

"How many of you are there?"

I counted in my head. There was me, my wife, two kids, Moose, and the cigarette lady. "Six of us."

He grinned, opened my bag again, and began pulling Bonita from his bag and throwing them in. "We have to give most of these away to someone when we get back anyway. Might's well be you."

While I watched in amazement, his friend and both sons opened their bags and began doing the same. They handed my bag back to me, filled to the brim. I thanked them profusely, got a good two-handed grip on the top of the bag, and, leaning backward, dragged the heavy bag back up the sloping deck to Moose. He stared down at it. I told him what had just happened. Then with a mischievous grin, he unwrapped another burlap bag, shook it out, took two fish out of the full bag, and threw them into the empty bag. He handed the new almost empty bag to me, gestured across the boat, and said, only half-joking, "Now go work the other side of the boat!"

When we got home that afternoon, Moose set up outdoors on the picnic table with piles of old newspapers and proceeded to dress out the fish. I had eaten Bonita before and been disappointed in the fishy flavor. But Moose very carefully removed certain parts of the Bonita that he knew gave it that fishy taste. "You've gotta take off every bit of the fat and the dark stuff before you cook it," he said, pointing out to me the bits he removed. We cooked and ate sumptuously that night. It was delicate and not fishy at all. We froze the rest and enjoyed many more evenings, even after his two weeks were up and they had returned to Arizona.

The Phone Call

I guess it was about six months or so later that our phone rang and I heard Moose on the other end. He talked to me for a few minutes then asked for his daughter. After the call, she told me that the cigarette lady had left Moose and moved in with her sister. I never did know exactly what their problems were, but she had made it clear to Moose that she would never come back to him. At least that is what she told him. He sounded sad and a little lost. He hinted that maybe he'd like to come visit us again for a while. When my wife called her sisters, she learned that he had made similar phone calls to them earlier in the day. For the next few days, the sisters talked at least once a day by phone, exchanging tidbits of phone calls with their father.

Then we got *the* phone call. Moose had killed himself. The three sisters made plans to fly to Arizona to make funeral arrangements and to dispose of Moose's belongings. They felt they needed a man to handle some of the tougher details, or maybe for some kind of moral support. The other two sister's husbands could not take time off from work, so I was asked to attend by default.

When we arrived, we learned that Mr. D'Angelo, an older Italian friend of Moose's, had found the body. Moose had called him that afternoon and instructed him to come to his trailer in one hour. "When you get here, just come inside. I want you to call my wife and tell her what you found here." He made Mr. D'Angelo promise to do that then said "See you later" as he always did when he hung up the phone.

One hour later, Mr. D'Angelo went to the trailer and knocked on the door. It was unlocked and partially open. He went inside. A recording of "Song Sung Blue" was playing on the small, 45 rpm record player that sat on the bookcase against the wall. Moose lay on the floor in front of it, a revolver on the carpet next to his right ear against his partially open hand. A pool of blood soaked into the carpet just behind his ear.

Moose had shot himself while lying down, listening to his favorite "Song Sung Blue." The record player was set on auto-repeat.

D'Angelo began to cry and, with trembling hands, called for an ambulance. Later that day, he kept his promise to Moose and called the cigarette lady. She called his daughters with the news.

The body was cremated. Moose often said that when he died, he wanted to be buried in the old family plot in Virginia. He always added, jokingly, that his ashes should be placed inside an empty Budweiser beer can first. The girls arranged everything as he had wanted, except for the beer can. They chose a proper container instead and made arrangements to take his ashes to Virginia after the funeral. A cleaning company was hired to clean the carpet so the trailer could be sold. Most of his stuff was sold off. Some things were saved for family members.

Moose had a great gun collection which included several collector grade rifles and one antique, in particular, of great value. All of the weapons, except the revolver he had used, were missing. Nora, one of the daughters, who I had nicknamed No-Nonsense Nora, asked me to call Mr. D'Angelo and ask about the guns. I did.

"He give me his guns a couple days before he die. He say he going away soon. He say he want me to have them *per recordo,* to remember him. Moose and me, we was best friends. I ask him, 'Why you gonna leave, where you gonna go?' but he no answer me. He just say he want me to have his guns."

Nora demanded the guns be returned. D'Angelo agreed to give them back if I would come over to get them. He could not bear to enter Mooses's trailer again. I left D'Angelo's trailer carrying an armload of rifles of various vintages and calibers.

The next afternoon, No-Nonsense Nora told me that she had been studying the rifles and she thought the valuable antique rifle was still missing. I called Mr. D'Angelo and asked if he had given me all the weapons. He said he had. Nora and I speculated that Moose must have given it to someone very special to him and we had no way of finding out who that might be.

The next evening, as we sat around Moose's kitchen table, the phone rang. It was Mr. D'Angelo. He asked me to come over to his trailer.

"What do you suppose he wants?" No-Nonsense Nora asked.

"He didn't say," I said.

Mr. and Mrs. D'Angelo were very nervous as they let me inside. While she wrung her hands, he poured us each a small glass of wine. I was in training for a series of ten kilometer races at that time. I avoided any kind of alcohol. I declined the glass.

"Please," he begged. "*Per piacere*, please take a small glass. I needa talk with you about something, but first maybe we share a little wine. Is very hard for me. Please, you have some wine."

I understood that he needed to feel he could trust me as a friend, and a sip of wine would signify that friendship. I took a sip. When I took a second sip, he began to quietly cry. With tears rolling down his cheeks he said, "Forgive me. I lie to you. Moose, he give me all the guns. Moose, he was my best friend. We laugh together. We cry together. We fish, we talk. Twenny years, we best friends. I know he is sad when his wife, she leave him. He come see me, I go see him, every night. He say, 'I go away soon. I wan' you have my guns. You remember me when I gone.'

"When he call me to come—I find him. So much blood. I kneel down. I call him. 'Moose! Moose!' But is too late. I call the 911. The police, they find me sit on the floor. After long time, they let me go home. I call his wife like he say, and tell her, like he—like he ask me."

D'Angelo reached to my glass and gently moved it toward me, his hand trembling, urging for a sign of understanding. I took another sip of wine.

"When you come here an' ask me for his rifles, my heart break. Is all I had left of him. When you take 'em away, I have nothing left of my friend. So I give 'em all to you, but I keep one—*solamente uno*—only one. I hide the one Moose love so much. He tell me how much he love thata one. I no know how much is worth to somebody else. But to me is worth lots because he like it so much. I have nothing else *per recordo*, for to remember him. So I hide it from you. But... I no can sleep. Rosina, she no sleep. We know is wrong to lie to you. We stay awake all night think' what we must do."

He stopped talking, wiping his eyes with a crumpled handkerchief. His wife wept quietly in the chair across from us, holding her apron over her mouth. Blowing his nose, he took a deep breath, and struggling to regain his composure, he stood and went into the other room. He came back with the rifle, wrapped in a blanket, cradled in his arms. He set it on the table, gently, in front of me, his hands trembling as he let it go. I gingerly unfolded the soft blanket that protected it and stared down at a beautiful, antique weapon. The metal was spotless, the stock highly polished. I could see all the care and affection Moose had lavished on this piece of history.

"Now you must decide. 'Is up to you. What you decide, we do. You tell me give back, I give to you now. You say I keep, I keep. *Per recordo.*"

I had listened to No-Nonsense Nora's argument that Moose was not in his right mind when he gave away the rifles. Moose was so upset about losing his wife he had made a bad decision that we should not honor. Besides, she added, Moose had a wealthy brother who telephoned that very morning from Virginia asking about this very valuable rifle. He wanted it for his collection. The wealthy brother should have been given the old rifle instead of someone not even in the family, she said.

Then I thought about Moose. What would he want? I couldn't ask him. Not now. Not anymore. But hadn't Moose already told me? Hadn't he told Mr. D'Angelo a few days before he listened to "Song Sung Blue" for the last time?

I wrapped the blanket around the rifle, picked it up, and held it out to Mr. D'Angelo.

"I think Moose would want you to keep it. I think it would mean more to you than to anyone else. Let's pretend we never had this conversation. Mr. D'Angelo, *va in pace.* Take Moose's gift and go in peace."

He gave me a tearful embrace and whispered, *"Grazie, amigo mio. Grazie tanto."* "Thank you, my friend. Thank you very much." His wife gave me a hug. We all wept.

"What did he want?" No-Nonsense Nora asked when I returned.

"He asked me to have some wine with him."

"What a strange little man," she said.

"Yes," I agreed, "what a strange little man."

Working the Other Side

By the end of the week, we had wound up just about all of Moose's business. The trailer was on the market. His ashes were packaged in an urn, ready to be shipped to family for burial in Virginia. It sat on the altar of the little church where we were to have the memorial service. All the daughters were there. Moose's wife, the cigarette lady, had come to town with her sister to take part in the service. Even his first wife, my mother-in-law, had come from several states away. Dozens of friends and neighbors who lived in his trailer park crowded into the small chapel. Mr. and Mrs. D'Angelo were there, softly weeping.

Shortly before it began, the daughters came to me and asked if I would say a few words about Moose. I said I would. They played the music we requested, which included "Song Sung Blue" in the background. The generic minister said a few hackneyed things, being careful to avoid being too sentimental because, as he had told us earlier, in sanctimonious tones, suicide is a mortal sin and we don't know where Moose will spend eternity. Then it was my turn. I took a deep breath.

I've known Moose for a much shorter time than many of you have. And I've been told a number of things that are worth repeating. Moose was loved by many friends and relatives. I've heard delightful stories from many of you. But he was loved most, perhaps, by his grandchildren. They looked forward to those summer visits between school years. He taught them so many of his talents and skills including fishing, hunting, and camping.

His sense of humor was a legend. His standard breakfast order in restaurants went something like this:

"What would you like, sir?"

"I'd like bacon and eggs."

"How do you like your eggs?"

"I like 'em just fine."

"Sir, how would you like them cooked!" she would say, exasperated.

"Oh, I'd like them better that way!" he'd say, his eyes opened wide in pleased surprise.

And no matter how many times he pulled that off, we would giggle in anticipation and laugh as if we'd never heard it before.

Moose left his mark wherever he went. As I walked through the trailer park, I saw dozens of those Road Runner weathervanes spinning on his neighbors' front lawns—weathervanes he made with his own hands in his little shed. He called them Arizona Buzzards and gave them to relatives and friends here in Arizona and in Washington DC, Virginia, and the Carolinas. We have one in California. For years to come, Moose's Arizona Buzzards will spin their bright yellow feet, point into the wind, and tell us, 'Look at me. I'm still here. I'm still here.' And we will think of him.

I told them the story about our fishing trip on the Redondo Special and how we tried to give away our tiny catch to the guys next to us and how they instead filled our bag with fish and how Moose gave me another bag with just two fish in it, handed it to me, and said, with grinning humor, "Now go work the other side of the boat." The audience laughed. Then I wrapped it up.

"There's been some discussion about the sanctity of life and our right to end it and about where Moose has ended up. I can tell you that Moose's ashes are right here in front of us today, in this urn. They will be buried in his family plot in the churchyard back in Virginia.

But I think that Moose, the Moose we knew and loved well, I expect he's up there right now swapping fishing tips with old St. Peter, the greatest of fishermen, The Fisher of Men.

And the rest of the time?

Why, he'll probably be 'working the other side of the boat.'"

The Arizona Buzzard.

43

Redondo Beach

Leaving El Porto beach behind, the Old Man soon spotted the popular Manhattan Beach pier just ahead. Maybe he would stop there, as he often did, and call the Italian Deli in Hermosa Beach on his cell phone. He'd order a sandwich, and it would be ready for pickup in the time it took him to ride the roughly two-mile distance. As he drew near the pier, he found the entrance too crowded with children. He continued on.

At Yacht Club Way, he turned and wended his way to the end of the driveway, past two guard gates to King Harbor Yacht Club. The tide was out. He parked his bike and walked down the sloping ramp to the dock below the two boat hoists. He knew that one or two Garibaldi fish—the California state fish—lived in the shaded waters beneath the hoists. Were they still there? He looked until he saw the reddish gold flash darting in and out of the shadows. Satisfied, he walked back up to his bike, mounted, and pedaled back out to the bike path and continued south.

The huge parking lot next to Ruby's Diner was crowded with cars, a few antique cars, and dozens of collector models from the forties and fifties. Pristine, restored, polished jewels that stirred memories in the Old Man's heart. Ruby's Diner hosted a monthly gathering of these gems, and luckily for him, today was one of those days. He dismounted and chained the bike to the stand outside the restaurant.

He was drawn to a 1951 Pontiac, green with white sidewalls, similar to the first car he had ever owned. He was a young kid, just graduating from college when he bought the used Pontiac. He had kicked the front tires, much to the amusement of the salesman. God only knew why he did that. He must have seen someone do that to wagon wheels in an old Western movie. Next to the restored Pontiac was a 1959 Chevrolet, a model he had also owned at one time. He traced the gull-winged trunk lid with a fingertip as he walked around it.

Scanning the lot, his heart skipped a beat when he saw the 1957 Chevrolet Bel Air, a two-door coupe, exactly—except for the color—like the second car he had owned. It was his first new car and the early love of his life. Walking slowly around this restoration, he drank in every feature. The excited feelings he had experienced that day, over half a century ago, came back to him. He bought that car, brand new, just as he was being discharged from the United States Army.

My first new car. It had a small down payment and a big finance package.

I was scared to sign that document, but she was so pretty.

I wanted her.

I pictured myself driving her past the sands along Malibu Beach, her twin hood ornaments flying through the ocean breeze.

Together we—she and I—would make new memories of new people and places.

It started, then, in 1957...

44

From 1957 Chevys to Louise Perry

She was a beautiful, deep metallic copper, so deep you could almost reach into it with your hands. The marketing experts at General Motors had dubbed it "Aztec Bronze," which made it seem even more exotic. Her long, narrow chrome side stripes transitioned smoothly into sleek chrome-sided rear fins. They blended with her "go fast" styling and made her look like she was cruising even when she was parked. Her white leather interior was richly ribbed, giving her that plush tuck-and-roll look the girls loved. And she was about to be mine. I had traded in my tired 1951 Pontiac for this brand new, younger, sexier, two-door hard top 1957 Chevrolet. She had twin hood ornaments that rode above her Blue Flame Six, 235.5 cubic inch, 140 horsepower, in line, single barrel carbureted engine that powered a two-speed Powerglide transmission.

I was seated in a sales cubicle in Paterno's Chevrolet dealership just outside Aberdeen, Maryland, holding in my hands the loan document consisting of seventeen pages printed on both sides with paragraph after paragraph of very fine print. I had painfully read through the first five pages while the salesman sat patiently, waiting for me to sign. Mr. Paterno, the dealership owner, stood outside the cubicle. He wore a natty gray, pin-striped, three-piece suit with a small red rose stuffed into the button hole of his jacket lapel. After some time, he slowly strolled into the booth and stood watching me.

Finally, he spoke to me. "You are reading the loan papers?"

"Yes," I replied. I stopped for a moment and looked up into twinkling eyes and his pencil-thin mustache.

"You mind I ask-a you a question?"

"No. Go ahead," I said, putting down the papers and leaning back in the chair.

"You gonna make all the payments?"

"Of course."

"You gonna pay on time?"

"Yes, of course."

He gestured both hands upward and shrugged his shoulders.

"Well, if you gonna make all-a the payments and you gonna make 'em on-a time, you no need to read all-a those things—just-a sign."

He smiled at me. Then he turned serious. "But if you no gonna pay every month on time, then... ah... you better read every single-a word."

I thought about what he said for just a moment, leaned over the document, flipped to the last page, and signed in three different locations. I stood up, we shook hands, and I drove her home.

A year later, she stood parked in my driveway on Orange Avenue, high in the hills of La Crescenta, California. General Motors had transferred me to California to help engineer the successful introduction of a relatively new, factory-installed automotive accessory, something called an air-conditioner. While here, I also monitored any and all problems that might arise with any GM heat transfer products.

GM had also launched a development program to replace the heavy, increasingly expensive copper radiators with cheaper and lighter aluminum radiators. That led to a field testing program of experimental aluminum radiators.

I visited Chevrolet and Corvette dealerships throughout California to find new car customers willing to let us place an experimental aluminum radiator in their new purchase. In exchange, the GM dealer would store the original copper radiator to be reinstalled in three years when our testing was done. I inspected the aluminum version every other month, at which time GM paid for the oil and filter change and a car wash. I located a dozen people willing to participate in the program. They were an interesting cross section of California drivers.

HARRY AND SALLY

Like the guy who lived in San Francisco, who drove an ambulance for the police department's homicide detail. "Call me Harry," he said when we met at the Chevrolet dealership on the day he picked up his new cherry red Corvette with tuck and rolled white leather interior. He was wearing a tan leather jacket with fringed sleeves over a black silk shirt and black jeans held in place with a thick leather belt and a bold, silver belt buckle. His shiny boots, of course, were black with silver tips. We signed some documents and installed the test radiator.

Two months later, I visited him for the first inspection. His Corvette was parked in a thimble-size garage in an apartment building in downtown San Francisco on one of those impossibly steep streets. His hobby was photography, and each time I called on him at home, Harry answered the door with enthusiasm and insisted on showing me his collection of color photos of his latest corpses before we went downstairs to see the car. One of his favorite photos was of a beautiful, full-busted, long-haired blonde sprawled across a white silk couch, wearing a white bolero jacket and capri pants. Blood had painted a rising sunburst splatter against the couch back. He had half a dozen photo albums of similar scenes and liked to fill in a narrative as he pointed to each photo.

Harry had a girlfriend, Sally, who lived in Oakland, and he sometimes asked me to meet him at her house to examine the Corvette radiator. She was a bottle-blonde divorcee with three young children. He was treated like royalty by this seemingly desperate woman and her children. I watched as they catered to his every wish and listened with wonder to his every word. Harry was single, had a full-time, exciting—though macabre—job, and owned a new cherry red Corvette convertible. He sat in the proverbial cat bird seat.

I lost track of Harry and Sally three years later when the test program ended and we replaced the aluminum test radiator with the original copper one. No more homicide scene photos.

LOUISE PERRY

My most memorable client, however, was Louise Perry. She was around sixty years old when we met and was about to retire from a position with the Los Angeles Department of Water and Power. Louise bought herself a new two-door 1958 Chevrolet Bel Air. We had spoken on the phone, and she had agreed to the radiator test program. I was waiting at the dealership on the day she came in to pick it up.

Louise walked in the door, and I knew it was her. She looked almost exactly as I had pictured she would from listening to her voice on the phone. The face was that of a very cute young girl who had aged gracefully. Her soft brown eyes and gentle smile were framed by wavy grey hair. She was slim and proper and wearing a black cotton dress, cinched at the waist with a starched white Peter Pan lace collar. She had dark stockings and short-heeled "sensible" black shoes that matched the small black purse she carried on her bent left arm.

"Mrs. Perry?" I asked, extending my hand and introducing myself.

"Yes," she said with a smile, shook my hand, and followed me to a cubicle where we would sign the necessary agreements.

"I see you live in Arcadia. That's quite a drive from downtown Los Angeles. It must have been quite a commute to your job at DWP."

"Well, yes. Mr. Perry and I built out there when we were first married in 1927. It was close to my husband's workplace. He was an accountant for a small winery."

"He's retired now too?"

"He passed away just last year," she whispered, her eyes downcast.

"Oh. I'm so sorry." We wound up our business and exchanged phone numbers.

After that, we became fast friends. Each time I visited her home to inspect the auto radiator, she invited me in for tea and cookies. She had no children, and her only living relatives were some younger cousins who still lived in Montana. Since she had no close family, I soon became a surrogate son. She called me for help when she had problems she couldn't handle, such as a leaking faucet or fetching things down from her attic. Among the latter was a good-sized cardboard box which held her deceased husband's dress white shirts. She asked if I would like to have them since I usually wore a white shirt and tie to work. They were yellowed with age and had a collar design that had gone out of fashion many years earlier. I said yes because I knew it would please her. I took them home to store in my attic.

When Louise decided to sell her large home and move to a smaller one, I spent a long weekend driving, loading, and unloading a rental truck. Louise's new home was a cozy one-bedroom, one-bathroom bungalow. Her tiny living room held only a couch and a replica Louis XIV arm chair. Lace doilies covered the arm rests. A black-and-white portrait of her husband graced one wall. A long horizontal mirror hung over the couch where I usually sat when I visited. She sat across from me in the armchair. Off to one side was a small kitchen

After I inspected the aluminum radiator and wrote a check to reimburse her for an oil change and a car wash, we sat, drank tea, and talked. She shared more about herself and her family history with each visit.

"I want to show you something very special," she said one afternoon. She stood, went to her bedroom, and came back carrying two flat cardboard boxes, one much larger than the other. She opened the smaller box and removed an embroidery that was framed and mounted behind glass.

"This is my sampler. I made it in 1904 when I was twelve years old." She placed it in my hands and waited for a reaction. It appeared to be made with colored silk thread sewn on a tight sheet of white linen. An intricate border pattern surrounded the letters of the alphabet, the numbers from one to ten, the name "Louise Hayden," and the date June 4, 1904. Intricate patterns and designs wove through and around the letters and numbers.

"I think I've seen this before," I said.

"You've seen similar ones on boxes of Whitman's chocolates—the Sampler series. I had to complete this for school when I was twelve years old and living in Montana. Hayden was my maiden name. Every girl in our little school house had to make one and get a passing grade by the time we finished the eighth grade." She was smiling proudly.

"It's beautiful, Louise," I said for lack of anything intelligent to say. "You are very talented."

"Well, thank you. It was pretty good for a twelve-year-old girl, I guess. But it can't compare to this other one." She set her sampler back into the box and set it on the floor. She carefully lifted the lid on the larger box and peeled back layers of tissue paper to reveal a glass-protected, larger sampler much more complex and intricately decorated. The rich colors had faded slightly, but that only added to the feeling of antiquity of the piece. Lifting it gingerly by its frame, she turned it toward me, balancing it on one knee.

"This was my great, great grandmother's. It lists the genealogy of her family starting with her grandparents up to her birth in 1819. She lived in New England when she made this. Here's the date," she said as she pointed to the corner, "May 11, 1830."

"It's beautiful. It must be very valuable."

"Indeed. A collector offered my mother a great deal of money for it, but she wanted to keep it in the family. When she gave it to me, she said I should pass it on to my oldest child. Since I don't have any children, I'll probably leave it to one of my cousins in Montana."

I thought briefly how great it would be if she were to change her mind one day and leave it to me. Then I forgot about it.

"So your family originally lived in New England. What brought them to Montana?"

"That was because of Daddy. After he graduated from medical school, he answered an ad in the newspaper looking for an intern for a small hospital in Butte, Montana. He and mother moved to Butte. When he finished internship, he started a private practice as a country doctor. He bought a small ranch outside of town and made most of his calls by horse and buggy."

I asked her what it was like to live on a ranch in Montana all those years ago.

"Well, you know, it was kind of nice. We had dogs and cats, some chickens, a goat, and cattle. Daddy had several ranch hands that took care of his small herd of cattle. They used to pay a lot of attention to me when I was little before I started going to our one-room schoolhouse. They lived in a separate bunkhouse that had a few beds and a table where they played cards when they weren't working. Mother insisted they keep that bunkhouse neat and clean. She'd stay right after them if they didn't make their beds every morning before going out to work,— except during roundup time. Then she allowed them to make their beds in what she called "roundup style." They got up so early and worked so late on those days she let them just toss their sheets and blankets across the bed and plop the pillow on top. They didn't bother to tuck in or smooth wrinkles during roundup time.

"Once I started going to school, I was pretty busy. We rode a bus to the school. It was a few miles down the road. We had one teacher who taught all the grades. She separated the grades by having us sit in small groups with just a little space between us."

"Sounds like you had a colorful childhood. How quaint that all seems compared to the way schools are today in the big cities. Teachers have a much rougher time now, I think."

"Well, yes. But we had our own problems too. One winter, our teacher took sick, and the town had a substitute teacher come up from Butte to fill in. Sometimes the little kids would act up— nothing serious, just silly and giggling. The new substitute made one girl stay after school for punishment. The regular teacher would have known better. On winter days when it got dark early, she always let all the kids go home early while it was still daylight and always on the bus. This substitute just didn't know. She was a city girl, or she would have known about the wolf packs. She let the one little girl—about eleven years old—leave a few minutes later after the bus had left. It was dark out. The last the teacher saw of her was as she walked out the schoolhouse door into the darkness. She didn't get home. They went looking for her and all they found was one of her shoes. They figured the wolves got her."

"What happened to that teacher? Today there'd be a huge lawsuit."

"Nothing much they could do. She just didn't know better. And people didn't sue each other so much back then. The substitute fell apart when she learned the child was missing and began to understand what she had done. She had a mental breakdown when they showed her the shoe. She ended up in a sanitarium somewhere in Billings, Montana. Nobody ever heard what happened to her after that. For a long time, when I heard the wolves howl at night, I thought about that poor little girl."

Our experimental radiator program ended after three years, but Louise and I maintained our friendship. I invited her to our home for dinner a number of times and visited her now and then or called to check up on her. She always accepted the dinner invitation, provided I would drive her there and back again. Her health was diminishing and she preferred not to drive, especially after dark. At our house, after dinner, we sat in my living room and she told stories of her childhood to my little daughters. They sat on the floor at her feet and stared, fascinated, as Louise reminisced.

"My favorite thing was when Daddy would hitch up the buggy and go into Butte to shop for groceries and such. Sometimes I'd go along with him. I was in my early teens and growing up fast. When we got into town, he'd hitch the horse and buggy to the rail in front of the general store and leave me sitting in it. Of course, in minutes I'd be surrounded by all the young cowboys in town. There weren't that many girls around, and I got a lot of attention. They'd squabble over taking turns giving me rides on their horses and teaching me rope tricks. I just loved all the attention, and it always seemed like Daddy got done with his shopping awfully quick when I was with him. He'd come out carrying stuff, climb up into the buggy, and call out, 'Time to go, Princess. Say goodbye to the boys.' And off we'd go while the boys would call out, 'What's the rush, doc?' With me looking back at the boys and they all waving their hats."

One evening, after dinner at my house, one of my little girls asked Louise why she left a ranch in Montana to live in Los Angeles. To the child's mind, it didn't make sense to leave horses and cowboys for dreary Los Angeles.

"Well, my Daddy sent me out here to college. When I graduated, I went back home, but I always wanted to come back here and get away from those cold Montana winters. When Daddy died, he left me some money, and I decided to come back to Los Angeles. Mother told me to invest it wisely and to send for her once I was working and settled down. I engaged a real estate person because I felt sure Los Angeles was going to grow. That was back around 1924. She showed me some acreage that was pretty reasonably priced and said that, in her opinion, it was in the path of commercial growth. I trusted her and bought ten acres at about $1,200 per acre. I got my first job and rented a nice place in downtown Los Angeles with two bedrooms. When mother arrived on the train at Union Station, I picked her up and we spent the first day just catching up and getting her settled in my house.

"'I want to see this property you bought with your Father's money,' she said. I told her we would go tomorrow to see it. The next day, bright and early, we walked to the nearest Red Car trolley stop. That was part of the Pacific Electric Railroad system. We took the number 17 trolley. It rumbled on and on, and mother kept saying, 'Where in the world are you taking me?' The small buildings along Wilshire Boulevard disappeared and the tracks went on another few hundred yards. The pavement ended where the trolley stopped to turn around.

"When we got off the trolley, she looked around kind of bewildered and said, 'Is this it?'

"'No, it's up this way,' I said. I started walking along the unpaved dirt road. It ran through dairy farms and bean fields. We walked close to another half mile until we came to surveyor stakes stuck in the ground. They were numbered. I finally found my numbers and pointed to the ones that marked the outline of my ten acres. There was nothing as far as you could see, except the beans and cows. My ten acres had been cleared off. It still smelled of cattle.

"Well, she was horrified! 'Your father would be devastated if he knew what you bought with his hard-earned money. Why, this is so far out in the wilderness no one will ever want it. I fear your real estate friend has badly used you and taken advantage of your naivety.'

"She kept on like that, on and off, during the next couple months. I said I thought the city would grow out there. She reminded me that all that empty acreage in Montana had been that way for a hundred years and would remain that way for another hundred and what made me think California would be any different. I felt very foolish, and it wasn't long after that I sold it and bought my first house and banked the rest."

I waited for Louise to finish the end of this story. She took her time, fussing with her teacup. Finally, she looked up at me and the children with a twinkle in her eye. "Do you know where that ten acres is located?"

"I can't guess. Tell me."

She shook her head slightly, pursed her lips tightly, and said, "It's in the heart of Wilshire Boulevard, smack in the stretch that became known as The Miracle Mile Development. It became one of the richest commercial properties in the world!" She paused a long time, stirring her tea, then she looked up at me, gave a little shrug, and said, "But who could have known back then, huh?"

When the bone cancer struck, it was with little warning. She failed rapidly. Before long, she had to have in-home hospice care. Her live-in caregiver called me one day and said Louise wanted me to come spend the following Saturday with her. When I arrived, she had a small package wrapped with a bow.

"I haven't forgotten your birthday coming up," she said, her frail hands shaking slightly as she handed me the package. "I don't know how long I have, so I thought I'd give it to you early."

I opened it and found a unique, looped belt hanger made of brass. "I've noticed you have many nice belts you wear with all those fine suits. I thought you'd get some use out of this." She looked up at me from the couch and said, "Now, if you would indulge an old lady, I want to take you to my special place. It is a place I love to visit, and I want to introduce you to it."

I helped her into my car and followed her directions to the Los Angeles County Arboretum and Botanic Garden in Arcadia, just a short drive from her home. I bought two tickets and we entered the gates. Just inside the gate were a couple benches. We sat down and she turned to me.

"This arboretum was opened to the public in 1956, just before you and I met. I loved to come here, roam the displays, sit and enjoy the fragrance and colors. They now also have the Queen Anne Cottage. That is in the National Register of Historic Places. It was built in 1885 or 1886 and has beautiful Victorian architecture. You should visit that too."

"Come," I said, "I'll get one of the wheelchairs and take you through."

"Oh, no, thank you. I'm not up to it. I'll wait here. I just want you to take a quick walk through this place then come and get me and we'll go back home."

"But I don't want to leave you sitting here alone."

"It's okay. I want you to see just enough so you will come back here after I am gone. I want you to remember me when you visit this place. Go. Look. It would please me."

So, choking back the feelings, I let go of her delicate hand and walked quickly through the main path, glimpsed the Queen Anne cottage, and hurried back to her.

When we got back to her house, she rested briefly in her couch then asked for my help to get up. "Take me to my backyard. I have something else for you."

Once in the yard, still hanging on to my arm, she walked to a cluster of plants that resembled a cross between begonias and geraniums. She told me the plant's name. I repeated it so I would remember.

"These are one of my favorite perennials. I bought them at the arboretum. They are hardy and well-known in the perfume industry. The sap is used as a base in many perfumes." I helped her as she bent and collected a small armful of cuttings. "Take these to that lovely backyard of yours and plant them. Then each year, when they bloom, think of me."

I took them out to my car and went back in. She was very tired and said she needed to take a nap now. I gave her a hug, and as I turned to leave, she asked, "Promise to plant those cuttings and visit the arboretum?"

"I promise."

"And think of me?"

"I will."

She walked to her bedroom, leaning on the arm of her caregiver. She looked back once. "Drive safely."

"I will, Louise."

One week later, Louise was gone.

The plant flourished in my backyard for years. When I sold that home and moved to another, I took cuttings with me. It still grows in my yard. I cannot remember its name.

Louise's antique samplers went to her cousin in Montana.

The brass belt holder still hangs in my clothes closet. Each time I use it, I recall my promise, and I again resolve that one of these days I must visit the arboretum and botanic garden in Arcadia, wander the paths, admire the flowers and the ambiance, and recall affectionate memories of Louise Perry, the delightful old lady who once owned the Miracle Mile on Wilshire Boulevard.

The Signpost

He left Ruby's Diner parking lot and the antique cars display. The wind was coming from the south with increased intensity. As he turned slightly off Harbor Drive onto the pavement above Delzano's Restaurant, he felt its stiff resistance. The bike path continued along the upper level and paralleled a wide pedestrian area with benches overlooking the International Boardwalk and the small boats at their docks down below.

He pulled over against the railing and stopped, one foot on the lower railing, to watch the tourists below. His eyes wandered to the tall signpost that rose from the lower level to his line of sight on the second level. He'd seen it many times before but had not paid much attention to what it said. He began to count. There were over twenty narrow, arrow-shaped signs pointing in various directions, bearing the names of famous cities and their distance in miles. This time, not being in a hurry, he read off the ones that faced him. He started with the lowest one on the pole. It read "Juneau 1,853." Just above that was "Taipei 6,792," and so on with each name more exotic than the one before: "Perth," "Kathmandu," "San Francisco," "Dubai,

"Tokyo," "Manila," "Hilo," "Kodiak," "Sidney," and finally, at the very top of the pole, "Seoul 5,965." It pointed southwest.

Imagine that. Almost six thousand miles to Seoul. More than twice the width of the United States, across the ocean, lay Seoul, Korea. Right out there. His gaze drifted past the boats tied below him, over the rock breakwater to the undulating waves beyond, and he lifted his eyes, slowly, to the far horizon.

Out there, he thought, *out there almost six thousand miles away is where Donald was sent.*

He is still there, someplace.

He did not come back.

He is still there.

Out there, he thought, out there almost six thousand
miles away is where Donald was sent. He is still there,
someplace. He did not come back. He is still there.

The Marine

D on lived on Third Avenue, about three blocks from me, in an upstairs apartment of a two-family house with his mother and younger brother. I knew nothing about his father. I never met him.

When our small group met each morning to walk to school, Don sometimes joined us even though it was a couple blocks out of his way. He hung out with us on weekends.

Don was a soft-spoken kid, a little taller than me, slim, and fair-complexioned with very light blonde hair and blue eyes. His ample forelock was always falling into his eyes, and I can still see his futile habit of brushing it aside as he spoke.

He was the first kid in our group to own a crystal radio set, and one day, he showed us how it operated. An antenna was pinned to the window curtain of his bedroom and extended outside the window. We could hear WIBX in Utica and sometimes WGY, "Your General Electric Station in Schenectady!" He pointed outside his bedroom window to another window directly across the alley where, on occasion, he watched the pretty lady next door entertain her boyfriend in her bedroom.

Don was not a stellar student. He struggled for his grades. If given a choice, he sat in the back of the classroom. When grades were passed out, Don was the guy who got the Cs and Ds and an occasional F or Incomplete. His modest scholastic performance seemed to be more a matter of choice than lack of intelligence. Don didn't seem interested in expending much effort on schoolwork. He was quiet in the classroom and unassuming during group discussions, even outside of classes. Still, his gentle presence, warm smile, and friendly manner made his company easy and welcome.

Our group usually talked about movies or cars or sports or school or girls. None of us were dating yet. Don was interested in a girl in his neighborhood. Actually, each of us had an interest in someone at one time or another, but none of the "relationships" had gone past a friendly smile as we passed in school hallways. The girls were more aggressive than we were. A girl might approach one of us and mention that her friend, so-and-so, wondered if we could come to her birthday party or would ask why we didn't ask so-and-so out. "She thinks you are cute."

How awkward and exciting. We weren't sophisticated enough to know how to react, except with mumbled attempted witticisms or foolish grins. Some of our older buddies were dating. Once in a while, a boastful pretender would imply that he had "scored." Then we would privately speculate about how exaggerated the claim was. Once, a pretty older girl in my homeroom had assured me, "Don't worry, honey, your time will come." Yep. That's what the four of us hoped. Someday, our time would come.

In our senior year, we speculated often about life after high school. Don had no firm plans. He wanted to get a job, get married, and raise a family, but his immediate concern was graduating from high school.

As we approached final exams, Don decided to join the Marines. He did not think he would graduate and believed he could complete high school and get a diploma through the Marines. He saw it as an opportunity to develop a career with multiple choices for the future. He would send his military pay home to help his mother and little brother. And someday, his time would come.

For the next few weeks, he learned all he could about the Marines and charted, in detail, his plans for the future. He was happy, and for the first time in the seventeen odd years we had known him, he seemed sure of himself. His new confidence made him seem taller and more handsome, and that stubborn blonde forelock added a special charm. A sparkle was in his eyes that I had never seen before. In a soft voice, he said good-bye to us one day and reported for boot camp the next morning.

A few months later, Don showed up at school during lunch period. He had completed boot camp and was home on a thirty-day leave. Wearing his sharp dress uniform with spit-polished shoes, he looked proud and capable and self-assured. His shaved head was sprouting new blonde sprigs that would soon plague his forehead again.

He met us again after school, and we walked home together. I remember how enthusiastically he talked about his training. This was something he knew well. In this he was an A student. He demonstrated how to place a clip of ammunition into the breach of a rifle without getting his thumb crushed by the powerful bolt that slammed shut behind it. He used a fallen tree branch to show us how to handle a rifle on the parade ground. He spoke of weapons and drill, of discipline and military protocol. We heard of the classes he planned to take, of where he was going to be stationed, and of the girl in his neighborhood who had begun writing to him.

We saw him daily at lunchtime and after school until his thirty-day leave expired. On that last walk home with us from school, we stopped at our corner and talked for a long time. He looked spiffy. He had let his hair grow out, and a small forelock was developing.

I wished him luck. He promised to stay in touch. We shook hands and joked and laughed and he walked away, down Mohawk Street to Third Avenue. Just as he reached the far corner, he executed a smart, parade ground about-face. He looked back at us, smiling, and saluted. We saluted back. He pushed aside his stubborn, budding blonde forelock and stepped out of sight.

A few months later, the First Marine Division was ordered to Korea. War had broken out in what was termed a "police action."

I was home from college for the holidays, reading the Sunday paper in the living room of my parents' home, when I saw the article on the front page of the *Utica Observer Dispatch.* There was a picture too. Donald Hobin was missing in action in what is today called North Korea, near the Hanchu Reservoir.

Some years later, I ran into Don's younger brother. He told me Don was still listed as missing in action.

From time to time, over the fleeting years, something sparks a memory of Don—a holiday song, a young man in uniform.

I wonder what he might have done with his life and if he would have married the girl in his neighborhood.

Would they have had children and grandchildren?

If so, might one of them been shy and soft spoken, troubled by a golden forelock that refused to stay in place above a gentle, fair-skinned, blue-eyed face?

The Ramp

He had been staring at the mileage signpost for a long time when his thoughts were interrupted by a penetrating voice.

"Are you lost, old-timer?" The query came from Richard Delaney, a very long-time friend and fellow bicycle enthusiast.

"Naw. I just can't decide which of those exotic destinations I want to ride to. What are you up to, Rich?"

"Just going out for a short ride. Maybe stop at the club. Which way are you going?"

"I'm just getting back from Marina Del Rey."

"Haven't seen you in a while," Richard said. "How've you been?"

"Oh, fine," he answered.

"And the family?"

"All good. All doing well."

Richard nodded, pursed his lips, and said, "Well, I guess I better get going. I had to park my car in that side street lot that locks up after sunset. I don't want to climb the fence like I did the last time I got back too late. See you later."

"See you later," the Old Man repeated even though they were not likely to see each other later.

How is my family doing? We give the same pat answer 'cause no one really wants to hear it all. Nobody wants to know—how it was and how it has changed.

The way it was... we owned two horses, a dog, and a cat. Then we bought two ducks on impulse—a male and a female—from a Mexican selling them on a street corner. The pair quickly produced ducklings. Tammy and Matty gave names to every animal, and the greeting ritual each day became lengthy. "Hi, Missy. Hi, Penny. Hi, Ginger. Hi, Smokey. Hello, Donald. Hello, Daisy. Hi, Huey and Dewey. Hey there, Louie. Hello, Mo!" They tried to hatch more duck eggs by building an incubation box with a lightbulb in it to keep them warm and took turns rotating the eggs, but all they succeeded in doing was cooking them, evenly, in the shell. That was just as well as it was doubtful we could have memorized any more names.

The half-acre yard and the home were full. Our lives were overfilled with busy things. Dance classes, horseback rides, birthday parties, and graduation ceremonies flowed smoothly into weddings and the birth of grandchildren. A lot of years went by. Things changed. I lost the wife. That happens.

The children grew up. That happens too. They moved away to find opportunities and follow dreams.

He rode past the signpost, ducking instinctively as he entered the low-ceilinged entrance to the parking garage structure. He came out of it at the far end onto Redondo Pier and continued, uneventfully, the last couple miles. He made a short U-turn at the end of the paved path in Torrance Beach just short of RAT beach and came back to the foot of the long, steep concrete ramp that rose up to the county parking lot where he had left his car this morning. He stopped the bike, about to get off, looking up the ramp, undecided.

I'm feeling pretty good today, all things considered. It sure doesn't look all that steep. I used to ride up it all the time until a year ago or so. I can make that. And if I decide to quit, why I'll just get off and walk.

So he got a rolling start with the bike, dropped it into a lower gear, and began the grind toward the top. He was about two-thirds of the way up the ramp, standing with his full weight on the pedals. His breathing was labored. His leg muscles burned.

I should not have tried this. But I think I can do this. I'll traverse.

He began to weave in short, uphill traverses across the ramp to reduce the climb rate and to make the last few feet easier to climb. That's when he saw the child's plastic bucket and the spilled wet sand. The front wheel bogged down slightly. He struggled to keep the bike moving. When the rear wheel reached the wet sand, it lost traction, spun freely in the wetness, and forward motion stopped.

Gravity took over. He pitched backward, downhill, and landed with a hard, unyielding impact, flat on his spine on the unforgiving concrete. His helmet-covered head bounced. The blow to his back knocked the breath out of him. For a few moments, he was disoriented. He felt no pain at first, and then it slowly spread upward from his lower back to the muscles of his shoulders and downward into his legs like piercing electric shocks.

He was afraid to move. There was no one nearby to help. Several hundred people stretched along the sands of the beach far below but not within shouting distance. He had his cell phone. He could call someone, if his limbs would respond. Who could he call? The nearest child lived five hours away by car. His closest friend is over an hour away. He didn't want to bother casual acquaintances. Most of them still work.

Funny how things end up, the way things have of changing.

It happens slowly, and then you become aware that they are all gone, leading all-consuming lives.

Maybe the grandson... maybe CJ. He would come...

...and through a feathery, coalescing mist, he saw it all again... that time when their first grandson, the one who still lived nearest, was born.

48

The Grandson

I have grandchildren and even a few great grandchildren. I love them all. They are a joy because, as every grandparent knows, we reap all the love and pleasure they can offer us and leave the worry behind with their parents. It was that way for me with all of them—all, that is, except for this one grandson. With this one—the first one—worry came right along with him because he lived with us for so many of his early years.

We knew he was due at any moment. His mother was at the end of her third trimester. We waited for the phone call, but it didn't come. That evening, no one answered our telephone calls. By midnight, we began calling hospitals until one of them confirmed that she had given birth to a baby boy.

We drove to the hospital and were ushered to a viewing room where a red-faced, wrinkled bundle lay inside a glass cocoon, wrapped tightly in blankets. He was in a neonatal intensive care unit. His new name was hand-printed on a piece of paper taped to the glass case. We shortened it to "CJ."

We've been pretty close since his birth. At four months of age, while living with me, he suffered from a severe chest cold and congestion. He couldn't sleep unless he was sitting up because the congestion would plug his breathing passages. So that night and the next, I sat up in a rocking chair, holding him upright, leaning on my chest, while he slept. We rocked all night while I softly sang a lullaby I made up using his name over and over again. For years later, I could get him to doze off by resting his head on my chest or shoulder and crooning that plaintive little chant.

Over the next several years, the new parents struggled with their personal issues, often at the expense of this tiny creature. We were allowed to step into the breach whenever they could no longer manage. Eventually, CJ spent more time with us than with his parents. He was a venturesome and athletic little boy, full of curiosity and surprises. Like all of our later grandchildren, CJ created a hundred little memories for the adults in his life.

FIP A OO-EE, UMPA

Driving CJ to his second grade class one day, we ran into a severe traffic snarl. A hundred parents in cars sought to drop their children off at the neighborhood grade school at the very same time. Traffic was stopped for two blocks.

"I should have turned down the last street. I should have come up the back way," I said to no one in particular. He was sitting on the center console cover of the front seat, a place that he preferred because it afforded him a full view out the front window. He turned to me and said, "Fip a oo-ee, Umpa!" He couldn't pronounce "Grandpa" yet so I understood "Umpa," but it took a moment to realize he was suggesting that I make a U-turn using an expression he had heard from some adult. The expression became a family standard. For years, everyone in the family referred to making a U-turn as "Fipping a oo-ee!"

Me Tough

I knew CJ's class had rehearsed what to do in an earthquake. He delighted in telling us how they practiced the duck-and-take-cover procedure, taking refuge under their desks. One day, while I was at work and he was in school, the South Bay area experienced a real earthquake. It was of pretty good magnitude, and I was anxious to hear about his experience. That afternoon when I picked him up from school, he excitedly jumped into the car and climbed up onto the center console. "Umpa, guess what! We had a real earthquake today!" he said. "We had to get under our desks until it stopped!".

"Were you scared, CJ?" I asked.

"Naw!" he boasted. "Me tough!" It became another favorite family expression. "Me tough!"

Let's Det Outta Heew, Umpa

He was asked to be the ring bearer in his aunt's wedding. We did little rehearsals at home that worked out very well. He carried the little velvet pillow that would bear the wedding rings across the living room right on cue. A few days before the wedding, I thought it would be a good idea to take him to the church and introduce him to the layout. The church was in the process of being repainted inside. Sheets of thick, translucent, four-foot wide plastic hung from the three-story-high ceiling to prevent paint spray from falling on church benches, walls, and windows. We had to push them aside to enter the church or to move from one section to another. Similar sheets hung between the vestibule and the entrance to the main aisle. The doors were all open to allow air to drift through so the paint could dry and the odor could dissipate. I walked him back to the vestibule.

"Here is where you will stand with your ring pillow," I explained. Then I showed him how to enter the sanctuary and walk down the aisle to the altar.

All this time he kept his head down, looking upward through his eyebrows at the ghostly thirty-foot-long swaths of hanging, translucent plastic that moved gently and hauntingly in the air.

I turned to him and asked, "Do you have any questions, CJ?" He ducked his head further, clutched my hand firmly, and said, "Let's det outta heew, Umpa!" He pulled me to the nearest doorway, his little legs moving as fast as they could without breaking into a run as we crashed through the terrifying plastic sheets that seemed to clutch at us.

On the day of the wedding, the paint job was not finished and most of the long, ghostly plastic sheets swayed menacingly throughout the church.

We stood in the church vestibule, just behind the bridesmaids. CJ's tiny tuxedo, patent leather shoes, and bow tie bound him stiffly. He held his arms out in front of him, holding the pillow with two rings loosely attached by thin thread loops. The flower girl was his older cousin, Ginny. She stood next to him with a bouquet of flowers. I stood behind them with my daughter the bride.

Wagner's wedding march brought out the usual goose bumps. The bridesmaids began their walk down the aisle. As the last one stepped out into the aisle, I tapped the little ring bearer's shoulder and said, "Now it's your turn, big guy. Follow that lady down the aisle." He looked through his eyebrows at the swaying plastic phantoms and the unclear shapes beyond.

"Go ahead, CJ. You're next," I said.

He froze, shook his head slowly from side to side, and whispered, "Let's det outta heew, Umpa!"

"Here," his aunt the bride said, "hand the pillow to Ginny." He did. Ginny, his eight-year-old cousin, stepped out into the aisle carrying the ring pillow with one hand, the flowers with the other, and did a magnificent job of balancing it all. I and the bride stepped out last, arm in arm, with the little delinquent ring bearer clutching my leg as we walked down the aisle in cadence with the music.

Once I sat down with CJ in my lap, his fear disappeared, and it was all I could do to hold him still through the balance of the ceremony. He twisted and turned and exhibited a brazen energy that led me to feel immense relief when the first strains of Mendelssohn's march sounded to end the ceremony. Everyone was elated but no one more than I.

BIRDS AND BEES

In the fourth grade, he brought home a descriptive brochure which explained an upcoming class that would explain *The Birds and the Bees*. I attended a screening of the movie which would be shown to the children. It described the changes that boys and girls could soon expect in their bodies and some of the simple things that the children should know about personal hygiene and reproduction. After the viewing, I signed an approval slip so my grandson could view this film. No specific date was scheduled yet. But a week later, when I picked him up from school and we were driving back home, he turned to me and, with a slightly gruff effort, said, "Umpa, does my voice sound lower?"

I smiled. "You saw the movie, huh?"

"Yeah. Does my voice sound lower?"

"Well, not a whole lot."

"Umpa, can we stop at the drugstore and get some de-do-do-rent?"

"You want deodorant? Is that what they said you should do?"

"Yeah. Cause we are gonna start to stink."

So we stopped at a drugstore. I explained to him that some deodorants came with the added feature of antiperspirant and what that meant. I said he could try it and see if it irritated his skin. The next morning, after his shower, he diligently applied deodorant with antiperspirant to his armpits. He carefully brushed his teeth and combed his hair.

That afternoon, I picked him up along with his closest buddy, Michael. They sat in the backseat and talked about all this new stuff as if I wasn't there.

"Did you get some de-do-do-rent?" asked the grandson.

"Yeah. I got that."

"Was yours aunty-press-pro-rent?"

"What's aunty-press-pro-rent?"

"It keeps you from sweating so you won't smell so bad. You should of got aunty-press-pro-rent de-do-do-rent !"

And so it went for a long time.

THE CRUSH

CJ had a crush on his student teacher, a young female adult who was in training with his classroom teacher. The student teacher was fond of him too. He brought her presents and described her as beautiful. He was jealous of his friend Alan who, he felt, was flirting with her. He told Alan, "You should stop acting like a fool and just be yourself. Then she will look at you the way she looks at me."

One day, she called us. She had received a beautiful amethyst ring from him. She wondered if we knew anything about the ring. We searched the jewelry box in our house. An amethyst ring was missing. What, we wondered, would motivate this sweet little boy to "borrow" such a valuable bauble and make a gift of it to this young lady? How had he become so enchanted? I stopped to retrieve it from her after school. I met her for the first time that afternoon. Her back was to me as I walked into the empty classroom after hours. I said hello. She turned and I understood immediately what he was feeling. The student teacher had large brown eyes, wore eyeglasses, had long, straight, dark hair, and a pretty smile. She was the spitting image of his absent mother. And he loved her.

Lucky to Have Me

I took him to his little boy events and participated in many school and athletic projects. Often his friends or teachers would tell him, "You are lucky to have your grandfather."

A time came when I was home in bed, sick with a very bad flu bug. I was alone with CJ. He had recently learned how to heat chicken soup and volunteered to open a can and heat some for me. I accepted. A few minutes later, he brought me a steaming bowl and a soup spoon. He sat watching me as I sat up in bed and ate the soup. Then with a very serious face, he said, "When you get old, I will take care of you." He waited a minute then added, "You are very lucky to have me."

"Yes," I said, "I am."

All the Days that Follow

The last decades have moved swiftly. The children and grandchildren have moved on, making a life for themselves. Their time is filled with endeavors and relationships. I am pleased.

When they stumble now, they pick themselves up, brush themselves off, and push on. I guess that means they have grown up. I don't see them as often anymore, but that is as it should be.

They never really belonged to us. They were placed in our care only temporarily.

Our responsibility was to assure that one day they would achieve independence, go out into the world—without us—and succeed in finding their own happiness. That day, it seems, has come.

And all the days that follow will be, must be, very quiet.

Sometimes, when all is still, I see a child's face and hear a child's voice.

It whispers to me—

We were lucky to have had each other... for a while.

Home

T he Old Man's thoughts returned to his predicament. How long had he been lying here? He was still on his back, one leg under the bike, the other on top of it, afraid to move. But he did, after a while. He feared he might have done some serious damage to something. *If I can just get home, I'll be all right,* he thought.

It took some doing to disentangle his legs from the bike, roll over, and get up to his feet. He managed to lift the bike back up onto its wheels and hobbled up the ramp, pushing the bike next to him. After a pause, he wrestled it onto the bicycle rack mounted to the rear of his car and drove home. The pain in his back was intense. He would wait until tomorrow and get to the doctor for x-rays or an MRI. Surely he could wait until then.

He found a bottle of Aleve and swallowed a few. It didn't seem to help much. It was going to be another long night. He lay in bed for an hour but could not find a comfortable position. Finally he found the pain eased when he lay back on the leather recliner in the family room. He tried to read, but his mind kept returning to the fact that he was hurt and alone. He would get over this injury. The back muscles were bruised, that's all. He'd be back to normal in a few days, he felt sure. It will just take time. Time, the most precious asset he possessed now—most precious because it was growing shorter.

One of these days, some part of his body would betray him. It eventually happens to everyone. It would happen to him.

What would happen after that? Would he suffer alone, like his aunt who lingered for so long, heavily sedated, only smiling briefly when he visited? Would he go quietly in his sleep, like his older brother had gone, asleep in his rocking chair, at home?

What happens after that? he wondered.

Wish I could ask Mom and Dad. Wish they could counsel me, tell me what to expect.

He gingerly got to his feet, shuffled to the desk in his office, picked up paper and a pencil, and began to write. He would write to them. It would pass the time, and strangely, it consoled him to be going through the motions of talking to his parents.

Dear Mom and Dad,

Well, your youngest child, your baby boy, is now eighty years old…

The Letter

Dear Mom and Dad,

    Well, your youngest child, your baby boy, is eighty years old. Seems like just a few years ago I sat on the edge of the kitchen table while you, Mom, dressed me in clean clothes you had washed by hand and hung out to dry in the summer sun so they smelled fresh and warm.

    Dad, was it that long ago that we listened to the Joe Louis-Max Schmelling rematch on that old Philco Super Heterodyne? That radio was the latest in broadcast technology and the same age as me—almost six years old—and just about the same height. On a good night, it was able to bring in four stations: WIBX in Utica; WSYR in Syracuse; WGY, "Your General Electric Station in Schenectady;" and WXNY in New York City. That night, the whole eastern seaboard was tuned to the New York City station to hear that fight. All the lights were turned off in our third floor apartment. Only the little yellow dial shone softly in the dark. We lay quietly on the floor of our parlor, in front of the radio, straining to hear every word through the crackle of static. The bell sounded the start of the first round. You leapt to your feet, ran to get a pillow for your head, and rushed back, set it on the floor, lie down, and placed your head on it just in time to hear the referee count Max Schmelling out. The "fight of the century," and you missed it. And they didn't have instant replay. We laughed about that many times, didn't we?

Where was my brother that night? I know he was there. He had to be lying there on the floor with us, but I can't see him in my memory of that night. Perhaps he sat on the couch next to the piano he practiced on every night. One of his favorite pieces was "Glow Worm." I hear it in my head today.

And Mom, you were in the rocking chair, in the dark, listening with us. The one you sat in while knitting a scarf or mending a sock. The rocker I fell against while playing as a child. The tiny scar is still visible on my right eyebrow, but you have to look very closely. See? Does it still show?

Life has turned out well but not always as I had planned. I made many good choices. I regret a few. But they all seemed right at the time.

What would have happened if I had picked different paths? Would the results have been better or worse? Would nothing be different? Can we influence destiny as much as we think we can? Maybe we end up right where we were supposed to be every time. It's funny how things turn out. I guess we just have to make the best of what we end up with.

Was I a good man? That's something to think about for all of eternity. Will we be able to think for eternity? Will we be busy doing things? Too busy to study the past and learn?

That will be a lot like life.

Nothing is certain in my mind. That comes with age, I suppose. There are none so certain of things as the young.

What happens next? You two are there. You know what happens next. Would you tell me, if you could? Will you be there to welcome me? Or does it all end the instant that I end?

Tonight I can see your young faces again in my mind. You were— you are—a handsome couple. I see you strolling, arm in arm, down Bleecker Street, on one of those pleasant summer nights in Utica. The night birds are chasing bugs we can't see, darting and swooping against the black, starry sky overhead. Soft streetlights are on, and it is dim in the spaces between them. Neighbors are standing around on the sidewalk, here and there, saying hello as you pass. We all know each *other. We each have our place in this painting of our street, in our town, way back then.*

I am visiting there tonight.

I am a child again.

I am looking down from our third-floor window, watching it all, again.

Love always,
Your son

The Philco Super Heterodyne Model 90 Lowboy Console
radio (ca 1932) that broadcast the Joe Louis – Max Schmelling
heavyweight championship rematch on June 22, 1938

Photo courtesy of Paul Turney of Paul@ tuberadioland.com.

51

The Dream

The Old Man lay back in his recliner, his head slightly to one side. He had fallen asleep reading the letter which he held loosely in his right hand, both arms resting across his chest. He dreamt, and the dreams caused him to smile.

He was riding along the beach. The sun shone warm and the sea air was salty and fragrant. He saw the dolphins just beyond the surf, leaping in couples that arched briefly in the air and slid smoothly back into the sea. They were playing, carving gracefully through the translucent green of the water. Brilliant droplets of spray sparkled in the sunlight, growing in intensity, melding into a radiant, gleaming chandelier whose lightbulbs were shaped like candle flames. The salt air acquired the rich smell of cooking. The murmuring surf resembled human voices and the dolphin's shadowy figures assumed human shapes, the sand the plush carpet of a dining room floor.

It was Thanksgiving again, and he was carving the turkey. It had always been his task to carve the turkey. The dining room table was expanded with all three extra leaves to accommodate the huge spread and all the family. Excited chatter and tantalizing aromas filled the air.

It was a happy dream. Everyone was there, as it used to be. The food was served. The room grew silent. They spoke in turn around the table, speaking of what they were thankful for. And when it came time for the children to speak, one of them—maybe it was a grandchild— said, "I am thankful that we have each other. We are so lucky to have each other."

He slept on, smiling in his sleep.

About the Author

J oseph N. Manfredo is also the author of *Only The Living*, a memoir, *After Midnight, poems and pontifications* and *The Trained Killers*. He is retired and living in Southern California.